"Few evangelicals have impacted contemporary psychology more than Everett Worthington. That alone makes the publication of his understanding of the relation between psychological science and Christian theology an important event. Suggesting that the relation is analogous to a marriage relationship and a dance, he argues for both their relative independence and the necessity that they be deeply engaged with and committed to each other. There is much to debate in this book, but the author's love of God, people and psychological science is evident throughout."

Eric L. Johnson, Ph.D., director, Society for Christian Psychology, and Lawrence and Charlotte Hoover Professor of Pastoral Care, The Southern Baptist Theological Seminary

"Everett Worthington is a significant scholar and researcher in the field of psychology who presents in this book a thoughtful and personal view of the relationship between psychology and Christian faith. In a winsome and irenic style, he argues for a relational partnership between theology and psychology that neither simplistically pits the fields in a struggle for authority, nor inappropriately intermingles their concepts and ideas. Most importantly, Worthington argues for the value of psychological research in this very important conversation about theological and psychological views of the nature of persons."

Warren S. Brown, Ph.D., professor, Fuller Graduate School of Psychology, and director, Travis Research Institute

"This is psychology for the intelligent Christian! Worthington turns integration into a dance with full participation from the science of psychology and genuine faith. Culturally relevant and full of the most cutting-edge psychological research, Worthington is true to both his faith and science. To those that struggle with reconciling theology and psychology, this book is a faithful guide with genuine respect for both disciplines. Communicated with a readable style a beginning student could appreciate. All previous books on integration will need to be rewritten to respond to Worthington's ideas."

Jennifer Ripley, professor, School of Psychology and Counseling, Regent University

"Past discussions of how psychology and theology are related have tended to be written either from the perspective of psychotherapists and counselors or from that of psychological scientists. In a remarkably well-informed, wide-ranging review of the literature, Everett Worthington argues that 'we are wise to look at all sources of information and wisdom we have at our disposal—and this includes both Scripture and psychological science.' This outstanding book is an invaluable, up-to-date reference source on issues at the interface of psychology and Christian belief."

Malcolm Jeeves, Emeritus Professor of Psychology, St. Andrews University, former editor-in-chief, *Neuropsychologia* and past president, Royal Society of Edinburgh, Scotland's National Academy

"Everett Worthington—accomplished psychological scientist, biblically rooted person of faith and professional writer—is the perfect person to assist Christians in coming to peace with today's psychology. With his conversational voice and dry wit, he introduces us to startling findings, differing perspectives, and evidence-based insights on faith and faithful living. Highly recommended!"

David G. Myers, Professor of Psychology, Hope College, and author of *Psychology* and *A Friendly Letter to Skeptics and Atheists: Musings on Why God Is Good and Faith Isn't Evil*

"This book will make you think! Everett Worthington is one of the most intelligent and influential Christians involved in scientific psychology. *Coming to Peace with Psychology* may not put you at peace with every dimension of psychology and theology, but it will definitely deepen your perspective and provoke you to consider ways that the science of psychology can enrich our understanding of God."

Mark R. McMinn, Professor of Psychology, George Fox University, and coauthor of *Integrative Psychotherapy: Toward a Comprehensive Christian Approach*

COMING TO PEACE

WITH PSYCHOLOGY

WHAT CHRISTIANS CAN LEARN
FROM PSYCHOLOGICAL SCIENCE

EVERETT L. WORTHINGTON JR.

IVP Academic

An imprint of InterVarsity Press
Downers Grove, Illinois

InterVarsity Press
P.O. Box 1400, Downers Grove, IL 60515-1426
World Wide Web: www.ivpress.com
E-mail: email@ivpress.com

InterVarsity Press® is the book-publishing division of InterVarsity Christian Fellowship/USA®, a movement of students and faculty active on campus at hundreds of universities, colleges and schools of nursing in the United States of America, and a member movement of the International Fellowship of Evangelical Students. For information about local and regional activities, write Public Relations Dept., InterVarsity Christian Fellowship/USA, 6400 Schroeder Rd., P.O. Box 7895, Madison, WI 53707-7895, or visit the IVCF website at <www.intervarsity.org>.

All Scripture quotations, unless otherwise indicated, are taken from the Holy Bible, New International Version®. NIV®. *Copyright 1973, 1978, 1984 by International Bible Society. Used by permission of Zondervan Publishing House. All rights reserved.*

Figure 2.1 on page 36 is reproduced from James R. Beck and Bruce Demarest, The Human Person in Theology and Psychology *(Grand Rapids: Kregel, 2005). Used by permission.*

Figure 3.1 on page 50 is from George A. Bonanno, "Resilience in the Face of Potential Trauma," Current Directions in Psychological Science *14 (2005). Used by permission.*

Figure 5.1 on page 80 is adapted from Francis Schaeffer, Escape from Reason *(Downers Grove, Ill.: InterVarsity Press, 2006). Used with permission.*

Design: Cindy Kiple
Images: Don Farrall/Getty Images

ISBN 978-0-8308-3882-0

Printed in the United States of America ∞

Library of Congress Cataloging-in-Publication Data

Worthington, Everett, L., 1946-
  Coming to peace with psychology: what Christians can learn from
psychological science / Everett L. Worthington Jr.
    p. cm.
  Includes bibliographical references and indexes.
  ISBN 978-0-8308-3882-0 (pbk.: alk. paper)
  1. Psychology, Religious. 2. Psychology—Religious aspects. 3.
Christianity—Psychology. I. Title.
  BL53.W68 2010
  261.5'15—dc22

                                                                  2010014226

P 25 24 23 22 21 20 19 18 17 16 15 14 13 12 11 10 9 8 7 6 5 4 3 2 1

Y 31 30 29 28 27 26 25 24 23 22 21 20 19 18 17 16 15 14 13 12 11 10

To my Cambridge connection:

Fraser Watts and Sir John Polkinghorne,
my intellectual ideals at the Centre

Nicholas Gibson and Liz Gulliford,
scholars and friends

Sir Brian Heap, Denis Alexander and Paul Luzio
at St. Edmund's College, my social motivators
and mentors in college life

John Barrow,
mathematician and Renaissance scientist
and cosmologist

Russell Stannard,
scholar, artist and public communicator
and always an inspiration to me

CONTENTS

Acknowledgments 9

Introduction 11

Part I: The Relationship of Psychological Science to Theology . . . 15

  1 Interesting Things About People 17

  2 A Tale of Two Cities 31

  3 What Information Can I Trust? 47

  4 Why You Might Not Believe What You
    Don't Already Believe 56

  5 The Methods of Disciplines 75

  6 A Relational Model 91

  7 Understanding the Relational Partners 106

  8 Dealing with Some Challenges 124

Part II: What Psychological Science Has to Offer Theology 147

  9 Psychological Science Provides a New Tool 149

  10 Psychological Science Is Limited 168

  11 Psychological Science Strengthens Theological Claims . . . 182

  12 Psychological Science Adds New Ideas to Theology 202

  13 Psychological Science Addresses Theologically Hot
     Social Controversies 216

  14 Psychological Science Helps Us
     Understand Virtuous Living 235

  15 Psychological Science Helps Us Live More Virtuously . . . 258

  16 Can Psychological Science Help Us Know God Better? . . . 272

Notes 281

Author Index 296

Subject Index 298

ACKNOWLEDGMENTS

I AM GREATLY INDEBTED TO Fraser Watts and John Polkinghorne, directors of the University of Cambridge Centre for Psychology and Christianity. They provided support, a haven and a stimulating environment at the University of Cambridge, Faculty of Divinity, that allowed me to write the initial draft of this book during the fall of 2005. The Centre staff, postdocs, affiliated faculty, graduate students and research assistants also provided feedback that helped me pull some of the ideas of the book together. When I began the book I had no idea of the depth and breadth of the dialogue between the sciences and religion. But the University of Cambridge—including the Centre for Science and Religion, the Faraday Centre and the Templeton Science-Spirituality Journalism Project—exposed me to experts and their ideas in what may be an unparalleled environment for tackling a book like this.

I also am indebted to Professor Paul Luzio, Master of St. Edmund's College. I was honored to be inducted as a Visiting Fellow at St. Edmund's during my visit. The College provided intellectual and social support and opportunities to share in its intellectual life.

I am also indebted to both the College of Humanities and Sciences and the department of psychology at my home institution, Virginia Commonwealth University. They provided the funds and freedom from many university, college and departmental responsibilities for a year, which allowed me the scholarly research leave at the University of Cambridge. Without the resources and freedom provided, I could not have completed this project.

I owe more than I can express to Mark McMinn, who gave some

straightforward feedback on an earlier version of the manuscript when I had lost hope that it would ever become a book. Whereas Mark certainly would not agree fully with my final product, he provided the objective perspective to allow me to jettison some very weak chapters and reshape many others. I know it is hard to give difficult feedback to a friend, and I thank Mark deeply for his courage and his intellectual rigor.

Kirby, my beloved wife since 1970 also helped me rein in excesses. Even more, she believed in me as I struggled with this book, and that is worth far more than its weight in gold. She suggested that I go to her brother's condo in Florida, where I could have time to write. And she was willing to sacrifice our precious time together while I was writing. Thanks to Wayne's generosity for making the condo available in his absence. Only there could I finally get this into readable shape.

There are countless others to whom I am thankful for the ideas—though perhaps none would agree with my whole case. Reciting a list of great thinkers on integration of psychology and Christianity would tax your patience and undoubtedly hurt people's feelings if I failed to mention them. Let me just say that intellectual curiosity is all about asking hard questions. I have been privileged to live as a psychologist from 1974, when I began graduate school in psychology, to now. This period allowed for over thirty-five years of asking and answering hard questions about whether and how Christian faith, theologies, and living could and should be intermixed with scientific theories, scientific studies, clinical science and clinical practice. Controversy has led people to different answers to those questions. In fact, I have embraced several different positions as times have changed and thinking has undergone new challenges. I have been blessed to participate in this conversation. I am intensely grateful to God and to the many people involved in this conversation about Christianity and psychology.

INTRODUCTION

THIS IS A LOVE STORY. It is about falling in love, being together in love at the end of time, but mostly about living and growing together in love. Like Romeo and Juliet, the lovers are star-crossed. Christians are from one house. Scientists from another. Often the members of each household try to keep these two apart. Sometimes there are even dagger fights, though the weapons are words and ideas.

Some people believe that science is at war with religion and no civil dialogue can occur. I disagree. In recent years the relationship between science and religion has—except in the political arena in the United States—come to be seen more as a dialogue or a conversation than as a war. In this book I will claim that we can know people better, and even know God better, by heeding psychological science. In fact, I'll suggest that the relationship between psychological science and Christianity is more like an emerging marriage than either a war or a mere dialogue. Although there may be marital spats, there is potentially an intimate relationship.

Seeing God more clearly by reading God's general revelation through the tools of science is not new. Galileo squabbled with the Roman Church.[1] Eventually, the power plays wound down, and more or less civilized conversations have ensued between scientists and theologians. For years, conversations have been cordial and helpful. There are only a few strident voices. Mostly, now, the two sides benignly ignore each other, and in doing so, ignorance of each other is perpetuated.

Rapid changes in science, social life, education, technology and health care have brought new emotion-laden issues into the political arena. Opposing sides have hijacked scientific data. They have shaped evidence selectively into hammers to beat on their adversaries and to fashion political and financial supporters. I don't intend to debate those hot issues, though I will refer to them periodically.

In the twentieth century Freud's talking cure spawned a variety of psychotherapies, which often helped people live more meaningful lives. A common emphasis on meaning brought psychotherapies into dialogue with religion. Psychotherapists, armed with what they had discovered about people, have created a body of literature promoting integration of clinical psychology and theology.[2] (I've even contributed to that literature.) Although I will refer to such literature, this book is not a summary and refers to little of it.

I won't focus on physics, politics, pastoral counseling or professional psychotherapy. I will, however, consider psychological science. Within the science-religion relationship, psychological science has had the least attention accorded it even though scientific advances have unleashed great potential for understanding people.[3] Among the sciences in today's world, I think that psychological science has the most potential to help people see God most clearly. Critics often cavalierly dismiss psychological experiments as artificial and trite.[4] They say that most experiments tell us, at best, about college freshmen. They say that experiments are contrived to answer questions that interest only academicians who must publish something—anything, regardless of how useful. People who make such arguments often have not actually kept up with modern psychological science. Both the American Psychological Association and the American Psychological Society regularly encourage, sponsor and publish science on practical issues, mostly with adults, adolescents and children who are not college students. The funding agencies in the United States—the National Institutes of Health and the National Science Foundation—and foundations typically do not fund research on college students. Rather they fund research on the hard-to-study samples of minorities, community members and people across the economic, social and political spectrums. Psychological science in the United States—and throughout the world—studies real people with real-life issues.

My theses in this book are that psychological science can help those who do and don't follow Jesus Christ (1) understand God's creation—in particular, human nature—more clearly, (2) know about God and actually know God more accurately through what we learn about people—who are God's handiwork—because people bear the image of God, (3) see some of the distortions of that image due to the pervasive effects of sin from the Fall of humans from grace, and (4) live more virtuously.

I believe that those who follow Jesus will experience the joy and benefits of redemption, and the fruits of that redemption will spill out into more virtuous living than they would experience without God's grace appropriated by faith. But I also believe that people who do not know and follow Jesus as Lord will be able to live more virtuously if they adhere to the principles revealed by both psychological science and Christian teaching.

Beyond integrating Christian and psychological truths, I hope this book uncovers new relationships between science and religion, helps address theological issues, and helps people understand virtue better and live more virtuously. Psychological science stands shoulder-to-shoulder with physics, biology and clinical science within God's general revelation to humanity. It therefore deserves a place alongside those disciplines in the relationship between the sciences and religion. That relationship has been rocky at times, but this whole book argues that it is now fully time that Christianity comes to peace with psychological science. If it does, psychological science can be a powerful part of God's general revelation, and it can move as an equal partner (though performing different functions) with theology.

This book is for thoughtful people who don't have to be psychologists to enjoy and learn from this book. Although I deal with some heavy topics, I also try to reveal interesting psychological findings that enrich life. I address enough theology that I hope you'll see—perhaps in a different and richer way than you do at the outset—how psychology can benefit theology and, in fact, all Christians. I think psychologists will find the book challenging because they are dealing with the relationship of psychology and theology on a professional as well as personal level. I pray that this book will stimulate questions that push thinking along and will, in the end, allow us to live redeemed lives that are virtuous and pleasing to God.

PART ONE

THE RELATIONSHIP OF PSYCHOLOGICAL SCIENCE TO THEOLOGY

INTEGRATION IS BELIEVING THAT PSYCHOLOGY and Christianity have things to say to each other and continue to be in dialogue with each other. The most common approach is to use a *filter* model in which Scripture is taken as the standard for evaluating the truth value of psychological scientific findings. But there are some difficulties with filter models.

On the other hand, a *perspectival* approach to integration suggests that psychological science and Christianity speak to people on different levels and must be seen from an inside perspective of each. Although we can learn from each, generally we learn about worldview from Christianity and about how to understand psychological functioning from psychological science. In the perspectival approach the two levels are not intimately integrated. In part one of this book, I will develop a way of looking at psychological science as being in relationship to Christianity that will serve as an alternative to filter models and to perspectival models—a relational model.

1

INTERESTING THINGS
ABOUT PEOPLE

IN THE EARLY 1990S, JOHN GOTTMAN, a clinical psychologist now retired from the University of Washington, upset most of the researchers who study marriage. He claimed that if he had ten minutes of videotaped interaction of a couple who were discussing a marital issue, he could with 94 percent certainty—not 93 percent, not 95 percent, but 94 percent certainty—predict who would remain together and be happy four years in the future.[1] What really got the goat of other researchers who studied couples was how he proposed to make the prediction. If the couple had at least five times as many positive as negative interactions with each other, Gottman said they will be together and happy four years from today. Ninety-four percent certainty. But with less than a five to one ratio, they had better pack their bags and save four years of bitter decline (or hope to be one of the lucky 6 percent who defies the odds).

"It ain't that simple," I chanted along with most of the researchers who studied couples. Even some long-term researchers who shared Gottman's behavioral perspective differed and were quite critical.[2] These included Scott Stanley, founder of Christian PREP, a program that trains couples in skills that help them prepare for and enrich marriage. Also included was the founder of the secular version of PREP, Howard Markman, who had coauthored a book with John Gottman previously, and Thomas Bradbury, another expert couple researcher. In the dispassionate (taken with a bit of tongue in cheek) method of scientific researchers, those researchers, myself and many others, set out to show that John Gottman was, well, an idiot.

The research accumulated. By 2005 I and others concluded that it was clear. John Gottman wasn't an idiot. Far from it. He could indeed make great predictions of marital outcomes on the basis of the five-to-one Gottman ratio.[3]

But it was also clear that his 94 percent certainty was a tad optimistic.[4] Research had uncovered a more nuanced story. For instance, imagine Dave and Sue, who have been having troubles but have sought counseling. Over the last four months their Gottman ratio has increased from 1 to 1 to 5 to 1. But imagine Kish and Tamara, who were blissfully happy with a 25 to 1 ratio for years. Then Kish lost his job and stayed home a lot while Tamara was bringing in the money. Over the last four months their ratio has slid to 5 to 1, and they seem in a downward spiral of increasingly frequent conflict. Both couples have a 5 to 1 ratio. What's your prognosis?

Or consider this. Maggie and Seth are a couple who spend months in nothing but positive interactions—250 without a negative interaction in sight. Then one day Maggie says something critical. That sets them off and they have fifty consecutive negative interactions that build in intensity until Seth moves out. Eventually the fight blows over and Seth moves back home. Walking on eggshells, they try to maintain a positive frame and succeed for another 250 consecutive positive interactions. Yet always lurking in the back of their minds is the next knockdown, drag-out verbal brawl they will inevitably have. That couple does not have a sterling future unless something radical changes.

So, although the five-to-one Gottman ratio allows for great prediction, it isn't nearly the whole story. Still, imagine this. If you could interview any couple for several hours or if you were told their long-term Gottman ratio, which would you choose to make the best prediction about their future together?

Logically, I know that I could make the best prediction using the Gottman ratio. As much as I am confident in my interviewing and discernment, I know for a fact that I can't predict anywhere near 94 percent accurately. But I would, nevertheless, almost certainly choose to interview instead of accept that one number. And you probably would too. The reason we would likely do that is a story for a future chapter. Right now, I want to look at how to make the best decisions. And one rule—or as they say in *Pirates of the Caribbean,* actually it's more like a guideline—is this: Get the most relevant information to make the best decision. But what is the most relevant information?

For instance, suppose you have to make a decision. The United States military is staging a $250,000,000 war game to simulate war in the Persian Gulf, and on one side is the entire U.S. military might, bolstered by its electronic and technological prowess. On the other is a rogue commander who has broken away from his government. He has support, but his resources are orders of magnitude less than the U.S. forces. Who do you bet on?

THIN SLICING CAN BE BETTER THAN LOTS OF INFORMATION

Malcolm Gladwell[5] has compiled a great book on the ways that people intuitively make decisions, sometimes using quick, unconsciously perceived information. Because the decision comes so quickly, he titled his book *Blink: The Power of Thinking Without Thinking.* One of my favorite chapters describes elaborate war games in the Persian Gulf that presaged the later invasion of Iraq. In spring 2000 the Pentagon organized the games, which they called Millennium Challenge '02, and the forces had two years plus to plan. The games were not staged until late July and early August of 2002. The planned scenario was this: there is an actively anti-American rogue military commander in charge of a military force somewhere in the Persian Gulf. He has broken away from his government, yet he has military support and threatens to drag the entire Middle East into a conflict. Among his supporters are many ethnic and religious extremists who are loyal to him and four terrorist organizations he is sponsoring and supplying.

The Pentagon settled on Paul Van Riper, a retired Marine with much command experience in Vietnam, to assume the part of the rogue commander. Van Riper was a soldier's soldier. He believed that battlefields were chaotic and foggy, obscured in emotion, smoke and chaos. He had come to this belief through his combat experience in Vietnam, where he was ruthless and tended to lead his men from the front rather than the back of the action. As an old-style warrior he was no longer in step with modern warfare. Yet he was a brilliant battlefield tactician. He seemed to be instinctively able to make good calls during the chaos of battle. So he seemed an ideal rogue commander to lead what were called the Red force against the modern, computer-equipped, technology- and information-heavy Blue force.

The Blue force was under the command of the Joint Forces Command (JFCOM). JFCOM was a military think tank, and their planning had been responsible for the shattering and rapid defeat of Iraq during the Iraq war of 1991—Operation Desert Storm. Technology was one of their main weapons. So, the Blue forces, under the watchful eye of JFCOM personnel, developed countercommunication technology to intercept and, when they wanted, to disrupt the communication of the Red forces. They also had developed the capabilities to take out the power grids of the opponent. Propaganda in information technology could be used to sew confusion and lower morale in the opponent's social-support network. Technology could be used to plan strategies to gain and use information. In fact, a massive array of dedicated and linked computers could connect with databases all over the world, and could crunch massive amounts of data. Within a matter of hours, scenarios of the entire environment of the Red team could be analyzed. It had become clear that modern warfare involved not only military actions but also political, social and cultural aspects, and the Blue team had that information locked and loaded.

They used what was called the Operational Net Assessment, a formal decision-making tool that analyzed separate systems of the enemy—military, economic, social and political. It created an interrelated matrix in which a computer assessment was made of the enemy areas that were most vulnerable to attack. Another tool at their disposal was the Common Relevant Operational Picture (CROP), which was a comprehensive map of the combat in real time. To keep the Blue team from getting stuck "in the box," they also had a tool called the Effects-Based Operations, which helped them think beyond simply identifying and destroying assets of the enemy, but to think broader about what the economic, social and political effects of various actions were. The

Blue forces were information rich. If a simple commander's view of the battlefield were a dollar, the Blue forces had the wealth of Bill Gates.

It's late July or August in Suffolk, Virginia. It's hot and muggy outside, much like it could be in the Middle East in spring or fall. The games were simulated from two war rooms at JFCON headquarters in Suffolk. *Simulated* is probably not the best word to describe the experience. There was great attention to detail, and sometimes when actions were ordered in the war room, actual exercises were carried out and sometimes videoed back to the war room. The Red and Blue forces literally couldn't tell what was real and what wasn't. It all seemed to be a real-time, actual battle.

Van Riper had at his disposal, relative to the Gates fortune, the informational wealth of a local business. He believed, like Napoleon wrote long ago, "a general never knows with certainty, never sees his enemy clearly, and never knows positively where he is." To the contrary, Van Riper was up against a Blue force whose brains were enhanced with the biggest and most sophisticated hardware and software in the world, whose electronics could see through the fog, mist and emotion that shrouds a battlefield, and whose geopositioning equipment lets it know exactly where every ship, every commander and almost every soldier is at every moment. Van Riper looks like he's going down in record time.

Let the games begin. On the first day of combat, the Blue forces dumped tens of thousands of troops into the Gulf. Even having home-field advantage, the Red forces' chances of combating the superbly equipped Blue forces was inconceivable. The Blue forces rallied an aircraft carrier battle group and deployed it offshore near the rogue commander's base. And not just one carrier—a fearsome war machine in itself—but a battle group. The firepower that could be directed to destroy the Red forces' base was almost inconceivable. With that show of force the Blue team issued an ultimatum—surrender or else. Any sane person would surrender. After all, the Operational Net Assessment had doled out all of the options for attack. The CROP had analyzed all of the Red forces' options for defense. Fighting the Blue forces was, in a word, inconceivable.

If you've seen *The Princess Bride*, based on the book ostensibly written by S. Morgenstern (but really written by William Goldman), I'm sure you see where I'm headed. You'll recognize Inigo Montoya's response to the Sicilian, Vizzini, who also kept using the word *inconceivable*. Inigo said, "I don't think that word means what you think it means."

Van Riper refused to surrender. The Blue forces did what they had planned. They knocked out the microwave towers and cut Van Riper's fiber-optics lines rendering land-line communication inconceivable. That forced the Red forces to use satellite and cell-phone communications, which could easily be intercepted through Blue forces' superiority in electronics.

Van Riper was not impressed. "Who would use cell phones and satellites after what happened to Osama bin Laden in Afghanistan?" Instead, Van Riper communicated by couriers on motorcycles. They used messages smuggled in written prayers. They avoided radio chatter between pilots and control towers, and instead used blinking lights as had been used to send messages in World War II.

The Blue forces must have thought, *This isn't going like we thought it would*. Then, they must have said to each other, like Butch and Sundance being pursued relentlessly by an expert tracker and lawman in the movie *Butch Cassidy and the Sundance Kid*, "Who *are* those guys?"

The huge Blue forces expected to be kowtowed to. Instead, Van Riper attacked. It began harmlessly enough. On the second day of hostilities, Van Riper launched a fleet of small boats to dog the aircraft carriers, cruisers and other large ships. Suddenly, Van Riper launched cruise missile attacks on some of the ships. Instead of shooting a few at each ship, which could have been easily handled by the sophisticated antimissile technology of the naval vessels, Van Riper, having done his homework, launched more missiles at fewer ships, shooting from land, sea and air simultaneously. "We probably got about half of their ships," he said.[6] And he got the big ones—one carrier, the biggest cruisers and five of the six amphibious ships. Inconceivable.

A Tasteful Study of Thin Slicing and Jam

With this anecdote about Van Riper, Gladwell showed that not all information is good information. In fact, too much information can slow down decision making or hang it up in perpetual analysis. My bet is that most of us would have chosen the Blue forces as the likely victor in this clash. But we would have been wrong. Common sense tells us that huge amounts of information is advantageous. But actual behavior often fools us.

Take the study done by psychological scientist Sheena Iyengar.[7] She invited shoppers to taste exotic jellies and jams in a hoity-toity grocery store in Menlo Park, California. Sometimes the booth had many choices, sometimes only a few. Of course, in the United States—and throughout much of the world—the consumer mentality says that people want more rather than fewer choices. Iyengar found, however, that when the booth had twenty-four jams to taste, only 3 percent of the tasters bought jam. But when only six choices were available, 30 percent bought jam. This isn't a difference of two or three purchases, which would be, as psychologists say, significant at the .05 level (but often practically not all that impressive). It's a tenfold difference. Perhaps you might have guessed that the six choices would outperform the thirty. (After all, this is a section on "too much information.") But did you see the tenfold difference coming? I never would have.

The point is not that too much information interferes with good decision making. Rather, though we often think we understand human nature, when we actually study it, it surprises us. Armed with a rich history of interpersonal interaction throughout our lives, with the wisdom of the ages transmitted in history and literature, and with a careful reading of Scripture and of theologians' reflections on Scripture, we still often cannot predict accurately how people will act. We need to put it to a controlled, psychological, scientific test.

What We Think Leads to a Good Decision Often Doesn't

Let me take yet another psychological study that has some surprising results tucked in among the validating results. Samuel Gosling and his colleagues wanted to find out how we judge people's personalities.[8] This might come in handy, of course, in picking trustworthy friends, selecting someone to date or marry, or hiring the best candidate for a job.

Gosling (and his team) found eighty college students, whom I'll call target people, and gave them each a questionnaire using an assessment of the Big Five personality factors. These five factors are the crunched-down essence of an unbelievable host of personality-assessment instruments. The factors are easy to remember because they can be represented by the acrostic OCEAN. O = openness to experience. This factor represents creativity, open-mindedness and (lack of) conformity to authority. C = conscientiousness. Conscientiousness is how responsible one is and how much one follows through in an organized and thorough way. E = extroversion-introversion. Extroverts are sociable and outgoing. They tend to be energized by lots of personal interaction. Introverts are loners, and when they must interact socially, they feel drained. A = agreeableness. These people are not easily upset, and they tend to get along with people. They are helpful, and it takes a lot to make them angry. N = neuroticism, which is an outmoded term only used because it has been historically used. This factor is really better captured by the term *emotional reactivity*. An emotionally reactive person is easily upset, and might respond with strong, negative emotion to an unpleasant happening. So, Gosling and his team gave the Big Five to the eighty students and developed a good understanding of the students' self-report of their behavior, which was expected to characterize them across many situations and over time.

Can friends predict their buddy's scores? Next the researchers recruited close friends of the eighty target people. Each friend completed the Big Five as he or she thought the target person would complete it. The results were not surprising. The friends could predict the responses of the target person quite accurately.

How about randomly selected strangers? Next, the researchers recruited eighty randomly selected college students who did not know the target. The strangers were armed with the Big Five and told that they were to complete it on a person they had never met. They were given access to the target's dormitory room *for only fifteen minutes.* Who was able to predict the target's behavior better—friends who really knew the target in lots of situations, or strangers with fifteen minutes to look around a dorm room?

Making your prediction. As a snap judgment, most of us probably think that friends ought to know their friend's personality better than strangers, no matter how long the stranger spent in the dorm room. However, my bet is that you are too clever to fall for that snap judgment. It might actually be correct, but you are probably thinking that the results show something surprising. (You've seen the way I've approached this topic thus far.) Before I tell you the results of the experiment, please write down your predictions. Compare whether friends could predict the target person's personality much better, better, equally, worse or much worse than could the stranger. Take each personality trait in turn: OCEAN. Make your predictions on table 1.1.

Table 1.1. Predicting Personality by Friends or Strangers in a Dorm Room

Trait	Write Your Prediction Here (friends relative to dorm-room observers: Much Better, Better, Equal, Worse, Much Worse)	Outcome (will be revealed below)
O = Openness to Experience		
C = Conscientiousness		
E = Extroversion or Introversion		
A = Agreeableness		
N = Neuroticism (Emotional Reactivity)		

Strangers were much better at predicting openness to experience than were close friends. Friends hang with each other in predictable situations. Part of being a friend is learning how the other person is likely to react in those situations. Friends don't often look for new situations, new ideas or new experiences. They enjoy the familiar ones. But dorm rooms are a repository of information about how many experiences people seem open to. Does the room tell a story of a person who lives each day as the same old, same old? Or are there a variety of books, music choices, videos? Do tennis racquets lurk in the corner of the room beside the violin? Do French impressionist prints snuggle comfortably next to Kandinsky, a picture of Marilyn Monroe and another of Barack Obama? It seems obvious, thinking back on it, that the dorm snoopers ought to be able to discern the person's openness to experiences better than close friends. But did it seem that way when you were predicting?

Strangers were also much more accurate at predicting the person's conscientiousness. This makes perfect sense now that we think about it. We don't often get to see how well our friends handle responsibilities and even how conscientiously they clean and care for their personal space. That is precisely what a dorm room might be expected to reveal.

Friends were much better at determining how extroverted or introverted their close friend is. Friends share lots of social situations with each other, and they observe whether friends are outgoing and energized by social interaction or whether friends struggle to get through social interactions and are drained by acting socially. Most people also spend time alone, coacting with others, and in intimate situations with others. The signs left around a dorm room wouldn't reveal much about whether such interactions were energizing or draining. But friends know.

Friends were slightly better than strangers at predicting agreeableness. Close friends have some sense of how agreeable their friend is. But actually friends mostly hang out in a limited number of situations, and friends by their nature like each other and tend to be agreeable with each other simply because they are friends. Close friends usually don't get to see how cross a friend is with the mechanic who takes too long, with someone who cuts him or her off in traffic, with teachers who drone on and on in lectures or give hard tests, with parents who are too distant or too intrusive. But sometimes the evidence of such interactions can seep into the dorm room through notes written in margins of class notes, piles of papers strewn about angrily, or e-mail or letters home.

Strangers were much more accurate at predicting the person's neuroticism, or emotional reactivity. People leave lots of evidence of emotional reactivity around. Journals chronicle ups and downs. Party memorabilia describes times of ecstasy. Wadded up or crushed printed e-mails reveal anger. Slashes of color, red marks and hostile notes reveal anger, depression and anxiety.

How did you do? Check yourself out against table 1.2 below.

Table 1.2. Results from Predicting Personality by Friends or Strangers in a Dorm Room

Trait	Prediction	Outcome
O = Openness to Experience		Strangers >> Friends
C = Conscientiousness		Strangers >> Friends
E = Extroversion or Introversion		Friends >> Strangers
A = Agreeableness		Friends > Strangers
N = Neuroticism (Emotional Reactivity)		Strangers >> Friends

The conclusion from the data is shocking. Strangers, by observing the living space of a person, come to know more accurately how the person will describe his or her own personality than do people who have had a long-time and close friendship with the person.

Looking in Reverse

In a way, my point is this. We each came at this task with a thorough background in human relations. We have a lifetime of experience with people. We have heard countless hours of talking heads commenting on the whys and wherefores of the psychology of behavior. We have heard numerous people talking about Freudian theory. We have perhaps taken a psychology course and read accounts of lots of psychological studies. We are also familiar with Scripture. We know what it says about human nature and why people behave the way they do. Yet, armed with all of this book-learning and practical knowledge, we still might not have been good at predicting this study. After I revealed the study's results, however, it's a different ball game.

After hearing the results, it all makes sense. Of course, most things make sense in hindsight. Predicting whether a person will accept a date with us is anxiety producing. After the person has made the decision, we see signs that had pointed to the outcome all along. One thing that psychology clearly shows us is that we aren't so good at making predictions—which is, after all, what often really counts in life. But we are great at formulating post-hoc explanations about events, because we really want to believe that life makes sense. So, we construct a rational account to make it make sense.

Job Interviews

Earlier, I mentioned that we might want to know the best information to look for if we were doing job interviews. At this point we ought to be skeptical that job interviews are necessarily the best way to select someone to hire. If close friends can't predict behavior better than a stranger armed with a clipboard and fifteen minutes in a person's dorm room, what does this say for the job interview? Job candidates typically put on their best behavior and give all the right answers at interviews. Of course, if they fail to show social intelligence—like belching and telling dirty jokes, or talking about their previous job in which they were fired for beating up the job supervisor, stalking the CEO and threatening their coworkers with violence—that certainly makes our decision easier. But how much can we trust the typical job interview?

Interviewer: Why do you want to work here?

Applicant: This company has a reputation as the best place to work in the United States, and it has always been my dream—since entering high school—to work here.

Interviewer: Tell me your greatest weakness.

Applicant: That's a tough one. I'd say, um, it's that I spend way too much time at work doing extra tasks on every job assigned. That means my life is simply not balanced. Besides having a rich life as a community volunteer and building houses for Habitat and feeding the poor, I also compete in triathalons, have a wonderful marriage and too many close friends (for whom I would do anything). But because of my extraordinary dedication to my job (and to this company—did I remember to say that it has an international reputation as the best place to work in the United States—this leaves me no time for watching CNN and completing *War and Peace*, which I've been working through for the past week or so—much to my frustration. Yes, my greatest weakness is definitely working too hard and being too conscientious.

Meanwhile, the savvy interviewer is not listening to much of this predictable impression management. Instead, the interviewer is trying to gauge (1) the personality of the job applicant and (2) the likelihood of success at the job from the answers to those predictable questions. The problem is that all too often the interviewer usually has fixated on the wrong information.

A Picture Is Worth a Thousand Bucks—I Mean Words

We have already seen that personality judgments are difficult at best, even when made by one's closest friends. But note this South African study by Marianne Bertrand, Dean Karlan, Sendhil Mullainathan, Eldar Shafir and Jonathan Zinman,[9] which was reported in Ori Brafman and Rom Brafman's book *Sway: The Irresistible Pull of Irrational Behavior*. A South African bank advertised via letter (junk mail) soliciting potential borrowers. They offered different monthly interest rates from 3.25 percent to 7.75 percent. However, there were some extras included in the letter. Some compared their rates to a competitor. Others offered lottery tickets for a monthly giveaway (e.g., ten cell phones per month). Others had a person's picture in the corner—smiling winsomely.

The results were interesting. Men who received the letter with the face of the smiling woman were, on the average, willing to take out loans at a rate of about 4.5 percent higher than no picture. They paid attention to the seemingly insignificant picture far more than the relevant information.

Now consider judging job competence. The picture is no more encouraging here. Each year, the draft for the NBA garners an amazing amount of attention in the *Richmond Times-Dispatch*. In fact, I understand that those drafts are now televised. (I "understand" this because I don't watch television. I spend all my time doing community service and working for Virginia Commonwealth University, the greatest place to work in the world.)

In fact, economists Barry Staw and Ha Hoang[10] have shown that teams actually don't always pick their players based on the available information. Furthermore, once the player comes to the team, playing time is still influenced by factors that are irrelevant to the player's performance. But more about Staw and Hoang's study in chapter four.

So, what makes for an effective interview? Not the blind-date style interview with predictable questions that help screen out only the most inept. Rather, the best interviews rely on objective data, to the extent it is available. These interviews are used to assess the relevant aspects that might be discernible from the interview. These include: Do you like the person? Does the person get along with team members? Is the person sincere and interpersonally adept? Is the person humble, or will pride and hubris be an issue?

SUMMARY

We have seen that we can learn a lot about people from psychological science—from (1) John Gottman's five-to-one ratio for marital happiness to (2) Paul Van Riper's thin-slicing defeat of the computers and computer jockeys in Gulf war games to (3) Sheena Iyengar's surprising finding that too much information can limit choices, not expand them, to (4) Samuel Gosling and colleagues' study of the prediction of personality by close friends and strangers in dorm rooms to (5) the studies that showed the way we often tune into the wrong facts when we are trying to make important decisions.

Using psychological science also tells us about creation and human nature above and beyond the considerable knowledge we already have. In making the many decisions we must consider in life, we are wise to look to all the sources of information and wisdom we have at our disposal—and this includes both Scripture and psychological science. We ignore either of these sources at our peril.

But perhaps this is preaching to the choir. Perhaps we already are convinced that psychological science is important. But how, we might wonder, does it relate to theology, which uses Scripture as one of its primary sources of data? That is the question we will tackle in chapter two.

2

A TALE OF TWO CITIES

It was the best of times, it was the worst of times.

CHARLES DICKENS, *A TALE OF TWO CITIES*

THERE HAVE BEEN A NUMBER of tales of two cities. The two that come most readily to my mind involve contrasts. In *A Tale of Two Cities*,[1] Charles Dickens compares and contrasts London and Paris, and two protagonists, who are twin brothers.

Another tale of two cities, however, is Augustine's *City of God*,[2] in which the earthly city is set in contrast to the city of God. The occasion for the *City of God* was the sack of Rome in 410. Critics argued that if the Romans had stuck with their many gods, instead of embracing the Christian God, Rome would not have been sacked, which came as the judgment of the gods. Augustine wrote in response to those criticisms. His work suggests that humanity is divided into two cities. One city seeks its happiness and fulfillment in earthly pursuits. And it worships false gods. Virtue, which the Romans so admired, often turned out to be the pursuit of power, the lust for domination, and earthly praise and glory. The other city, the city of God, worships the triune God. Its hope lies not in peace on earth but in eternal life in fellowship with God. At present, argued Augustine, the two cities are without borders and coexist on earth, indistinguishable until the final judgment. Adam's fall set the two cities in motion, and the stain of the consequences of sin has led to the imperfect nature of the world today and the possibility of a future city of God lies only through redemption.

It is impossible to estimate how much influence Augustine's *City of God* has had on Christian life since his time. A characteristic of Augustine is the turn inward. Until Augustine, thinking about Christianity had been mostly about the relationship people had with the church, the sacraments, the teachings of the church leaders and (to a lesser extent) the Scriptures (which were not available to common people). Augustine turned attention toward the heart and its sinfulness, and to the sovereignty of God. And in focusing our attention on the earthly city and the city of God, he dichotomized social life and encouraged people to think about which city each human enterprise was part of. With Augustine's inward focus, the same enterprise could be an activity of the earthly city for one person and an activity of the city of God for another.

For example, Martin Luther thought that political activity for a Christian was separate from the activities of the city of God, but his contemporaries Ulrich Zwingli and John Calvin believed politics should be integrated with Christian activity. Calvin subsequently established in Geneva, Switzerland, perhaps the most intentionally Christian government that has ever existed.

People have brought this same Augustinian mentality to the scientific enterprise. For some, science is alien to the city of God. Following the pathway of science is a sure road to perdition. For others, science is redeemable. If practiced correctly, it can be integrated with Christianity and thus be a part of the city of God.

I advocate the integration of psychology and theology, but my approach differs in some substantial ways from previous writing on this topic.

THE ORIGIN OF THE INTEGRATION DIALOGUE

Origins always present a dilemma. We could see the early Greeks as writing about science and theology if we wished. Certainly, the gods, and how they dealt with nature and with people, were the cause of much of the Greek and Roman literature. Although modern science, per se, did not exist then, one could make a conceptual stretch and liken the study of nature and people to today's natural sciences and psychological sciences. But because they were not writing about Christianity and were not dealing with science as we know it, we will not begin our discussion there.

The Scientific Revolution

During the Renaissance, Galileo, Francis Bacon and Isaac Newton certainly engaged in serious writing about how science and religion intersected.[3] But though they were dealing with early modern science, they also did not study psychology as we understand it today. What they called psychology would not be recognized as such in the profession of psychology today.

The Integration of Psychology and Christianity Begins in the Counseling Room

For most laypeople, the interaction of psychology and Christianity begins in counseling. Christians sometimes worry about the wisdom of receiving counseling from psychotherapists who are not Christians. People who feel vulnerable because they are depressed, anxious or stressed-out are often concerned that secular counseling could undermine aspects of their faith. This concern peaked in the 1960s, which is where our discussion of the integration of psychology and Christianity begins.

The counseling method of Carl Rogers,[4] based on nonjudgmental listening, was occurring simultaneously with the 1960s rejection of a traditional Christian worldview. Vietnam and protests were in the news. Authority, legitimate and illegitimate, was on everyone's mind. Young people of my generation were debating protests, seeking self-imposed exile in Canada to avoid the mandatory draft, joining the military and seeking military deferments. Those were times of intense stress characterized by shame. Protesters of our national policy and priorities were ashamed of the United States. Traditionalists were also ashamed of the open dissent in society and over the flagrant rejection of traditional values. It seemed too that while the rejection of traditional values was to some degree a national phenomenon, the bulk of the rejection of traditional values was among the young and the more highly educated—like university professors, psychologists and counselors. That distrust of secular intellectuals reached deeply into American society, including the church. Is there any surprise that typical

Christians in the pew, who have their share of mental-health problems, look askance at counseling? *Counseling, after all is done by those intellectuals*, they thought at the time. *You can't trust intellectuals.*

In those times when many psychologically vulnerable people felt like they had lost their mooring, they unfortunately saw the mainline church to espouse an almost anything-goes approach to Christian belief, which had arisen from over one hundred years of intellectually driven German biblical criticism. Christians who were troubled psychologically couldn't find an anchor in society. *The only anchor available is Jesus Christ himself*, most thought. Spiritually that could not be better. It showed our permanent need to depend on Jesus alone. But in other ways the metanarrative that most people heard throughout the 1960s was that life is not stable, and we must have some stability. Shaky foundations lead to strident demands for *some* stability.

The Christian community cried out for explicitly Christian counseling that was centered on biblically consistent beliefs and values— traditional theology that one could count on—and on counselors who took Jesus Christ seriously, prayed in sessions, spoke openly about spiritual concerns and assigned homework centered in stable truth, the Bible. In the 1970s, Christian psychotherapists who had been trained in secular clinical psychology responded. Several suggested ways to integrate clinical psychological theories with a generally Reformed Christian theological worldview. (*Reformed* here means some variant of Calvinistic conservative theology—not reformed traditions of worship.) These clinical psychologists became the early integrationists.

Most of the Early Integrationists Held to Reformed Theologies

In the late 1960s and through the 1970s, the theology of most of the psychologists who began the integration movement derived from Calvinistic, Evangelical Free Church or Baptist Reformed theologies, or conservative theologies within mainline Protestant churches. Pioneers included trailblazers Clyde Narramore, Bruce Narramore, Paul Tournier, Gary Collins, James Dobson and others. These writers were mostly concerned with how counseling might occur if a counselor had an integrated conservative Christian theology and psychology.[5]

Mostly, the clinical psychology of early integrationists held a traditional Christian view of people derived largely from their religious framework. However, because there were no explicitly Christian training programs for Christian psychotherapists, when they formulated their *counseling* theories, most adapted the secular psychotherapy theory in which they had received their training. For example, Freud's theories formed the basis of the integrations proposed by Clyde Narramore and later Bruce Narramore. However, other theories were also influential. Existential theory was integrated with Christianity in Paul Tournier's and Gary Collins's writings. Carl Rogers's listening skills and basic humanism (using the word not as a secular philosophy but as a value for human individuals) were included across the board. James Dobson even used many behavioral psychotherapeutic methods.

Filter Theories

What drove all of these theorists of psychotherapy—or in Dobson's case, popular applied counseling—were implicit or explicit filter theories. The religious tradition was the mold, and the secular theory of psychotherapy was fit into it. Theorists tried to knock off some offensive edges of their secular counseling theory so that a biblically consistent theory of Christian counseling remained. I call this a filter theory (even though there are many variants) because the secular counseling theory is essentially poured through a theological filter. Psychologist James Beck and professor of Christian formation Bruce Demarest, both of Denver Seminary, wrote one of the better integrative books on human nature.[6] They tackled four topics—(1) origin and destiny, (2) substance and identity, (3) function and behavior, and (4) human relationships and community—with an approach respectful of the theological and psychological disciplines. In their book Demarest first wrote about theology, then Beck covered modern psychology. Finally, they jointly constructed an integrative chapter on the areas of agreement and departure about an integrated theory of human nature. In the final chapter, they say,

> The principal sources of information concerning the human person can
> be represented by three concentric circles: authoritative Scripture being

the inner circle, voices from the Christian past the middle circle, and the social sciences, including psychology, the outer circle, as below. (See figure 2.1, reproduced from Beck and Demarest, 2005, p. 397.)[7]

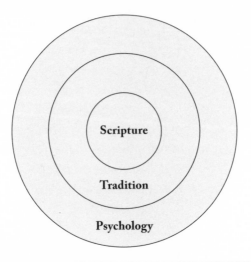

Figure 2.1. Sources of information about the person

Often the sources of information about God and creation have been called God's special revelation (taken to be Jesus and Scripture) and God's general revelation (taken to be what God revealed through creation). Beck and Demarest explain their privileging of Scripture over psychology using various arguments. But they come back to one argument several times.

> The following caution must be noted with respect to natural, or general, revelation's contribution to our knowledge of the human person, particularly its nature and destiny. The truth content mediated by general revelation proves less perspicuous in these regards than the truth content mediated by special revelation. Thus disciplines that build largely on the former are exposed to varying degree of error. The Swiss theologian Emil Brunner offers a helpful insight here in his "law of closeness of relations," which states: "The nearer anything lies to . . . man's relation to God and the being of the person, the greater the disturbance of rational knowledge due to sin; the further away anything lies from this center, the less is the disturbance felt, and the less difference is there

between knowing as a believer or as an unbeliever." The principle inherent in Brunner's law infers that disciplines such as psychology and philosophy—that deal with the core issues of the human person—contain insightful truths mixed with misjudgments or errors. This means that the pronouncements of these disciplines must be carefully evaluated in the light of authoritative Scripture insofar as it addresses such issues. Our task as responsible investigators is to welcome all that is true in psychology (or any other discipline) while rejecting what is inconsistent with biblical teaching.[8]

There was a prominent voice shouting in opposition to such filter theories. Jay Adams, of Westminster Theological Seminary, had written a number of books that adamantly denied the worth of psychology.[9] This is ironic because when we examine his *Christian Counselor's Manual*,[10] which I happen to think was the best practical Christian counseling book of the 1970s, it is clearly behavioral. While Adams's practice seemed to be based on a filter model, his writing and preaching railed against it.

Larry Crabb's writing hit the scene in the mid-1970s.[11] Although Crabb's early theology was in many ways similar to some of Adams's, Crabb was not a separatist like Adams. Crabb was trained in a secular cognitive-behavioral program in clinical psychology at the University of Illinois. Cognitive-behavior therapy was just becoming influential in secular psychology. Popular evangelical approaches to theology, such as Francis Schaeffer's (1990) influential writings in the 1970s,[12] were easily reconciled with cognitive-behavioral approaches to psychology. Both were heavily rational. Crabb's writings spawned a variety of therapists writing Christian theories from cognitive or cognitive-behavioral points of view.[13]

Crabb[14] suggested a four-category system (see table 2.1) for the integration of clinical psychology and Christianity. First, the *separate but equal* approach represents those who believe that spiritual and theological levels of analysis, which are based on Scripture, are separate from psychological and counseling levels of analysis. Second, the *tossed salad* approach advocates drawing willy-nilly from both theology and psychology, with expediency as the guiding rule. Crabb cautioned that this can result in contradictory propositions within a belief system or in practice. In fact, he argued that the philosophy of materialism and other beliefs within psychology that exclude God will inevitably cause internal conflict within a tossed-salad model. Third, the *nothing buttery* approach teaches that psychology is secular and impure, and is best ignored altogether by Christian practitioners. Because God can handle all problems, psychology is seen as irrelevant, unneeded and a source of error. Nothing but Scripture is needed. Crabb spoke against this approach, arguing that the power of God can be manifest even if one accepts psychology. (On the other side, some secularists also advocated nothing buttery, claiming there is no room for God within psychology.) Finally, *spoiling the Egyptians* (reminiscent of book 10 of Augustine's *Confessions*) suggests that Scripture should be the primary evaluative standard against which psychological findings are measured. True integration occurs, say the adherents of spoiling the Egyptians, only when we incorporate psychology that is consistent with biblical teaching and principles—a filter model.

Table 2.1. Larry Crabb's Categories Regarding God's Special Revelation and God's General Revelation as Reflected in Psychotherapy

Separate but equal	Psychotherapists treat psychology as authoritative in secular matters, but Scripture is authoritative for religious matters. The two are not seen to mix.
Tossed salad	Psychotherapists draw relevant information from both Scripture and psychotherapy without privileging either.
Nothing buttery	Psychotherapists, especially those who treat Christians, are urged to draw all principles of helping from Scripture alone. A similar approach would involve secular psychotherapists who do not draw any helping principles from Scripture.
Spoiling the Egyptians	Psychotherapists employ a filter model, using Scripture to filter and reflect which parts of secular psychology that are taken to be valid.

In a landmark book on the integration of Christianity and psychotherapy, John Carter and Bruce Narramore[15] presented a model similar to Crabb's but more reminiscent of H. Richard Niebuhr's writing *Christ and Culture*.[16] They endorsed an "integrates" model—another filter model similar to Crabb's "spoiling the Egyptians"—in contrast to Crabb's three alternate models, which they reject. The "against" model views Christianity and psychology as incompatible and in conflict. The "of" model secularizes biblical propositions, reducing the supernatural to naturalistic and materialistic causes. The "parallels" model recognizes both psychology and Christian theology as legitimate but makes no attempt to integrate them.

Newest Voices in Integration

Robert C. Roberts. In recent years, other opponents of integration have emerged. Robert C. Roberts is a philosopher from Baylor University who takes a uniquely philosophical approach to integration.[17] He begins by describing psychology as not involving data at all. Data, he argues, flying randomly at us like confetti on a ticker-tape parade, would have no more effect on us than the confetti does. Rather, data comes at us organized. It might be loosely organized, such as a general approach to a science (e.g., a materialistic worldview) or as a theory that embodies assumptions about human nature, personality and reality (e.g., Freud's theory or cognitive theory). Or it might be tightly organized (e.g., Antonio Damasio's theory[18] of embodied emotion). Because the science is in essence a worldview, then it can be examined as an explanatory worldview against other philosophical and theological worldviews. It should then yield to philosophical or theological analysis. (I must say, while philosophers and theologians might put stock in that analysis, not many psychological scientists would. This approach is basically philosophical, not psychological.)

Eric L. Johnson. Recently, in *Foundations for Soul Care: A Christian Psychology Proposal,* Eric L. Johnson[19] has described what he calls a Christian psychology. Johnson's approach is aimed at remaking psychology to accept Christian theorizing. We might see his effort as taking Roberts's approach more into psychological science. Roberts aims mostly at personality and clinical psychology, but Johnson's approach, still largely concerned with counseling, is broader and *could* include psychological science. Johnson insists, however, that Christian theological worldviews be put forth to understand the data of psychology.

While I believe this approach would be wonderful for journals like the *Journal of Psychology and Christianity* and the *Journal of Psychology and Theology*, which accept Christianity, I fear that his proposal will have no hearing in mainstream psychology—either clinical or psychological science. It would, I believe, be flatly rejected. And even if it were to be accepted, it would marginalize Christian psychology, taking it out of the mainstream and creating Christian psychology backwaters in which it would float inertly.

David Powlison. David Powlison[20] has taken up the mantle of Jay Adams, but has carried it to a far more sophisticated position. Adams was the radical proponent of the "nothing-buttery" approach, as it was characterized by Crabb.[21] Powlison does not argue that psychology is worthless. He notes many worthwhile uses. In an article in *Comment* magazine, Powlison says, "Research is the part of psychology that intuitively seems the most objective, the most neutral and the most scientific. . . . There is no doubt that scientific methods have reaped an incalculable store of facts, findings, information and correlations."[22] However, he continues to emphasize the primacy of Christian Scripture as the lens through which we should understand psychology—not through psychological theoretical lenses such as evolutionary psychology. God, who knows people the best (perfectly, in fact), gave us Scripture to richly portray human experience. The Bible seeks to help us develop "a transformed orientation and transformed intentions."[23] Its revelations about people are secondary. "We might say," says Powlison, "that the psychological riches revealed are 'by the way,' a secondary spin-off from primary purposes."[24]

Psychological science can provide a massive data base about human nature—which is often organized according to a conceptualization that emphasizes an interaction between nature (e.g., the neurobiological, genetic, physiological and developmental aspects of our bodies) and nurture (e.g., the child-rearing environment we grew up in, our current situation and its triggers and pressures, and dispositional learned characteristics). It is important that we think theologically about data (including critiquing psychological theories and conceptualizations), cautions Powlison. And when we do, the individual person enters the equation. "The human factor is a decisive element in the complex of final causation," he says, making his main point. "Nature and nurture significantly influence and constrain, but they don't finally explain. In an essential way, why you do what you do always comes down to *you*."[25]

We will come back to this point later when we discuss some of the research of Daniel Gilbert (see pp. 66-71). For now, though, let's look at one thing Powlison is claiming. He suggests that Scripture should be used as a filter through which psychological data and theory must pass to be considered consistent with Christianity. This filter model has generally been the argument posed by most integrationists—myself included (see Worthington[26]) through the history of the movement.

Psychologists in the Broader Field of Science and Religion

The integration approach between psychology and Christianity must be seen in its proper perspective as part of the relationship between science and religion in general. Voices from psychological science have been underrepresented in those discussions, and when they have appeared, they don't cross-reference people in the integration movement that I have already discussed.

There were early appearances of experimental psychologists in the debates and discussions about science and religion. The prestigious Gifford Lectures have addressed *natural theology* or *natural law* each year from one or more of four venues in Scotland—Universities of St. Andrews, Glasgow, Edinburgh and Aberdeen—since 1888-1889. (Natural theology or natural law is the idea that we can learn about God or God's laws from observing nature.) The 220-plus lectures boast several psychologists among their distinguished lecturers, including William James[27] (in what became *The Varieties of Religious Experience*), arch-behaviorist John Watson[28] (proponent of classical conditioning) and John Dewey[29] (psychologist and educational philosopher).

A few psychologists have written about psychological science and religion. These include, foremost, Malcolm Jeeves, honorary research professor at the prestigious St. Andrews School of Psychology. David G. Myers, psychologist at Hope College, has written solo works and other works jointly with Jeeves. Also important is Professor Fraser Watts, who is at Cambridge University.

Malcolm Jeeves. Malcolm Jeeves[30] began writing about Christianity and science in 1968, *The Scientific Enterprise and Christian Faith.* He continues to address contemporary issues in their overlap (see *From Cells to Souls—And Beyond,* 2003). Jeeves has consistently written that psychology and Christianity are different ways to explain reality. This is what Baylor philosopher Steven Evans calls the *perspectivalist* view.[31] That is, science and religion have different perspectives on truth, agendas, goals and objectives, data, and methods. Thus, we must treat each from its own perspective. Sometimes this is called the levels-of-explanation model. The models of science and religion are thought to be linked at some places, and to ask different questions at others. But they seek to provide answers to different levels of questions. To oversimplify, religion asks and answers *why* questions, and science asks and answers *how* questions.

In *Human Nature at the Millennium,* Jeeves asks whether Christians and non-Christians might expect a different scientific understanding of brain physiology or developmental psychology. He answers that the theories should be the same. Beliefs should not intrude into the scientific theories in those areas. On the other hand, in personality theory and psychotherapy, Jeeves thinks that it is not as easy to keep the Christian and scientific content apart. People-studying-people is categorically different from people-studying-things. People have presuppositions that often affect the way they understand human nature. This is especially true when people are explicitly trying to influence others, as in psychotherapy, or are trying to measure more subjective aspects of a person, as in personality.

Jeeves has been an arch-foe of reductionism. He has championed a view of people as having a physical presence that undergirds but does not determine personal characteristics like beliefs, values and experiences in consciousness. People's subjective experiences are linked to their bodies, but are not determined by them. People's experiences, especially mental experiences, exist on multiple levels. Both bottom-up and top-down causality exist. Different properties are evident at different levels of analysis.

David G. Myers. David Myers[32] is the author of the all-time best-seller *Introduction to Psychology.* He also is a prolific writer within positive psychology, examining happiness and well-being. He has been involved throughout his career in giving psychology away to the masses, and his publication efforts have reflected that stance. Myers strongly believes that psychology uncovers true aspects of human nature. He has worked hard to show that such findings can fit within and contribute to Reformed theology and personal Christian faith. Myers articulates a levels-of-explanation view that gives more weight and attention to scientific psychology than to the theological side of integration. He argues that psychology and theology share "humility before nature and skepticism of human presumptions."[33] He suggests that psychological science is uncovering lawful principles that we must use continually to reform our understanding of theology. He is strongly committed to the position that we must follow the data of psychology and, if it warrants, allow the data to correct points of theology. At a minimum he expects that data should correct the attitudes and behaviors that people derive from their theology. This viewpoint asserts that theology contributes its understandings of human life at one level, and that psychological science contributes its perspectives at a different level. Myers urges a reevaluation of our theological and biblical understandings if a seeming contradiction emerges. He cites numerous times how the church erred in its understanding of scientific matters and the frequency it has had to retract its understanding of the Bible in the face of overwhelming evidence to the contrary.

Fraser Watts. Fraser Watts[34] is a distinguished cognitive neuroscientist who is also ordained and trained in theology. He holds the prestigious endowed Starbridge Lectureship in the divinity faculty at the University of Cambridge. He has written steadily on psychology and Christianity (and more generally science and religion) for nearly the past twenty years. In the introductory chapter of *Science Meets Faith,* Watts outlines his position on the dialogue between science and faith. He describes common misconceptions that there were substantive philosophical and historical conflicts between science and faith. He suggests that the substantive conflict is not that science and religion give different answers to the same questions, but they give different answers to different questions. The philosophical conflicts have often arisen due to extreme positions in religion (like fundamentalist assumptions about separating faith and the world) and in science (like scientists who hold materialist and positivist assumptions). Watts suggests that rationality and empirical evidence play a part in both religion and science, but only up to a point. At that point there are differences in perspectives between the two disciplines.

Finally, Watts traces the history of the relationship between science and religion, and finds little evidence for a prolonged history of conflict but finds no more evidence for a prolonged history of mutual support— though there have been periods of each. Instead, most scientists and theologians, he argues, try to keep the domains independent of each other as much as possible. However, both science and theology are concerned with truth (although different kinds of truth) and with explaining life. Inevitably, then, the disciplines cannot be kept completely separate. He argues that for mutual benefit, the disciplines must stay in contact and conversation with each other. Watts describes faith as fundamentally a matter of personal commitment, even though it can mount a rationally supported view of the world. Knowledge of God comes through God's revelation to people, and Watts distrusts scientific efforts to provide knowledge of God. "Knowledge of God," he says, "is not based on observation in the same way as the conclusions of natural science, though it can be expected to be consistent with observational knowledge."[35]

In *The Psychology of Religious Knowing*, Watts describes different ways of knowing. He likens religious knowing in many ways to knowing in a psychotherapeutic relationship. These positions seem to capture Watts's general approach between science and religion. They are different but related perspectives on similar but not identical phenomena.

CAN PSYCHOLOGICAL SCIENCE CONTRIBUTE
TO THE FIELD OF SCIENCE AND RELIGION?

I think modern psychological science can add to the discussions among scientists, theologians and people of faith. John Polkinghorne,[36] eminent physicist, ordained clergyman and Cambridge professor, has described scientific approaches in general as being like theology. Both disciplines search for truth. Both disciplines use inference from their different data to draw conclusions. However, Polkinghorne argues, science is different from theology in that there is a cumulative quality to physics, natural sciences and the life sciences that is not true with theology. Namely, science tends to invade an area and map it out, "conquering" and "understanding" it. Once science has understood the area, it turns its attention to new areas along its boundaries.

Theology is not cumulative in the same way as science. Theologians rarely settle more integrative issues once and for all. The same fundamental human-God issues keep coming up as the centuries pass. Thus, the theology of Augustine stands shoulder to shoulder with that of Thomas Aquinas, Karl Barth, C. S. Lewis and Francis Schaeffer. There is no reason to presuppose that Augustine's theology is inferior to Aquinas's merely because he wrote earlier. The arts and humanities speak to different contexts in time and space, and are thus more contextualized than is science. "Different generations gain different forms of spiritual insight, and we have to be humble enough to be willing to apprentice ourselves to the past in a manner that is not necessary in science."[37]

Psychology straddles several disciplines. It is a science by employing the scientific method and embracing scientific values. But it is contextualized. People are partly a product of culture, and culture changes over time. Thus, the way people act and think and behave changes over time. In a way, psychological science is positioned so that it might bridge a gap between the sciences and theology.

SUMMARY

I began this chapter examining the relationship (or not) between the city of God and the earthly city. Whereas some people would like to equate theology with the city of God and psychology with the earthly city, I cannot buy into that metaphor. The two cities of science and theology—or in our case, psychological science and Christian theology—are interrelated. Psychological science can be a valid avenue to learning more about God and knowing God better, but it needs to be used properly. (Conversely, although it is not my focus in this book, Christian theology can aid psychological scientists in knowing more about people.) For psychological science to tell us validly about God and help us know God, we must use psychological science in combination with theology and recognize that both disciplines have enough weaknesses and impurities to raise the necessity of humility in deciding how the two fit together.

I keep using the term "psychological science," because I believe that to learn about human nature from psychology, we are wise to draw more from psychological science than psychotherapy. While psychotherapy is a valuable tool for what is sometimes called soul care, it is not as good for revealing human nature as is psychological science. Finally, we will never be certain about the truth of the outcome of integrating faith and science. But uncertainty does not prevent us from making judgments and analyses. However, we must accept them only tentatively and with humility.

When incongruities arise in the conversation between psychological science and Christian theology—as they inevitably must—we can resolve some simply by checking for discord against Scripture as we understand it. But for some disagreements arising from different findings in theology and psychological science, we must pursue two-sided conversations to try to resolve the discord. We are going to have uncertainties as we try to decide whether to believe a theologian who says one thing or a scientist who says its opposite. Whom do we trust? What can we be sure of? These are some of the questions I will address in chapter three.

3

WHAT INFORMATION CAN I TRUST?

WE HEAR ABOUT TRAUMA DAILY. Soldiers on long deployments face loss of life and limb or brain damage from exploding homemade bombs. Then, upon returning home for a few months, they are sent back into the fray. Natural disasters like Hurricane Katrina devastated New Orleans and the Louisiana and Mississippi coasts, traumatizing hundreds of thousands. The attack on the twin towers in New York City traumatized millions of New York residents, and perhaps the country, if not world. *Who is safe*, we think, *if New York City can be attacked and the subways and buses of London bombed?* It seems our threat level is permanently orange.

I begin this chapter by talking about people's reactions to trauma— something most of us believe we understand. But as I'll show, we do not necessarily observe in real life all of the things that seem to make a lot of sense as we reason about them. What "makes sense" to us does not always turn out to be true. With this chapter, I am laying the groundwork to suggest that relying on scientific studies of people's psychology may be more reliable than relying on some of the observations of psychotherapists, who seem to have much experience in how people act. But first, let's look at trauma.

TRAUMA

What Is Trauma?

Potentially traumatic events threaten people's existence or identity. People who experience traumatic events will sometimes develop post-traumatic stress disorder (PTSD). PTSD is characterized by (1) worry,

(2) vivid flashbacks that rehearse the experience, (3) sudden emotional experiences such as depression, anxiety and anger, and (4) attempts to protect oneself from the possibility of future dangerous and existence-threatening experiences. Epidemiological research has shown that the vast majority of adults will be exposed to at least one potentially traumatic event over his or her lifetime. I say *potentially traumatic event* because not everyone reacts with a PTSD response.

Clinical Experiences of and Logical Thinking About Trauma

The clinical wisdom in dealing with trauma has come to us through psychotherapists' experience and observations of traumatized people. Psychotherapy reveals that some events are so shattering to a person's sense of stability and identity, they usually provoke trauma. If they don't, psychotherapists have noted, it is likely because the person is repressing true feelings. (Repression is defensively "forgetting" because feelings are too threatening to deal with consciously.)

Resilience in the face of trauma is rare. Usually, two types of people appear resilient. The very psychologically healthy seem to be truly resilient. But some people are so troubled that they are unable and unwilling to face the trauma.[1] Such psychological defensiveness is due to repression, which is an unconscious defense that can be described as forgetting the incident and then forgetting that one forgot it. Repression leads to a slow adjustment to the trauma, and its symptoms show up as psychological problems in a few (sometimes quite a few) years.

To avoid repression, psychotherapists (or sometimes pastors, friends or family members) need to help people process the trauma. This process is not to be rushed into by stripping away the person's coping defenses without concern for what will happen when the psyche is shorn of protective defenses. Two types of treatment might be needed—first, supportive psychotherapy, and, later, uncovering or interpretive psychotherapy. The psychotherapist must discern the appropriate tact, timing and dosage of interpretations of resistances to help the person progress through the trauma. In general, though, it is probably helpful, early in the aftermath of a trauma, to talk about the experience, which should provide some emotional catharsis (which Freud likened to blowing steam from a kettle to relieve pressure), assuming the therapist is careful not to probe too deeply and set off a second trauma.

Who Wouldn't Be Traumatized by That?

This is the clinical picture. It was formulated by wise clinicians who have treated many people experiencing trauma. So is it a trustworthy picture?

Research gives us a different picture. George Bonanno, a professor of psychology at Teachers College, Columbia University, has investigated potentially traumatic events for over fifteen years.[2] He began this study by reading of the work on resilient or indestructible children. Children of Kauai, Hawaii, for instance, who were in extreme poverty and experienced otherwise potentially harmful events, had been followed by researcher Emmie Werner for over thirty years. She found that many of the children eventually recovered from trauma, and she identified important protective factors associated with resiliency. These included social support, presence of a close mentor relationship and high ego resiliency. Bonanno wondered whether adults who were exposed to potentially traumatic events would also include some who were resilient and others who weren't, and whether he could identify the protective factors that predispose adults for resiliency and PTSD.

In many studies Bonanno and his colleagues identified four prototypical patterns of response to potentially traumatic events. If we were to graph the degree of disruption of normal functioning for two years after an event, we could see how much people are changed by the event. Importantly, we are not choosing a sample of people who are "psychologically healthy" at the time of the event. The sample includes highly functioning and barely functioning people. This is a sample of plain, everyday folks.

Bonanno summarized his findings on a graph (see fig. 3.1).[3] All of the lines jump around a bit due to (1) normal fluctuations in day-to-day functioning at the time various measurements were made and (2) different responses by different people in each group. But there turn out to be four patterns. There are those whose behavior becomes more disrupted after the potentially traumatic event, and it essentially stays *chronically disrupted* for three years. These people represent from 10 to 30 percent of the people, depending on what trauma is being investigated. There is a pattern of *delayed disruption* that occurs in 5 to 10 percent of the people. These people seem to have moderate disruption during the first year. Then at about the start of year two, things become progressively worse. A third group of people—from 15 to 35 percent of the sample—experience a trajectory of *recovery*. They start out with substantially disrupted lives, and they slowly recover. By the end of the first year their disruption has declined to occasional and mild disruption, and by the end of the second year, they are virtually operating at the pre-event level. The fourth group is *resilient*. That is, they respond to the event with mild disruption, but within a few weeks their lives are virtually as they were before the event. This group makes up 35 to 55 percent of the sample! A minimum of one-third of people are resilient on the most difficult and potentially traumatic of events, such as the 9/11 terrorist attacks or being present when a loved one is murdered. Within merely a few weeks they seem to be experiencing normal levels of positive emotions and generative experiences—like engaging

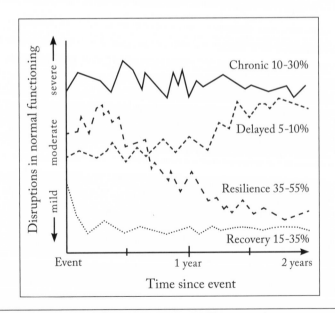

Figure 3.1. Four patterns of response to potentially traumatic events

in new creative activities, seeking new relationships or engaging in new challenges at work.

While it has usually been assumed that the most common response to a potentially traumatic event is eventual recovery—initial disruption followed by a slow recovery over a year or so—this was not in fact the case. In all studies, resilience was more prevalent than recovery. After 9/11, Bonanno, Galea, Bucciarelli and Vlahov[4] conducted a random-digit phone survey of New York City residents. Over 65 percent were considered resilient six months after the attack, and even among the people most centrally involved in the attack (i.e., loss of a close relative or friend, or personal escape from one of the towers), at least 50 percent were resilient.

Of course, it is important to show that findings like this are due to resilience and not to denial or repression. Bonanno and his colleagues[5] have shown in several studies that people were not just denying but were engaged in truly positive behaviors and fulfilling lives. Objective, structured interviews as well as reports of people's close friends and relatives corroborated people's self-reports of good functioning.

A third finding from Bonanno's research program is that there are multiple and sometimes unexpected factors that might promote resilience. These include supportive relationships and personal capacity to adapt flexibly to challenges—no surprises here. But Bonanno, Papa, LaLande, Westphal and Coifman[6] found that the ability to express or suppress emotions when the situation demanded was related to resilience. Note, it isn't just expressing emotion that is cathartic. Resilience required having some ability to discern whether the person needs to express or suppress emotional experiences and expressions, and then to control those emotions as the situation dictates. Remember too that Bonanno doesn't find superhumans to participate in his research. These are folks like you and me who can control their emotions.

Other protective factors that contribute to resilience and recovery include personal *hardiness*. This is a personal characteristic of being committed to finding meaning in life, having some sense of control, and a belief that one can grow from both positive and negative life experiences. In addition, other factors included the trait of *self-enhancement*.

Namely, people who habitually emphasize their strengths tend to do better when they need to exhibit strength. *Repressive copers* also tend to be more resilient. These people try to stifle emotional expression, especially in the presence of others. *Positive emotions* and laughter also help people be resilient or recover fast. When people get into a morbid funk after a potentially traumatic event, it is hard to recover.

It is important to note that in general much of this research has involved relatively discrete and potentially traumatic events, such as disaster, riots, motor accidents, violence, death of a loved one or the like. However, Bonanno finds similar results in dealing with the protracted loss of a chronically ill loved one.

George Bonanno's work on trauma shows that we cannot always use common sense or rely on the observations of clinicians to predict what will happen. It reveals how theories derived from clinical practice might be excellent for people who have developed a chronic and serious psychological malady. But we would be unwise to build a theory of human nature on clinical experience, no matter how well it described what went on in a psychotherapist's office.

My point is this: the best information is not necessarily what we believe to be the best information—we need to back it up with systematic, scientific observations. This is true when we listen to therapists who describe human nature, but it is also true in other arenas.

HEURISTICS: THE DIAGNOSTIC FALLACY

Social psychologist Solomon Asch conducted a classic experiment when he had to miss part of class one day.[7] He took that opportunity to do an experiment on his students. He "forgot" to tell them, of course, that he was doing an experiment—a definite no-no in today's world of psychological studies. He said he had arranged a guest lecturer for the last part of the lecture when he had to be away, but he also said, "You'll like this guy. He gave a lecture in another of my classes, and here is what the students said about him." He passed out the student evaluations. The evaluations consisted of seven descriptive adjectives. Asch's students didn't realize, of course, that the lists were slightly different. Six of the adjectives were the same—involving qualities like industrious, critical, practical and determined. In fact, Asch had extracted them from the horoscopes in the newspaper that day. However, tucked in the middle of the six other words was the word *warm* on half of the descriptions and *cold* on the other half.

The lecturer entered the room and was introduced by Asch. After Asch left, all of the students listened to the same lecture. At the end of the period the lecturer left the room and a graduate assistant administered student ratings. You would think from the ratings that those students who had read the word *warm* had received a bag of M&Ms and were on a chocolate high. And the students whose list included the word *cold* seemed as if they had received a painful electric shock. The ratings were opposite. The "warm" professor was rated as good-natured, considerate, sociable, friendly, humorous and humane. But the "cold" professor was self-centered, irritable, ruthless, unsociable, unpopular and humorless. The students confirmed the "diagnosis" they received in advance by observing data from the lecture that supported it, which led to completely different ratings by students who listened to the same lecture by the same professor.

We are all subject to such biases. For example, you have come to this book with an idea of how psychology and theology relate to each other. You might have come to that opinion through years of careful study, or perhaps someone offered an offhand assessment of theology and psychology in a sermon, Sunday school class, university lecture or casual conversation. As far as our perceptions are concerned, once we have started down a road, it is hard to get off it. We notice evidence that seems to support our position, and we fail to see evidence that does not support it. This is the way people's minds work.

We all want to be able to predict what is going to happen. This is natural. When I walk up to a crosswalk and see the walk symbol light up, I predict that I can step out with confidence. My mind, with a desire to predict, sets up rules of thumb that cover most of the cases. By paying attention to the rule of thumb, I don't really have to pay close attention to every little action, and my mind is freed to think about important things. This is an efficient way for us to live. The problem with these *heuristics*, which is what these rules of thumb are called, is that they don't take into account that situations and times may change. If you've been to England and looked left before stepping into a crosswalk instead of looking right (traffic runs on the opposite side of the street in England), then you know that heuristics, good as they are, can let us down.

Another problem is whether our heuristic is good. We all make rules of thumb to govern our choices. Sometimes these are not based on good data but on assumptions or what seems like it should be logical. It is hard, but we must not necessarily trust our assumptions and received beliefs. Some of the things we believe are scientifically supported but others are not. Take Bonanno's studies. I believe that most people would have laid good money on the received view (based on much clinical experience) that few people are resilient after a major, potentially trauma-producing event. But when a broad sample of people were measured—not the ones who visit a clinician because they have already developed problems—it turned out that 35 to 55 percent were resilient, and another 15 to 35 percent experienced a fairly fast recovery. To discern the truth about human nature, we need to look not just to assumptions about what we think is scientific or to statements from theological systems that go beyond what the Scriptures actually say. We must keep seeking the best data—theologically and scientifically—and keep asking whether the data support or disconfirm our assumptions and logical conclusions. The data can enrich, expand and at times eviscerate our theology.

WHAT ABOUT INCONSISTENCIES?

Note, too, the other side of this equation. When an observation is not in accord with a theory or theological system, that does not mean we throw out the whole theory or theological system. Philosophers of science spend a lot of time thinking about what happens when scientists find inconsistencies. Imre Lakatos has shown that scientists rarely jettison a good theory just because an experiment was surprisingly different from what was hypothesized. Rather, scientists protect the core of their theory. Some aspects that are peripheral to the core of the theory can be easily given up due to inconsistencies, but an accumulation of inconsistencies is needed before a scientist will give up a theory believed to be effective at explaining life. The same is true of our theological beliefs. If I believe God loves me but a few bad things happen to me and my loved ones, I don't chuck my belief—at least not at the first little trouble. Some peripheral beliefs can be readily given up in the face of a scientific finding opposed to a theory—or a life event opposed to a theological belief—but it takes much more than that to make us give up our main theories or theological beliefs.

SUMMARY

Our idea of how psychology and faith relate often depends on listening to counselors and psychotherapists describe how psychology fits with Christianity. (I have written several such books on that topic from a clinical framework myself.) However, I've chosen some examples that challenge our sense that integration is best done from the clinician's chair. Clinicians are excellent in helping people who wish to solve problems in living. Clinical science shows that people get better faster when they go to counselors than if they don't. I am a firm believer in Christian counseling.

My cautions are aimed at what we believe about human nature, and I hope I have shown that what we start out thinking often determines what we end up thinking, blinding us to data in front of our noses. Why is this so? This is the topic of chapter four.

4

WHY YOU MIGHT NOT BELIEVE WHAT
YOU DON'T ALREADY BELIEVE

YOU PICKED UP THIS BOOK WITH BELIEFS about how psychology and Christian theology relate. For example, you already had an idea about whether psychology or Scripture can tell us truth about people and about which, if either, is more authoritative. You already had an idea about whether psychology could help you know anything valid about God and whether it could help you know God better and love God more. Regardless of whether you accept the lordship of Jesus, you likely hold to opinions, attitudes, beliefs and values that will make you more or less open to what I write. To the extent that I say anything new to you, you might not believe what I say. And your acceptance or rejection of my ideas might have as much to do with non-rational factors as with my (or your) reasoning. Let's consider some of the reasons for this.

INITIAL EXPECTATIONS

Our initial expectations may blind us to being open to experience, affecting belief and perception. In chapter one I briefly mentioned Barry Staw and Ha Hoang's study[1] of the National Basketball Association draft. The NBA draft process is ideal for examining how people make choices. Not only that, statisticians keep detailed records on virtually every aspect of pro basketball. There are statistics on shooting percentages from the field, behind the three-point arch and from the free-throw line. There are stats on the number of layups, points per game, points per career and points per minute of playing time.

Some statistics deal with toughness, including rebounds and blocked shots per minute. Some deal with quickness—assists and steals per game, per minute and per career. And because defense must be man-to-man rather than zone in the NBA, there are stats on how well a player limits his opponent's scoring. I'd guess there are even stats on the number of times any player argues with a referee. (I'd have to go with Kobe Bryant here.)

College players amass statistics also. As a pro team prepares to select a player in the NBA draft, the team must judge the player's future as he plays against pros rather than rely on the player's stats when he played against college players. Besides selecting the player on mere ability, though, the team must consider its own team, the ages of the returning players and their likely future, total payroll, possible resentments of more established players, and personality match of the rookies with other players and the coach. The choices are many and difficult.

Sometimes choices can be embarrassingly poor. Take the Portland Trail Blazers, who had second pick in the 1984 draft. The first-round choice was Hakeem "The Dream" Olajuwon, who went to Houston. But as Portland stared at the remaining choices, they saw a smorgasbord of possible future NBA all-stars—including Michael Jordan, Charles Barkley and John Stockton. So who did Portland pick? Sam Bowie. Bowie was an excellent player, though he was prone to injuries and never reached his potential. But who knew? Who would willingly pass over Michael Jordan, Charles Barkley or John Stockton?

Staw and Hoang weren't really interested in the draft per se but in the effects of players' draft numbers on identifying the superstar players. They developed a statistical system using shooting, toughness and quickness to quantify the best players. They could predict that players selected high in the draft, for the most part, were excellent throughout their careers in shooting, toughness and quickness.

But then they turned their attention to playing time. We would logically expect that a player who was high in shooting, toughness and quickness would spend a lot of time playing. They threw the data into a regression equation, along with time on the injured reserve, trade status (was the person about to become a free agent or had the person just been traded to a new team) and original draft number. They found that, indeed, scoring predicted playing time. However, surprisingly, neither toughness nor quickness mattered at all. And more surprisingly, draft number was by far the strongest predictor of playing time—even overshadowing scoring.

Over the season, getting drafted first rather than second predicted playing twenty-three minutes longer per season. Getting drafted first rather than twelfth was responsible for playing 253 minutes more— over four hours! That is a lot of court time. I'd rather be drafted first.

Here's another consideration. Owners and coaches might also have had an eye on the money. First-round draft choices put people in the seats—at least for a couple of years until the novelty of having a new and promising player wore off. But Staw and Hoang anticipated that. Draft status continued to be the strongest predictor of playing time even to the player's fifth year in the league—a time when we would logically expect performance to matter a lot more than the draft that took place five years earlier.

Once Staw and Hoang found how important a high draft number was, they kept crunching those numbers. They first removed the variance due to a player's skill—scoring, toughness and quickness—and with people statistically equated on skill, they found that being picked early in the draft usually meant little chance of being traded. In addition, again after equating players on skill, someone picked in the first round (regardless of draft number) usually stayed in the NBA over three years longer than someone selected in the second round.

What are the implications of this study? First, teams might be better if they focused on the scoring, toughness and quickness of the players instead of their draft number. But the coaches were to some degree blinded by their initial expectation, which is shown by the player's draft number. And the 1984 Portland Trail Blazers learned that a high draft number doesn't always mean a player will be a superstar.

As you come to this book on integration, your ideas might be just as firmly entrenched as the draft number in the mind of the NBA coach. The fact is, you might not accept some new information because of your initial expectations.

HIDDEN FACTORS

Expectations are usually right in front of our eyes, but we don't notice them. As a result, we might make decisions that aren't the best. Many hidden factors can influence our decision making. We discount or ignore those factors because it doesn't seem they would make any difference. Yet they do.

Mountain Talk

The other day Katy Anna, my youngest child, now twenty-six, started teasing me about my language. I grew up in East Tennessee, raised by parents right out of coal-mining communities. My dad was from Lake City, Tennessee (formerly called Coal Creek), and my mother was from LaFollette, Tennessee. Growing up, we talked mountain talk. "Way-ell, I cain't hep it," my dad would say. I picked up the mountain dialect, and I sounded like someone "rite outta the mountains. That's whar I wuz drawin' my lainguage frum. I'm frum East *Ten*nessee and dang proud of it." And all through college at the University of Tennessee, I was called Sonny.

That lasted until I went to MIT for my master's degree in nuclear engineering. Most of those professors had worked at Oak Ridge (just down the road a piece from where I grew up) during World War II, and they had stories of the mountain folk of East Tennessee. The point of the stories, which they told in class even though I sat there and got more than my share of teasing, was how backward people from the South are.

I worked hard to get rid of my mountain twang. The generic Southern drawl is always going to be part of me, but I tried so hard to eliminate the multiple mountain diphthongs and nasal twang that when I came home after spending four years in the navy, my brother accused me of going over to the dark side and being a Northerner. So, when Katy Anna teased me about saying "a hundERD" instead of "one hunDRED," I was properly ashamed. It appears that I could take the boy out of East Tennessee, but not East Tennessee out of the boy.

Cultures of Justice and Honor

When I began to study forgiveness, I found that there are big differences in the way people around the world react to injustice. In much of the United States, injustices are treated as just that, a violation of justice that needs to be redressed. However, in some other countries injustices are taken more as violations of honor. This can affect how people share their faith in different countries. In cultures of justice, like Europe, we can freely use justice metaphors. We can say, "People violate the law of God. God is a just God whose demands that injustices must be paid for. So Jesus had to pay the penalty for our violations of God's law."

In a culture of honor, though, an injustice is not just something that needs repayment. It is also a violation of honor. Honor is more about reputation than about mere offense. Reputation is all-important; saving face when offended and restoring a victim's face when we offend him or her.

In the South, we lived in a culture of honor. Cultures of honor usually develop among people who are nomadic or who depend for their livelihood on raising animals. Animals are mobile and can be easily stolen. What keeps people from stealing is the sure and certain knowledge that if one animal is stolen, the reprisal will be swift and violent. Getting the animal back, which would be strict justice, is sneered at. That would merely encourage others to take any animals they could drive off. So, the reprisal must also take care of the damage done to one's reputation. It must be out of proportion to the crime. "If someone steals my pig, I will hunt him down, kill him and his family up to the fourth generation." That reputation maintains honor.

The South, especially the Appalachian spine and some of the mountains inland of that range—on the Cumberland plateau and in Kentucky—was settled by people from the borderlands of northern England and southern Scotland, and the Scot-Irish from Northern Ireland. Their common bond was the herdsman mentality. On the Appalachian spine the immigrants maintained the lifestyle they had enjoyed in England and Scotland.

Farm cultures tend to be more peaceful than animal-rearing cultures. Farmers usually have plenty to worry about in terms of climate and natural disasters, but they don't have to worry about someone illegally harvesting all of their crops at night. Their farms aren't going to walk away if they don't severely punish the thief.

We learn our cultural heritage even if we don't pay conscious attention to it. These cultural factors are present in all of us. We carry with us things we learned just like I learned mountain talk growing up. We don't pay attention to those hidden factors, yet they can exert a huge impact on our behavior.

Experiment on the Effects of Southern Culture in Michigan

University of Michigan professors Dov Cohen and Richard Nisbett[2] took students who were either Michigan-born or from the South but had migrated to Michigan to attend school. They randomly distributed the Michigan-born and Southern-born university students into a group that did or didn't get personally insulted.

Here's how they were insulted. They were sent down a narrow hallway with a cart in the middle of the hall. A worker (a confederate of the experimenter) was working at the cart, and there was little room to squeeze by. In fact, the worker had pulled out a drawer making passage impossible. As the students walked down the hallway, the worker, in obvious cranky mood, was showing all the signs of extreme frustration. The college students usually stopped and politely waited for the worker to step aside and let them pass. But the worker delayed. Finally, with a sigh and churlish attitude, the worker slammed shut the drawer, and as he stepped aside he called the college student a name. Cohen and Nisbett had done some preliminary research to determine the name that was guaranteed to provoke the most hostility in the most people.

The insult really did make most of the college men mad relative to the students who were not insulted. On the average, their cortisol and testosterone levels went up. They later shook hands with a stranger harder than those not insulted. Their palms were sweatier. They also had to write the ending of a story about a fictitious couple, Jill and Steve, who were going together. At a party, Jill complained to Steve that Larry had tried to kiss her twice already. Five minutes after Jill returned to the group, Steve noticed that Larry was leaning in, trying again. What would Steve do about this? The students who had been insulted were more likely to say that Steve would be physically aggressive.

Were there differences between the Southerners and the Michigan-born students? In response to the insult, the Southerners' testosterone

and cortisol levels were much higher. The Michigan-born men sometimes controlled their emotions so much that their cortisol and testosterone went down. When shaking hands the Southerners became
knuckle-grinders, crunching harder on the stranger's hand. And in the
Southerners' fictitious ending to the saga of Steve and Larry, well,
Larry was often lucky if he walked away to flirt another day. Michigan-
born men did not react as aggressively.

The researchers then did a final test. They set up a game of chicken.
Once again, they sent the students down a narrow hallway to squeeze
past the cart. But this time the worker wasn't around. Instead, walking
toward the opening and timing his approach to precisely coincide with
the student's approach to the cart and wall was the Bouncer. The
Bouncer was about 6'3" and was 250 pounds of muscle. He had played
college football and literally worked as a bouncer in a local bar. The
Bouncer walked toward the slot in "bouncer mode." Namely, he gave
off all kinds of vibes that said, "Step aside or take the consequences."

First, all students stepped aside. (Hey, they were, after all, smart
enough to be students at the University of Michigan.) But the key variable was how close each student got before chickening out, stepping
aside to let the Bouncer pass. The Michigan-born men bailed out at
eight to nine feet before reaching the cart. The Southerners—less than
two feet. That is the average, so many went eyeball to eyeball with the
Bouncer before stepping aside.

The Southern students—who weren't directly out of the mountains
but were usually well-to-do, adventuresome, serious college students
at a university with a great academic reputation—were willing to go
nose-to-nose with someone who could put them in the hospital. Why?
Because *someone else* insulted them ten minutes earlier. The culture of
honor in which they were raised but no longer lived was having its way.
Furthermore, it is a sure bet that none of the students, if asked to explain their behavior, would think to refer to their Southern or Northern roots.

These studies reveal that more often than we care to imagine, how
we think people will act—based on our informal psychology, which is
informed by Scripture, Christian tradition and common sense experi-

ence—turns out to be wrong. We usually more accurately uncover how people actually act through psychological science.

ADVERTISING

The reason these hidden factors have such a big effect on us is that we don't pay attention to what is relevant. We operate on the basis of our logic, assumptions and common sense, and can arrive at logical conclusions that *sound* very true, but aren't.

In *Yes! 50 Scientifically Proven Ways to Be Persuasive*, Noah J. Goldstein, Steve J. Martin and Robert B. Cialdini[3] recall one of the best public-service advertisements in history. In the 1970s the Keep America Beautiful Organization showed a Native American canoeing on a pristine lake. On the shore, amid litter, he looks at the camera, and a single tear runs down his cheek. (Cue the violins.) That ad became a driving force for stopping litter.

Years later the same organization revisited this idea. In the new ad, people stood at a bus stop. They were reading the newspaper, smoking, drinking coffee. When the bus arrives, it obscures the bus stop, but as it pulls away, we see cigarette butts, empty coffee cups and discarded newspapers. The camera pans over the scene and lifts to a poster of—you guessed it—the Native American with a tear in his eye. As the scene faded, the words appeared, "Back by popular neglect." This clever ad makes sense: It seems like it would be an effective antilitter ad. But this ad did not have people rushing to the litter bin. Why? Perhaps you can figure it out. What was going on that the advertising field didn't predict?

It conveyed the message that everyone litters. It is popular to do so. The ad fell victim to a principle of persuasion called negative social proof. The message underneath the surface is that everyone is doing it, so it's all right.

Cialdini is from Arizona, home of the Petrified Forest National Park. Signs throughout the park proclaim, "Your heritage is being vandalized every day by theft losses of petrified wood of 14 tons a year, mostly a small piece at a time." One of Cialdini's graduate students visited the Petrified Forest with his fiancée—a completely scrupulous citizen in all respects. When the woman read the sign, she nudged her fiancé in the ribs and said, "We'd better get ours now."

This gave Cialdini an idea. He decided to test whether his research team could design a more persuasive sign (in the direction of not stealing the pieces of petrified wood). They marked two trails with either of two signs. The negative social proof sign said, "Many park visitors have removed the petrified wood from the park, changing the natural state of the Petrified Forest," and it was accompanied by a picture of several park visitors taking pieces of wood. The second sign showed a lone visitor picking up a piece of petrified wood, with a red circle-and-slash indicating not to do it, along with the words, "Please don't remove the petrified wood from the park, in order to preserve the natural state of the Petrified Forest."

Signs were placed at the head of two trails (randomly alternated on different days) that had marked pieces of petrified wood scattered along each trail. A survey of the number of remaining pieces of petrified wood was made daily, indicating how much had been stolen on each trail.

> In a finding that should petrify the National Park's management, compared with a no-sign control condition in which 2.92 percent of the pieces were stolen, the social proof message resulted in more theft (7.92 percent). In essence, it almost tripled theft. Thus theirs was not a crime prevention strategy; it was a crime promotion strategy. In contrast, the other message, which simply asked visitors not to steal the wood and depicted a lone thief, resulted in slightly less theft (1.67 percent) than the control condition.[4]

Armed with this finding, Cialdini and his research team set out to see whether they could design effective public service advertisements to promote recycling. They designed three ads. In one intentionally campy ad a *Leave It to Beaver*–style, gee-whiz family was in a neighborhood with several neighbors standing in a driveway.

> *Child:* Over here, Mrs. Rodriguez, it's our week to take the recycling down to the center. [Child hands a paper bag filled with newspapers to his mother, who places it onto the flatbed of a truck. Mrs. Rodriguez does the same.]

Child: Gee, Dad, where's Mr. Jenkins? [Mrs. Rodriguez rolls her eyes.]

Dad [disappointed]: Well, son, you see, Mr. Jenkins doesn't recycle.[5]

The camera cuts away to a hammock, where Mr. Jenkins lies napping in his back yard. He is covered by newspapers, cans and trash. The camera cuts back to a close-up on the child's face. A single tear rolls down his cheek. The camera fades to a geographical shape of the state of Arizona, which encompasses pictures of faces of many people and the words "Arizona Recycles."

Public Service Announcements (PSAs) are considered successful if they can move 1 to 2 percent of the people to act differently. Cialdini did a field-test of the PSAs, comparing some communities not assigned to see the public service announcements to others that saw one of the three commercials. They measured a 25.4 percent advantage in the tonnage of recycled materials for communities seeing the ad relative to the control communities.

THE BEST WAY TO ACCURATELY PREDICT OUR OWN BEHAVIOR

In chapter two I recounted an admonition by David Powlison. He argued that it is important to think theologically about psychological scientific data, and when we do, the individual person enters the equation. "The human factor is a decisive element in the complex of final causation. Nature and nurture significantly influence and constrain, but they don't finally explain. In an essential way, why you do what you do always comes down to *you*."[6] This argument is a caution and a constraint on psychological science. Science tries to predict as much of life as possible—recognizing that we will never be able to predict perfectly. Let's note that there is nothing wrong with predicting and controlling life—as long as we don't come to believe that we have so much control that we don't need God, which would be tragic. However, we need to know that when we drive down the street, people will stay in their own lanes. We need to be able to predict our own and others' behavior, and we need police to help control it. The number of times we must predict and control behavior each day is enormous.

I think Powlison's conclusion that humans are unique is correct.

Scripture tells us we are unique, and psychology tells us the same thing. The case from Scripture is easy to make. We are known by God in our mother's womb. We are fearfully and wonderfully made (Ps 139:13-18). God knows every hair on our heads. We each need a personal relationship with God for salvation, and we each desire to better that personal relationship.

The case from psychology is somewhat complicated. But it bears on the whole project of psychology, which helps us to predict those specific events and decisions that Scripture might only provide general moral guidelines for. (For example, Scripture doesn't tell us to drive on the right side of the road and stay in the lanes.)

Perhaps the best case for the uniqueness of humans comes from the body of research by Harvard psychologist Daniel Gilbert. In *Stumbling on Happiness* he says, "You will be heartened to learn that there is a simple method by which anyone can make strikingly accurate predictions about how they will feel in the future. But you may be disheartened to learn that, by and large, no one wants to use it."[7] His contention is that if we want to know how we will feel when we experience something in the future, we should find someone who is experiencing that thing right now and ask the person how it feels. Then we can guess about our own feelings on the basis of this knowledge.

That sounds crazy, you might say. Why would I want to ask *someone else* about his or her experience when I can guess very accurately my own experience? Unless the other people are my clones, sharing my DNA, and have had the same experiences as I, their experience will be different from mine. After all, I am unique. I realize that my experiences aren't always consistent, but I'll take my chances guessing based on my own past experiences rather than rely on a stranger's experience.

Gilbert might reply that this is very reasonable. But let's look at some studies.

When we want to predict how we will feel in the future, we use our God-given imagination. But imagination tends to be inaccurate for at least three reasons.

1. Imagination is often inaccurate because it tends to fill in and leave out details because it focuses on the now. When students are asked just

before a big football game how sad and disappointed they will be two days after the game if their team loses, they estimate that they will be very sad. They rarely are. They forget about all the intervening events—doing homework, going to class, phoning their parents to ask for money, doing the laundry (we hope). Routine events of normal life stabilize emotions quickly and dampen the disappointment of a devastating loss of the big game.

Three studies illustrate the problems of imagination. Study one includes three conditions for the participants. In one condition, people are called *reporters*. They are given a prize—a gift certificate to the equivalent of Gelati Celesti (that's our award-winning, local ice-cream parlor)—and then asked to do a long, boring task—sorting shapes on a computer or sorting papers. When they have completed the task, they rate how they feel about the prize. They might give it the average rating of 3 on a ten-point scale.

The second group of participants—the *imaginers*—are told they will be given a prize and afterward will complete a long, boring task. They are then told that the prize will be the gift certificate to Gelati Celesti and are asked to imagine how they will feel about the prize after they complete the task. Most say they will feel really good (say, 7 on a ten-point scale). But after doing the task, they don't feel so positive about the prize because that long, boring work intervened. So they rate their feeling about a 3. In other words, they actually felt four points worse than they expected to feel.

The third group is the *psychological information* group. This group was treated just like the second group, except that they were not told what the actual prize would be. However, they were told that someone selected randomly from the first group (the reporters) and rated their feelings toward the prize after doing the boring task as x—maybe 3, maybe 4, maybe 2, they fluctuate around a mean of 3. So, with that evidence, people in the third group predict that they will feel x. Having made a rating, they are then given the actual gift, do the boring task and finally rate how they feel. Most of the time their actual rating was somewhere very close to x. So, it turns out that guessing on the basis of imagination leads to an inaccurate prediction (overestimating by 4 the effects of a positive gift) of one's feelings in the future, but basing a guess on research findings yields an accurate prediction.

2. Imagination is often inaccurate because it projects the present into the future. When we guess how the future is going to be, many of the details are often missing. So, the imagination looks to the present and inserts those details into the way we think the future is going to be. Imagine this study. Volunteers from group 1 (reporters) ate a few potato chips and reported on how much they enjoyed the chips (let's say about 7 on a ten-point scale). Volunteers in group 2 (imaginers) were loaded up on salty snacks—pretzels, peanut-butter and cheese crackers, tortilla chips, melba toast and bread sticks. They were then asked to predict how much they imagined they would enjoy eating potato chips tomorrow. Not very much, most said—about 2 on a ten-point scale. But when tomorrow came, they liked the chips about the same as group 1 did (about 7). They underestimated their liking for the chips because they brought the present (feeling full) into their imagination about the future. Group 3 (psychological information) was loaded with the same snacks as group 2 and told they would have to eat a snack tomorrow. They were not told what the snack would be, but they were told that a randomly selected person out of group 1 rated it x. How much, then, did the person think he or she would enjoy it? Why x, of course. The next day, the psychological-information group members were given chips and their predictions were quite accurate.

3. Imagination is often inaccurate because it fails to realize that things look different once they have happened. Namely, bad things look better once they have happened than we imagined them to be, and good things don't look as good after they have happened. For example, when I imagine being "downsized," laid-off, it looks tragic. But afterward, I might find that this gives me the courage to go back to school or enter a new line of work. On the other hand, repeated studies of lottery winners have found that one year after winning the lottery people experience about the same happiness as they had before winning the lottery. To test this in a study, Gilbert took a group of volunteers, group 1 (reporters) and told them that the experimenter would flip a coin. If it came up heads, the volunteers would win a gift certificate to a local

pizza parlor. The coin was flipped. *So sorry.* It was tails. The volunteers reported how they felt. Not too bad, really. They started with nothing and ended with nothing. People in group 2 (imaginers) were told of the game and about the pizza parlor prize. They were asked to estimate how they would feel if it came up tails. They predicted that they would feel pretty badly. Flip. *Sorry, tails.* Then they rated how they felt. But it actually wasn't that bad. They had overestimated how badly they would feel. Members of the third group (psychological information), of course, were not told what the prize would be but were told of the rating of a randomly selected person from group 1. Those who received psychological information again were very accurate in predicting their actual feelings once they did lose the flip. Again, individual imagination was an inferior predictor to learning about actual psychological experimental results.

From Gilbert's research, we know that we could make better predictions about our own future experiences if we used a stranger's actual experience instead of our imagination. But now imagine this. Suppose a strange psychologist offers to pay your admission to a concert if you can predict in advance how much you will enjoy it. Would you want to (1) see the program of the concert, or (2) have a randomly selected person's rating of his or her experience at the concert? If you are like most people—me included—you would want to see the program. Unfortunately, if you are like most people, me included, you would end up buying your own ticket.

Having psychological information about how a group of strangers act—the participants in a study—is what psychological science provides. Yet we are strangely reluctant to use the research. Why?

Gilbert presents a great explanation. Basically, science gives us information about the average person, but we don't see ourselves as average. Ninety-four percent of college teachers see themselves as better teachers than the average.[8] Ninety percent of drivers see themselves as better drivers than the average.[9] Most business managers see themselves as better managers than the average.[10] It isn't that we are all narcissistic egomaniacs. (In fact, if tested, we probably would believe that we are more narcissistic than the average person.) But we have a general tendency to see ourselves as *different* from other people. For example, most of us see ourselves as not as good at chess as the average person[11] or as doing more selfish acts than others.[12] We don't always see ourselves as better than others, but we do see ourselves as unique.

Even when we do what others do, we believe we are doing it for unique reasons. We might think, *I didn't volunteer for the hard task at work because I have too much stress due to my kid's broken leg.* Others didn't volunteer because they were lazy (or they were too smart to want to appear to be kissing up to the boss). Or we might think, *I voted for Obama because I couldn't stand McCain's war posture, but others voted for Obama because they saw him as a charismatic leader.*

Why do we feel so unique? Gilbert lists at least three reasons. First, we know ourselves in ways we don't know other people. We actually experience our own internal processes, but we have to infer others' processes. "There is a difference between making love and reading about it, and it is the same difference that distinguishes our knowledge of our own mental lives from our knowledge of everyone else's."[13] Therefore, we gather different amounts and types of information about ourselves than about others. Furthermore, we only see others when we are with them, but we are with ourselves 24/7. We have lots of different information about ourselves. Thus, we conclude, we must be unique. Second, we enjoy thinking of ourselves as unique. When we show up at a party decked out and find two other people wearing the same outfit, we suddenly think the party is a bust. Third, we believe we are so special because we believe other people are unique. This makes complete sense. Most of our lives are spent trying to distinguish one person from another. If I go to a scientific meeting, I want to notice which of the people I meet is Dr. Jekyll and which is Mr. Hyde. If I go to a dance, I want to remember that this is Delores and that is Cheung. Social life is about being able to distinguish people from each other, so we look for the few distinguishing characteristics that help us sort out individuals. I look for the aspects of Delores and Cheung that make them different, not similar. Delores is taller than most, has the red dress and does a great cha-cha. Cheung is wearing that sparkling dress, has that cute crooked tooth in front, which makes her look endearing, and is terrific at waltz. I don't pay attention to the thousand ways that Delores and Cheung are similar to each other—both women, same hair color and body shape, both speak English, both bright conversationalists, both Christians and so on. Because we spend so much time thinking about differences—between ourselves and others, and among others—we tend to value the differences and think mostly about how unique each person is.

Thinking about it rationally, however, we can see that if we bite two apples and try to tell the difference between the two according to subtle differences in taste, we overlook the many ways that just knowing they both are apples could help us distinguish their taste from almost all other foods.

That is what psychological science tries to do. It tries to tell how virtually all people will act in a particular situation or, more generally, in a type of situation. Though knowing a lot about apples in general helps us enormously in planning our diet, it doesn't help us distinguish that apple 190 tastes slightly different from all other apples because it has a little ding on its side and the bruise changes the flavor slightly.

We can see why people might not want to use psychological science to predict their behavior. They value and believe in their uniqueness. That uniqueness exists, is important and could (in principle) never be eliminated by a psychological science. Psychological science is about big numbers. It describes our "appleness" but not our individual uniqueness. Our uniqueness is much less than we ever want to admit, but it is, after all, the difference that makes all the difference.

Do We Need Science for Telling Us About People?

We don't really need science to tell us about people. There are many ways that we learn. We can learn extremely valuable truths about people from the Bible. However, that is not the principal message of the Bible. Powlison says the Bible helps us develop "a transformed orientation and transformed intentions."[14] Its revelations about people are secondary. "We might say," Powlison notes, "that the psychological riches revealed are 'by the way,' a secondary spin-off from primary purposes."[15] We also can learn about people from philosophy, which attempts to generalize about the human condition. The arts and literature attempt to take a single case or story and help people generalize from it. In addition, we can ask our friends for help understanding people.

All of these methods might tell us things that are true about individuals, but they suffer several disadvantages relative to psychological science (which has its own disadvantages, such as being unable to investigate some of the issues that can be addressed in literature, arts, theology and philosophy). First, based on people's impressions and logical reasoning, armchair theorizing is not always accurate. Second, sampling bias, which means that each writer, artist, philosopher and theologian has a limited data base, limits the information people use on which to base their reasoning. (So does psychological science, but it self-consciously attempts to ask its questions broadly, and recognizes that we should never trust a single psychological study—only a body of studies using different methods and different samples.) Third, writers can have an agenda other than being truthful.

Let's examine the television reality show *Who Wants to Be a Millionaire*. The rules of the show are simple. The contestant answers a set of multiple-choice questions that get progressively more difficult. The first are slam dunks, such as

> How many points is a three-point shot worth in the National Basketball Association?
> 1. Two
> 2. Three
> 3. Four
> 4. It depends on who the home team is

Well, maybe they aren't quite that easy. But as the money increases, the questions become more difficult. Perhaps a later-round question might be, "In the period after the storming of the Bastille, how many nobles were executed inside the city limits of Paris?" If the contestant is uncertain, he or she can ask for help from one of three lifelines. The contestant can phone a friend for help, narrow down the possible answers or poll the audience.

Henri had cruised through the first couple of questions but suddenly sweat broke out when the host of the French *Millionaire* show asked, "What revolves around the earth?" The alternatives were (1) the moon, (2) the sun, (3) Mars or (4) Venus. You are probably thinking, "Well, duh," but Henri was befuddled. He reread the question and hemmed and hawed. The host suggested, "Don't rush. If you need help, you can always use a lifeline."

Henri polled the audience. That presumably was a good choice. After all, even if some people in the audience miss questions, most are usually correct.

But the results were astounding. Only 42 percent indicated the moon, which of course is correct. Two percent picked Mars. A full 56 percent, however, chose the sun. Poor Henri. But the audience had an agenda. They had weighed Henri's intellectual capacity and thought, *Get this bozo off the stage.* And they did.

This is an obvious warning about nonscientific sampling. People we come into contact with everyday do not behave in carefully controlled ways. They have agendas that bias the information they give us. Artists do not paint truth, they paint their perceptions of truth filtered through their skill and experience. So do novelists and philosophers. Science attempts to control those biases.

Scientists have the same personal, sinful, pride-filled, power-grabbing agendas. We are, after all, human. But good science cuts down on much bias. Science, of course, is not completely objective. Scientists subjectively choose the topics they want to study, identify the variables, decide which methods to use and what they will call data. Then they select the statistical methods to analyze the data and choose the way to conceptualize the results within a larger theoretical framework.

But science follows a prescribed method. All of those subjective choices are made within a disciplinary matrix. That is, scientists can't pick any sample, measures, statistics and theory to use to give some contextual meaning to the findings. Scientific studies have to undergo peer review, in which other scientists judge whether the study is within the disciplinary matrix of science. Furthermore, studies are the basic data of science, but studies can still be biased—even after going through peer review. So, psychological science depends not on single studies but on reviews of bodies of studies that try to study the same phenomena but do so with different variables, methods, outcome measures, statistical methods for analyzing data and interpretive frameworks. Those meta-analyses or qualitative reviews of the literature are the real stuff of science. Studies are merely ways of getting to the stuff of science.

SUMMARY

You came to this book with a point of view about theology and psychological science, which is unlikely to change dramatically. In this chapter I have suggested many reasons for this. We examined how initial expectations bias future decisions we make (e.g., NBA draft numbers). We saw that there are hidden factors we don't see as important (e.g., being raised in a culture of honor). We simply don't pay attention to much of what is relevant (e.g., Cialdini's influence studies). We often commit to a course and fixate on it.

The irony is that we actually have a good way of making personal decisions—use the results of psychological science, which tell us about ordinary people. But we often don't avail ourselves of this method of making personal decisions. Our irrational belief about the degree to which we are unique is drummed into us by modern American culture.

But culture has opposing pulls. Living within our skins, we are wired to be skeptical of psychological science. But we also are wired by culture to respect science. While our culture can also push us to distrust religion, we often find communities of Christian believers who share our Christian worldview and support those beliefs, values and practices. The various strands of our religious and psychological contexts suggest that we need a way to keep Christianity and psychological science in conversation. We need some model, to which we turn in chapter five.

5

THE METHODS OF DISCIPLINES

I WANT TO SEE GOD MORE CLEARLY. Psychological science can help. "Now we see but a poor reflection, as in a mirror; then we shall see face to face. Now I know in part; then I shall know fully, even as I am fully known" (1 Cor 13:12). One day, we will speak face to face with Jesus, have complete fellowship with God the Father and be fully surrounded and indwelt by the Holy Spirit. In the meantime, our life *should* be consumed in knowing God more deeply. But I confess that mine isn't always.

Like most of us, I struggle with self-control, which shows up in choosing what to eat; when to exercise; how to balance work, leisure and family activities; and other lifestyle choices. And like most of us I struggle with more morally pernicious issues. How can I reign in complaining or gossiping, control my anger, judgment and criticism, and show mercy, grace, love and forgiveness? Can I be appropriately humble and control my pride as it runs amok?

Pride is a great illustration. I recall visiting a scientist who told me at length about his research, but he didn't ask about mine. As time passed, I felt the pressure build to describe my accomplishments. I hinted. I asked leading questions. But nothing brought the conversation around to me. Finally, I found myself bragging and emphasizing my importance. Even as I did it, I realized that pride was intruding in our relationship. I should have been content to honor him. I knew it, but couldn't control myself.

In Romans 7, Paul laments, "For what I want to do I do not do, but what I hate I do. . . . Who will rescue me from this body of death?"

(Rom 7:15, 24). Jesus, of course, is my deliverer. But how? If only I could see God more clearly. If only I knew the all-encompassing sovereignty of God more sharply. If only I knew the humble Jesus better. If only I allowed the Holy Spirit to work unimpeded in my life more often. If only I realized and lived out the knowledge of just how much God loves me. If I knew God better and loved God more. If only . . . then, maybe I could be more self-controlled.

Fortunately, I don't have to launch a program to reach God. The tower of Babel was a human attempt to meet God. We know how that turned out. Instead, God reaches out to meet me, revealing the divine character and God's relationship to me.

GOD'S PROGRAM TO RELATE TO US

As we know, the Scriptures (both the Hebrew Scriptures and the New Testament) comprise God's *special revelation*. They tell us directly of God and how the triune God and people relate.

God also provided *general revelation*, which reveals something about God and humans through nature. God's general revelation has been well studied. Humans have studied the order of creation through natural philosophy for thousands of years. But with the advent of modern science, our knowledge of creation has increased enormously. We have studied novelty, personality and relationships in humans for thousands of years and have learned about humans and some things about God through these disciplinary studies. But the social sciences, and particularly psychological science, has significantly increased our knowledge of humans over the last one hundred years and provides ways to know God better, if we look closely.

Though the triune God reaches out to reveal God's divine character to me (it's God's nature to reach out to all humanity), I have a part in this two-way relationship. I must try to discern what God has revealed to us. To see God more clearly, know God better and love God more, I must consult God's divine revelation. The more I consult, the greater chance I have of knowing God better.

I can also consult God directly using methods refined in the church to discern God's special revelation—the written Word and Jesus within me. I can seek the advice of wise Christians. I can study theology. I can attempt to discern the truth personally through disciplined reflection. I can use the spiritual disciplines developed by Christians throughout the ages. For example, in my battle to exercise self-control, I might find Scripture verses about self-control and seek to understand them within the context of my life. I might meditate on God, Jesus, the cross, the psalms or other Scriptures to discern how to be more self-controlled. I might let Scripture speak to me about self-control using *lectio divina*. I might invite others to pray for my self-control. I might seek accountability within small groups at my church or work.

To see God more clearly, know God better and love God more, I might supplement God's special revelation (and associated practices in the church) by consulting God's general revelation. I can reflect on self-control within human nature as revealed by clinical psychology, sociology, anthropology, economics, political science or psychological science. Or I can reflect on human nature as revealed by other disciplines.

CAN SCRIPTURE ANSWER ALL OF MY QUESTIONS ABOUT SEEING GOD BETTER?

Scripture is sufficient for informing me about the necessities of salvation. Scripture is "God-breathed and is useful for teaching, rebuking, correcting and training in righteousness" (2 Tim 3:16). But it is not *the only* resource needed for every purpose. The wisdom from most corners of Christianity says that sources besides the Bible are helpful. C. S. Lewis said,

> That is not how Christianity works. When it tells you to feed the hungry, it does not give you lessons in cookery. When it tells you to read scriptures, it does not give you lessons in Hebrew and Greek, or even ordinary English grammar. It was never intended to replace or supersede the ordinary human arts and sciences: it is rather a director which will set them all to the right jobs, and a source of energy which will give them all new life, if only they would put themselves at its disposal.[1]

Here's another example. Both Jesus and the disciples healed others.

If I truly believed that Scripture alone is sufficient for all physical healing, then I probably would never consult a physician. Today, when we
are ill, most of us pray, and we also consult a physician.

Furthermore, revelation is progressive. Theology changes. Church
practices in the twenty-first century are not the same as they were in
the eighteenth. Similarly, science grows and refines knowledge. If we
had consulted a physician for an infected hand in 1900, we might have
had our limb cut off. That rarely happens today because medical science has advanced. We know more about how the God-designed human body functions, malfunctions and heals. Science has informed
medicine. Science can also inform theology, church practices, and individual faith and piety.

Whether we heed C. S. Lewis or our own experience, the voices sing
in unison. We do consult sources other than Scripture or God in our
efforts to know God better.

IS PSYCHOLOGICAL SCIENCE A PROFITABLE SOURCE TO CONSULT?

Here are some ways I might try to know God better. I might read some
church history, interview a few exemplars of Christian devotion within
my church, read selected biographies of the saints, join a closed Christian community, or devote myself to prayer and worship every hour. All
of these traditional Christian sources are ways that I can often know
God better.

Sampling

In each case, the quality of my knowledge of God, however, depends
on an undisciplined *sampling* of experiences. My reading of church history depends on which sources and which periods I read. I learn different things about God if I read only from the Reformation period and
ignore the Middle Ages. My sampling of Christian exemplars might be
suspect—especially if I happen to not have a good sense of who might
really know God or if I hang around with people who really aren't close
to God. I can sample biographies of the saints. Who were the biogra-
phers? Do they have any wisdom to impart? Are they promoting their
agenda? Even sampling from Christian communities and joining one

might not provide the knowledge of God I seek. Attending services of a nondenominational Bible church, traditional Roman Catholic parish, Pentecostal congregation or Russian Orthodox church shows different sides of God's character. And even sampling people to pray for me might backfire if I (or the pray-ers) do not properly discern godly motives. My point is this: consulting "Christian" sources has its own validity problems in providing a true and full knowledge of God.

Psychology is a *scientific* discipline. As such, its method is prescribed. Like medical science, theology or any discipline, the method of discovery in psychological science is fixed. In science, the scope of information that is available is narrowed by agreeing to a particular scientific method. But the method allows a depth of understanding that we cannot get from nonscientific disciplines.

Truth does not unveil its beauty because psychological science employs a rigorous method. Psychology is a huge field. We will still have the difficulty of sampling from an unwieldy collection of articles, chapters and books. But at least the "canon" of psychological sources is limited by confining it to scientific studies and theories.

Psychological science can tell me about people, their minds and behavior. As such, its subject matter is about the inner workings and outward environments of people. But if my objective is not merely to know people but also to know God, then there must be a connection between studying people and finding out about God from studying people.

CAN STUDYING PEOPLE TELL ME ABOUT GOD?

Francis Schaeffer pointed out that there were complex relationships between animals, humans and God (see fig. 5.1).[2] On one side of figure 5.1, there is a great chasm between God and creation. God is omnipotent, omniscient, transcendent and eternal. God's creation is none of these. We are like the animals in being utterly different from God in these respects—created, not Creator; limited, not limitless; finite, not infinite; fallible, not infallible.

Yet, on the other side of figure 5.1, God and humans share personhood. They differ from the rest of creation. Both are personal. They can communicate, think, emote, pursue goals and interact spiritually.

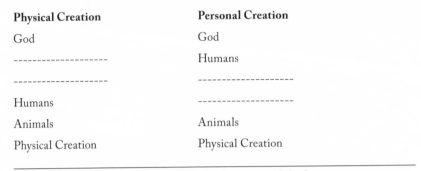

Figure 5.1. Relationships among animals, humans and God

Furthermore, God has made humanity God's personal receptacle for Jesus' incarnation. Humans are therefore special in a way that animals can never be. There is a great divide between the personal and the impersonal. If God were impersonal, we could not know God. We could know only other humans. But because people and God share the personal, it is possible to know God in a way that neither animals nor created matter can.

I could learn about God's character by studying divine creation. There is a beauty, order and elegance in nature that bespeaks of God's joy at creating. The same beauty, order and elegance are revealed in the creation of humans, but the Scripture tells us that God did something special with humans. Humans bear the divine image. This suggests that we can learn about the image of God—in terms of both its structure and the essential relational quality—through the study of humans. Psychological science is one way of conducting this study.

WHAT IS THE BEST WAY TO STUDY PEOPLE?

Studying humans, their qualities and interactions with others or with created things, can be a reliable way to learn about God—because we are indeed similar to God. By seeing how humans act, we can tentatively extrapolate to how God might act. I say "tentatively" because the Bible informs us that unlike God we are fallen and sinful creatures. Being creatures and not the Creator, we are limited in ways that God isn't. We are limited in time and space. We can know only our own experience (and some would argue we have access only to a small portion of that) and not the experience of others. And we can be remarkably inconsistent. So, we are similar to God because we are creatures made in the image of the Creator God. But we are also dissimilar because we are fallen creatures. Sin permeates our lives and it twists what we see and how we interpret it. The Fall distorts the pure goodness in people and in nature (Gen 3). Distortion can occur because people are blinded to the truth (Jn 9:25), but it also can occur because humans have a heart that is hostile to God (Rom 8:7-8). The degree of this distortion of the divine image within that is due to sin is a matter of some disagreement (see chap. 8 where I discuss this in detail).

Nevertheless sin distorts communication of God's divine revelation to humans. By analogy, my communication with my wife can sometimes run aground. Yet most of the time, despite human sin on both of our parts, we can understand the essence of each other's meaning. We can never be sure we understand completely, but that doesn't stop us from having meaningful and loving communication.

But there are many *ways* to study humans. These include the humanities, arts and social sciences. The best way to learn about God through people depends on what I want to learn. Often I want to learn how individuals think, act and feel, which are precisely the areas that psychological science studies. I might extrapolate to how God thinks, acts and feels about humans, or more specifically, about *me*.

So if I am vexed about my inability to exert godly self-control, can I get help from psychology? Can psychological science tell me anything about my moral muscle and how to strengthen it? Has psychology learned anything since the apostle Paul's time that can help me live more virtuously? Can psychological science help me know God better and love God more?

I believe the answer to all four questions is yes. Psychological science has revealed much that helps us know God better. Most people are not aware of many of these advances because scientific data are shared first in psychological journals. But the amount of God's general revelation that is discerned through psychological science has grown rapidly. I hope to

convince you that we can know God better through the study of psychological science. I will show you some of the things you can know—just in
case you aren't aware of the latest research in psychology.

WHICH FINDINGS TELL US SOMETHING ABOUT GOD?

Discernment Is Needed

The body of psychological findings is vast. To know God better, we
must be discerning. First, we must discover which findings are important. Then we must figure out which ones tell us about human corrup-
tion, which ones reveal truth about humans yet do not tell us about
God, which ones tell us something about God, and which ones actually
help us to know God better?

Disciplinary Importance

Findings should first pass the tests of disciplinary importance. They
should be published after being reviewed by other psychological experts, preferably in high-quality psychological journals. They also
should stimulate others to use the research and to do additional related
research.

Usefulness

Scientific findings should (eventually) be useful. Sometimes basic scientific research takes many years before its applications are known, and
sometimes its usefulness is merely to advance other basic scientific research that is more practically helpful. Judgments of importance thus
must first pass through a scientific filter. But after that, theologians,
pastors and laypeople judge the importance of scientific findings based
on the usefulness.

Rational and Spiritual Discernment

To discern whether psychological findings reveal God's character, both
rational discernment and drawing on the Holy Spirit for spiritual discernment are needed. Rationally, we ask, does this fit with the implications we could draw from Scripture and theology? Spiritually, we ask,
Lord, does this edify? Does this allow me to know God more person-

ally? Thus, there is a way of determining whether science helps us know God better.

PSYCHOLOGICAL SCIENCE IS NOT MERELY THINKING ABOUT THE PSYCHE

Some Limits on Scientific Knowledge

There are limits to psychological knowledge—and therefore to what you can learn about God from it. Psychology is a *discipline* defined by both its subject matter (mind and behavior, including animal behavior) and its method (the scientific method). Insights about human minds and behavior that come from theology, art, the humanities, philosophy, the Bible or just armchair theorizing—and not from psychology— may be true. I do not denigrate the value of these insights. However, they aren't psychological science. They do not use the scientific method, which is part of what defines psychological science. (A scientific study of physics uses the scientific method too. But it doesn't deal with the subject matter of mind and behavior. Thus it isn't psychology either.) Psychology requires both particular methods and particular subject matter.

Importance of Disciplinary Methods

For example, the great philosopher Aristotle surmised that heavier objects would fall faster than lighter ones. It makes sense. That belief ruled for two thousand years. But Galileo conducted empirical tests (through observation) on Aristotle's belief. Galileo discovered that heavy and light objects fell at the same rate. Sometimes relying on informal observation and armchair reasoning is wrong and even dangerous. Aristotle philosophized about scientific subject matter, but he didn't do modern science. He did not subject his hypotheses to scientific tests.

Similarly, I can describe my philosophy of life, but I am not doing the discipline of philosophy because I am not using philosophical methods. As a layperson, I can describe my beliefs about God and the relationship of God to creation, but no theologian will equate what I am doing with the discipline of theology, because I am not using theological methods. While those philosophical and theological musings can be profitable, they are not practicing the disciplines.

Why Am I so Uptight About Method?

Maybe I seem to be making much ado about nothing, creating a tempest in a teapot. But there is a reason. We cannot always believe our undisciplined psychological observations.

For example, let's take a psychological belief that seems perfectly logical. What about "look before you leap"? Fools do indeed rush in, don't they. Yet aren't there also times when we should "strike while the iron is hot"? Now that we think of it, weren't there times when we hesitated and lost golden opportunities? These opposites seem true when we examine them one at a time from our armchair. We can also reach back into our past and recall many times when each was true.

Three helpful (and sometimes not so helpful) heuristics. Psychological insights derived from nonscientific methods are often overgeneralizations. They seem to be verified by our experience. But our verification inevitably looks mostly or solely at those aspects of our experience that confirm our beliefs. We don't naturally look for evidence that refutes our beliefs. Experiments in psychology have shown how we all have this *confirmation bias*. This is coupled with *belief perseverance*. Even in the face of contradictory evidence, we often continue to hold onto outmoded beliefs. This makes sense, of course. If we believe that our mother loves us, and one day, she yells at us, it would not make sense to abandon thirty years of experience with a loving mother because of one bit of evidence to the contrary. We also have *belief bias*. When we read something that supports what we already believe, it makes sense. When we read something we disagree with, it is easy to see flaws. People who observe a presidential debate almost always believe their candidate won the debate.

Confirmation bias, belief perseverance and belief bias, all discovered by cognitive psychology, tell us that we have a *self-serving bias*, a bias toward evidence that confirms what we already believe. Self-serving biases help us predict what might happen. So, we formulate beliefs, look for evidence that we are right and ignore evidence that is contrary to those beliefs.

This tendency to maintain beliefs and retain orderly perceptions has theological implications. Once we have a childhood "theological belief system" and formulate a concept of God, chances are high we will be reluctant to change them. Contradictory evidence seems to bounce. Under normal living we require either an overwhelming amount of contradictory evidence or a very emotionally engaging experience to change our theology. *If we trust an undisciplined method*, our confirmation biases, belief perseverance, belief biases and other self-serving biases will rule. We will create a god in our own image. We might say, "My God wouldn't do that!" We read studies that support our beliefs, spend time with friends who agree with us, memorize Scriptures that prove our point, and attend churches that feed us the scriptural food that tastes good to us because we are familiar with it. We try to manage our experiences so that we do not have to leave our comfort zone.

However, scientists who adhere to a professional or scientific discipline subject themselves to its method. That method provides guidelines that protect us from many whims of undisciplined, self-serving thinking. It corrects the biases that simultaneously warp our understanding of God and make us certain we are correct.

But We Never Are Limited to Only One Method

Scientists, of course, still retain their judgment. Scientists do not limit information to *only* one discipline. So the scientific method does not have absolute rule over us. Nonetheless, when I put on my white psychologist lab coat, I cannot in midanalysis switch into my artist beret, historian glasses or theologian robe. I subject myself—at least for the duration of my analysis—to the scientific method and its white-coat rigors. Only after science is done can I employ thinking from other disciplines—and that is not part of science. This is not to claim that the scientific method eliminates biases and subjectivity. It doesn't.

When I put on my black theologian's robe, I similarly subject myself to a method. The theological method gives priority to texts and to ways of working with the material in those texts. If I were to don the philosopher's toga, I would think hard about the logic, analysis and rules of argumentation, and apply them rigorously within the discipline of philosophy.

The Relationship Between Two Methods

As a Christian psychologist I employ two different methods—scientific methods acceptable to psychological scientists and theological methods acceptable to Christian theologians. That sets up a competition. The competition could be treated as a life-or-death, only-the-winner-survives competition. I could see psychological science as the mortal enemy of theology. Or (as I do) I can see the competition as friendly, in which the two disciplines move together. The competition is about who is leading and who is following *at a particular moment.*

I approach this book as a psychologist first and theologian second. I am seeking to show you how psychological science can inform professional and lay Christian theology. It certainly would be possible to write a different book on how theology could inform neuroscience, social psychology, personality psychology or the psychology of religion. The disciplines can converse and mutually edify each other. I did not choose to write that book.

Are theology and science at war? Volumes have been written about the history of the interaction between science and religion. Let me simply assert that some people find a warfare model useful politically and socially. But for most, there is increasing dialogue developing between science and religion. In particular, a fruitful dialogue between psychology and Christianity has developed, though most of the speaking has been done by the clinical psychologists—of which I am one. I think, though, that neither the warfare nor the dialogue model is best for capturing the complexity of the interaction.

A RELATIONAL MODEL OF PSYCHOLOGICAL SCIENCE AND CHRISTIAN THEOLOGY

I like to portray the relationship between science and religion as more like an ongoing relationship. One metaphor is that the relationship between psychological science and Christian theology is like a marriage—

with periodic conflicts but also a lot of shared intimacy. Sometimes it seems like an arranged marriage. The marriage was arranged when God put the divine image within humans. That joined the divine and human natures, and thus two ways of studying them—theology and psychology—into the one flesh of marriage. In that spirit, let's examine whether we can see God better through psychological science and its interface with Christianity.

Can We Know God Better?

I can know God in ways similar to how I know my wife, Kirby. As I do with Kirby, I interact with God. I communicate with God directly, in prayer, and discern God's communication to me. As with Kirby, I share with God times of excitement, comfort and intimacy. Also as with Kirby, sometimes God and I share disagreement, conflict, anger and disappointment. But we work out these differences.

I can know Kirby better by reading books and letters Kirby has written about herself. I can also read God's Word. I learn about the experiences God has had with others, of the love and passion experienced by those, throughout history, who have known God. I too can know God by reading the book of creation.

I know Kirby, the mother of my children, by observing her children. By seeing the children do things that I know Kirby taught them, I know more about Kirby and I know her in a deeper way. I also know God because I know God's children. They tell me of their experiences with God, and I know aspects of God that I might not have experienced myself. The more I know, the more I appreciate and love God.

I know Kirby because I know her work and living space. I know too the world God has created, the pictures God has painted and the way God has populated the world. God populated it with beautiful people and glorious creations—both artistic and functional. Each reflects God from a different angle. By studying each, I can know God better, which helps me love God more. The different disciplines—theology, the humanities, the arts, the physical sciences, the life sciences and the social sciences—help us see different aspects of God through different aspects of the divine creation.

Different Data

Psychological science draws on different data than does theology. Theology uses the data from Scripture, which include historical, poetic, prescriptive and metaphorical data. Psychological science uses the data from experiments, studies and systematic observations that are usually quantified. In psychological science, the data from Scripture are sources of hypotheses and sometimes standards against which findings are tested.

Psychological science draws on different data from clinical psychology. In psychological science, data are from people in general, but in clinical psychology, most data are from clients, who are admittedly troubled and are seeking to return to normalcy. Psychological science includes clients of psychotherapy because psychological science typically studies all people. However, clinical psychology does not generally include people who do not volunteer for some psychological treatment.

Personal in a different way. Psychological science is *personal* in a different way than the other disciplines, as well. Theology deals mostly with the relationship between God and humans from the perspective of God. Second, it deals with the relationship between humans and God from the perspective of humans—how humans can more closely apprehend God. Third, it deals with the relationship among humans in light of God's sovereignty.

Clinical psychology deals with the human psyche and human interactions, as does psychological science. But the purpose in clinical psychology (at least as practiced by Christians) is to heal people of their sicknesses and sins, and restore them to a right relationship with God, and consequently with humans. Or, at a less ambitious level, it is to heal people because we are commanded to love our neighbors and to be compassionate—not just to evangelize our neighbors or make disciples.

Psychological science tells about human experience in general. It deals with the personal experience within the person, the way it goes wrong and becomes abnormal, the social experience in relationships, the development of people from womb to tomb, and even the psychology of religion. Psychological science is a story told from the human perspective. We can thus draw inferences about the relationships between God and humans, and God and creation (by observing humans' treatment of creation, including the environment and animals). Psychological science—as a psychology committed to methodologically materialistic explanations (even though psychologists might believe in many nonmaterialistic causes and effects)—deals with human, animal or environmental variables. Sometimes these include perceptions of the divine, and God's influence, but the perceptions are still within the material explanatory system. Thus psychological science is limited to drawing inferences about God rather than trying to "measure" God or prove God's existence.

Psychological science also does something unique. It can deal with the mind and behavior of animals, which neither theology nor clinical psychology does. It can learn from the animals because humans and animals share similarities (see fig. 5.1).

I believe these disciplines can enrich and cross-pollinate each other. Theology provides checks on scientific findings. Psychological science provides checks on theological interpretations of scriptural (and other) data.

As in any relationship, psychological science and Christian theology attempt to communicate. But this is difficult because psychological science uses one language system and Christian theology uses another. (Actually, there are many theological language dialects.) These two parties must share some language in order for communication to occur. I hope to show how the language of psychological science can help us know people and God better.

SUMMARY

In chapter 1, we saw that psychological science could show us fascinating aspects of people that we might not have been able to guess by drawing on other sources. In chapter 2, we saw some tensions within the historical dialogue between science and theology, and I suggested that psychological science was an underrepresented participant in that dialogue. In chapter 3, I argued that psychological science was a trustworthy source of truth about people and human nature, at times more trustworthy than clinical psychology. In chapter 4, I showed why this might be the case. However, I showed too why this might be difficult to accept, especially if you come to this book trusting in the validity of clinical psychology. In the present chapter, I compared the disciplines of psychological science and Christian theology with an occasional nod toward clinical psychology. I zeroed in on the distinctive methods of the disciplines, both of which tell us about humans and their relationships with each other and with God. Because both address human nature (albeit with different methods and different data), I suggested that a good metaphor to describe their relationship with each other was as a marriage. This requires theology to come to peace with psychology. In the following chapter, I will expand this relational model of the interaction of psychological science and Christian theology.

A RELATIONAL MODEL

"Why, Lord?" I have heard that plaintive cry thousands of times from friends, clients and colleagues. I've uttered it myself more times than I can remember. Haven't we all thought, *Lord, this suffering would be much more bearable if I just knew your purposes. Why are your purposes so opaque?*

WHY IS THE MIRROR DARK?

God Wants It That Way

In our less emotional moments, we think more clearly. We know that God made the window into the divine mind opaque. Perhaps we couldn't stand the empathic suffering we'd encounter if we could fully think God's thoughts and feel God's feelings. Perhaps we would become too puffed up with pride if we thought we could whistle up an explanation from God anytime life didn't go our way. We regularly would have God as defendant instead of judge if we had our way.

The story of Adam and Eve in Genesis 1–3 implies that humans might once have had that direct access to God's thoughts. Adam and Eve walked and talked with God in the Garden. To the best of human ability they communicated with God without a veil between them. But the Fall bent human ability to understand God. Since then, humans have passed down that fatal flaw, that fallen nature. Our human nature is partially redeemed at the new birth but will only be fully redeemed in the new creation.

Then we recall Job. God told him in no uncertain terms that Job was answerable to God and not the reverse. That's a hard word when we are suffering. But if we can grasp the truth of it, we see that it conveys that we have an all-powerful and trustworthy God. God has divine purposes, and God will do good. That is the kind of God I want to worship—not a God who is beholden to me. The Scriptures are clear that God is love, grace, mercy, compassion, sympathy, empathy, forgiveness and kindness. But God has standards also. In fact, God's character defines the standards.

Complex, Intertwining Levels of Causality

In addition, there are multiple levels for explaining causes for disappointment and suffering. Those levels seem independent but sometimes aren't. Suppose I strike a nail with a hammer. I could explain the motion of the nail by considering the physics of force and motion. However, I can also explain the cause of the motion of the nail by referring to my will (i.e., my purpose was to drive the nail into the wood) or my psychology (I have pent-up frustrations, unconscious hostility that is being displaced onto the nail). Even limiting myself to the physical world does not eliminate the interdependence between levels of explanation. Suppose I could explain all of the forces that act on an electron. Psychologist Roger Sperry[1] observes that we might still not be able to understand the motion of the electron if we do not know that, at the level of analysis of physical shape, the electron is in a metal wheel and is rolling down a hill. The level of analysis of rolling down a hill is different than the level of analysis as the atomic forces.

Philosopher of science Michael Polanyi[2] put forth yet another level-of-analysis argument. Suppose you begin to scribble randomly on a paper, doodling, lifting the pen, doodling and lifting. Suddenly, in mid-doodle, you begin to write a sentence expressing your thoughts. This is a higher level act. At one level I could explain the physics of the ink bonding to the paper caused by both the doodles and writing. But from a thinking, communicating person's perspective, there is a vast difference between meaningless scribbles and actual communication.

There are two problems that different levels of analysis suggest. First, we are not on a level with God and will never see things as God does. Second, we cannot know fully different levels of truth.

What Can We Conclude?

There are at least three reasons why the mirror is dark. First, the mirror is dark because it might not be good for our faith if we could see more clearly than we do. Seeing with complete clarity would feed our pride. Thus, one reason is moral. We are fallen and thus morally corrupt. There are effects of the Fall that twist our motives and morals. The second reason is ontological. We are confined to a level of analysis that cannot have total access to the mind of God. As mere creatures, we are different from God. Third, we can share a portion of God's thoughts, if God reveals them to us. But we do not have the attributes of God and are incapable of knowing things as they truly are from God's perspective. Thus, the third reason is epistemological.

Faith or sight? We are confined on a plane of physical existence. We are forced, as Paul argues, to walk by faith, not by sight (1 Cor 13:12; 2 Cor 5:7). Clearly, Paul says it is better to walk by sight. We will rejoice when we do see God face to face. But while confined to earth, we should walk by faith. We must realize there is an unseen world that interacts with this world. So, we do not confine our "sight" to the seen world.

The causes of events. Explaining the causes of events is a matter of different levels, but not just a case of parallel noninteracting planes. It is tempting to separate the natural and supernatural levels of existence and say that they are independent, which avoids many conflicts. But Scripture makes it clear that there is a connection between the natural and supernatural.

God can affect creation. C. S. Lewis[3] argued that the motion of pool balls bouncing around a pool table might, in principle, be completely predictable from calculations using Newtonian physics. However, if someone watching the pool game suddenly reached onto the pool table and caught one of the balls, things would change radically. The laws of physics would not be violated. But an agent acting on a closed physical system (i.e., the balls confined to the pool table) could disrupt the natural flow of the bodies within that system.

In the Scriptures we find that God has repeatedly stepped into our closed system (i.e., the natural world) and intervened. In effect, God caught the pool ball: parting the water for the Israelites, consuming Elijah's offering, causing a virgin birth, doing the many miracles through Jesus, raising Jesus from the dead, and providing a Scripture that faithfully reports God's historical acts. God has acted within creation. God still interacts with and will interact with physical existence as long as it exists.

Humans affect the supernatural world. Scripture tells us that God wants us to pray (Mt 5:44; Lk 18:1), and our prayers have power (Jas 5:16). God listened to Abraham ask mercy for Sodom (Gen 18:21-33). He listened to Jesus (Mk 6:41), and he listens to us today. James 5:16 tells us: "The prayer of a righteous man is powerful and effective." God thus responds to our prayers and life is affected as a result.

God is immanent. God is working continually to sustain creation (Col 1:15-17; Heb 1:1-3). And nothing is made without Jesus' hand being involved (Jn 1:1-3). God's work is on a different level of causality than human action. God's can be active within creation without violating natural causality. But in God's sovereignty, God might violate natural causality in the physical universe. Of course, these truths entail a couple of implications.

Implications. First, nothing can be predicted with 100 percent accuracy. At times past, present and future, God miraculously reaches into time and space and changes what humans expect to happen. Second, science often attributes to chance things that cannot be scientifically explained—such as motion of molecules within a container. These small variations are not miracles but part of the unpredictability inherent in science. The same unpredictability is inherent in genetic mutations and natural selection in biology, which describe the mechanisms of evolution. In humans, the same apparent randomness is attributed to free will. Third, most causes are natural at the level of science and simultaneously supernatural on the level of God's causality. Science seeks to explain how material objects relate to each other in a way that helps us understand, predict and (perhaps) control nature. The Scriptures reveal why life is as it is and demonstrate that life's objective is the glory of God. Scripture's main purpose is not to answer the *how* questions. Science does not answer the ultimate *why* questions. Yet psychological science answers some why questions by dealing with motives and emotions, cognition, attitudes, and attributions (i.e., ways people explain the cause for events). But those are on the natural level, not the supernatural.

In principle it is impossible to discern how much of a deviation in physical or human processes is attributable to miracle, random variation or free will. However, if a scientist were to say that he or she excluded God from doing the unexpected in nature, as well as in human-divine and human-human interactions, that would not be a scientific statement. It is as much metaphysical in nature as if a scientist were to say he or she were including God.

EXPANDING THE MARRIAGE METAPHOR

An Analogy to Relationship Development

I am going to carry the marriage metaphor of chapter five a bit further. In my relationship with my wife, I see the things she does, creates, organizes and reveals. This is not merely an intellectual exercise on my part. I am not just making a propositional statement *about* Kirby when I observe a painting she made. I also react emotionally. What I observe becomes meaningful to me.

When we first met, I wanted to know more about Kirby. I asked her friends about her. Each person revealed a different aspect of her character as he or she had perceived it through different interactions with her. Her tennis partner told me how well she played tennis. Her friends said she was warm and caring. Her college Sunday school class leaders told me of her faith. Those she talked with about their problems spoke of her compassionate character.

When she communicated with me, she showed me that she cared for me. Our communication stimulated my love for her. I revealed myself to her. She kept our confidences as a treasure. She did not embarrass me by revealing them inappropriately. On dates I found her to be bright, energetic and fun. Through careful observation, I discovered that her friends' reports were true.

At some point our relationship changed subtly yet profoundly. Biologists might call the change "emergent." Until I allowed her acts to become personally and relationally relevant, she was just a human object to me. As I grew to know her better and we connected more emotionally, she became more than an acquaintance; she was my friend. Then we started thinking about ourselves as a couple, and one day we married. That marriage has developed, changed and grown throughout its duration.

Similarly, the relationship between theology and psychological science, if they work together, can have emergent properties. Together they can know more about people and God than either could know separately. The combination might be more fruitful than the sum of the individual contributions. And then, with that transformation in the relationship, the adventure begins.

Knowing the One You Love

There is never enough time to know and love a woman. Every angle from which I see Kirby reveals something new. I've been married to Kirby for more than forty years. Without our lifelong marriage relationship, I would not be able to know her half as well or love her half as much. We talk, we share our feelings, and we know that our commitments to each other are equally deep. Because we communicate personally, we know and love each other. I also know her because I have read things she has written—books, letters, e-mails and notes of love she has written to me and to our children, her extended family, her friends, her students and acquaintances.

I know her because I know her children. Of course, they are my children too. But I can see bits of Kirby in Christen, Jonathan, Becca and Katy Anna. By studying Christen, I see Kirby's heart for children. By studying Jonathan, I see her outgoing, engaging love of others. By studying Becca, I see Kirby's sensitivity. By studying Katy Anna, I see Kirby's eagerness to experience life, flitting from experience to experience. Most of our children have autoimmune struggles. By understanding their physical problems, I know more about Kirby's. I also know Kirby because of what our children have told me about their interactions with her.

I know Kirby better because her students have told me about her. She sparkles as she teaches. Strangers stop me in the store and tell me about how much they love Kirby's teaching. They thrill to her zest for life that comes out when she is in front of students. They are more energetic because she is so energetic.

I know more about Kirby because I study the things she created. She draws. Her art adorns the walls of our home. She likes to draw scenes of Florida shores. She has created a haunting black-and-white ink drawing of a tree emerging from the fog. She has drawn a rocky outcrop of a Northern California shore and boats beneath a bridge. She even has drawn an abstract image that conveys a kneeling figure being illumined from above. I know more about Kirby because I see what she has created. She has dabbled in pottery. She makes mobiles. Her creative works reveal her creative nature and show me some of the things she values.

The way she decorates our home reveals her life and her personality. We have a simple, peaceful living room and the lived-in comfort of the family room, where toys, videos, rugged but comfortable furniture and books about God and children abound. The kitchen is well organized but tends to collect a bit of clutter around the edges. There just isn't enough space to put everything. Notes to herself and to-do lists drape over the table beneath the phone. The bedroom is simple and comfortable. Bookcases and storage areas that line the walls suggest that children, learning, and knowing God are important things that sneak into our intimate times, enriching them. Her office is a converted children's bedroom. It is a room of passion. She collects materials that she uses when she gives workshops to parents. She shows them how to work practically with their children. Materials are everywhere. Socks for sock-puppets. Toilet-paper tubes with finger holes cut in them to make dancing figures. Tennis ball cans cut apart and reconstructed to hold bottle caps, ribbons and brightly colored objects that fascinate infants. Materials sit atop the carefully organized plastic bins, each of which contains the makings for a workshop. A computer sits in one corner. It isn't state-of-the-art technology but a glorified word processor. That reflects her personality as well. Technology takes a lower seat to creativity, love of parenting and practicality.

I expect change from Kirby. Some people are absolutely predictable. Their steadiness is a virtue. Kirby is steady in the important areas like love, but she is always changing in interests, always evolving in activities.

I know about her love and care for people who are distressed. She is a comforter. She brings healing and counsel to her friends. She is altruistic and kind.

Loving the One You Know

So I find that for a thousand reasons, I love Kirby. I know this woman because I have learned about, interacted with and shared intimately with her the relationships she has had with those who know her. I know her because of the objects with which she has populated our world. I love her because she is unique in all the world, and she loves me.

I have described my knowledge and love for Kirby at length. This is not only because I'm an incurable romantic deeply in love and I want to tell you about it. Nor is it merely to illustrate that Paul's metaphor of the church as the bride of Christ is a good one (Eph 5:24-33) or to show how much the love of our spouse is like the love of the triune God. It is all of those things. But for our purposes it is because many of my specific reflections are applicable to the relationship between psychological science and Christian theology. Through psychological science we find that humans are orderly, logical, creative, original, unique, beautiful, unpredictable, loving, compassionate, caring, empathic, personal and relational. Theology reveals a sense of story, personality and relationality as well.

For me there is a parallel between coming to love Kirby more through knowing her better and coming to love God more through knowing God better. This suggests to me a relational model of the interaction between psychological science and Christian theology.

DANCE AS A RELATIONAL MODEL

The Dance

In a ballroom dance, which involves partners in a handhold or close embrace, one dancer leads and the other follows. Yet this does not take away the autonomy of either partner. Similarly, we dance as partners with God, who leads. This dance involves suggestions, direction, confidence, movement, patterns, improvisation and flair. We submit. God shows off the divine creation.

In understanding our relationship with God, the academic disciplines of theology and psychological science make contributions as dance partners. Initially their relationship is a dance between strangers. At first, a man and a woman might be hesitant to dance. They see each other across a crowded room and wonder, *Should we dance?* They can enjoy their solitude or try to see if they can move as one. When strangers engage, it is often initially awkward. They might step on each other's toes, bump knees, hold each other in uncomfortable, strange and new ways.

The dance is aided if both partners have a good dance frame. A dance frame is firm without appearing stiff. Both partners stand with good tension in both arms. If the man steps forward, the woman does not let her arm collapse. If she does, the man will step into her personal space. But if the woman has a good frame, she feels pressure from the man's movement, and she steps back as the man steps forward. They move together. If the man steps backward, the woman does not let her arm be pulled forward, leaving her body behind. If she does, they will pull apart. Instead, she lets her entire frame step forward, and again, they move together. The man might try new steps that the woman hasn't learned. Usually, that isn't much of a problem if the woman's frame is firm and she keeps her feet moving to the rhythm of the music.

In the dance between theology and psychological science, these same moves happen. Each discipline has its personal time and space. But will they dance together? Initial attempts are awkward. But each discipline has a frame—a firm method of approaching its subject matter. If the frame is maintained, then they can sustain engagement without invading each other's personal space and treading on toes, or without pulling away and losing contact.

The more partners dance with each other, the smoother they dance. Of course, on occasion partners have fundamental differences and break the partnership. But usually, practice makes the partners better able to anticipate each other's moves and work together with each other's styles. They recognize each other's strengths and compensate for each other's weaknesses.

Engaging

Sometimes, the dance will change to a personal and intimate relationship. When romantic relationships develop, they usually do so predictably. Bernard Murstein[4] described a theory of relationship formation called the Stimulus, Values, Roles (SVR) Model. In his theory partners examine different aspects of the relationship as it matures. Unsuitable partners are dropped at each stage of relationship development.

At the initial stage people are attracted to each other because of their stimulus characteristics. They like the way each other looks, sounds, feels and smells. They like their looks as a couple. They compare each other on similarity of socioeconomic status, clothes and other external characteristics. A partner who passes through the stimulus filter is then examined at a deeper level.

At the second stage people explore each other's values and priorities. They talk. They discover their likes and dislikes. They talk about the things that are important to them. What are their religious beliefs and practices? What are their goals and ambitions? What are they trying to do with their lives? Again, a relationship might cool off or end if the dissimilarities between the partners is deemed too great to overcome or not potentially rewarding enough to merit the effort to overcome differences. Those relationships that survive the values filter move to a deeper level.

By the time partners know each other's values well, they have had considerable experience at interacting with each other. They might begin to seriously entertain the idea of marrying. Thus they think a lot about how they act in each other's presence—their roles with each other. Can they be intimate with each other? Or does the interaction stay on a social level? Do they enjoy talking about the same things? Can they resolve differences amicably? How do they like to spend their time? Do they have the same drive for intimacy or sexual interaction? Relationships fall by the wayside often because the partners are not compatible in such roles.

Murstein's SVR model can apply to the formation and deepening of any relationship, but it might be especially useful in two. It can tell about how a person's personal love of God can develop. It also can describe this relationship between theology and psychological science.

Engagement

The culmination in the courtship between science and religion—or particularly Christian theology and psychological science—is formal engagement. During the engagement, mutual commitment builds. Psychologist Caryl Rusbult[5] has studied the elements of commitment. We become more committed to a loved one if we have more satisfying experiences and invest more in the relationship, but also if we do not pursue alternative people or activities. Our relationship with God grows when we experience joy in worship, God's love of us, God's care for us, comfort in times of distress and learning when we seek more knowledge. If we put effort into knowing God and if we put ourselves on the line as public Christians (rather than as undercover agents for God), then those investments will build our love. Augustine argued in the *Confessions*[6] that his belief enabled him to love and know God more—not that his love motivated his belief as we often understand it. Yet psychological science has shown, as one of its fundamental truths, that behavior strengthens belief just as beliefs motivate behaviors. So most of us find that Augustine's observation fits us. The more we commit in faith to Christ, the more we know God. Faith is an insider's experience rather than an outsider's. It is difficult to simply learn *about* God and from that come to know God. It is easier to come to God first. We will then learn not only about God but also know God personally.

Similarly, the fields of Christian theology and psychological science will become more committed to each other to the degree that we are satisfied with the union, invest in the union and don't play around with alternatives (such as a conflict model). I believe that, in fact, psychological science and Christian theology are already married. In some ways it is like an arranged marriage. Because God reveals the divine character through both special and general revelations, the two disciplines are joined together. The question we face is, how committed will each discipline be to this arranged marriage? Like our relationship with God, we will experience a more personal relationship between psychological science and Christianity the more we enter into an insider's experience. If you are primarily a theologian, pastor or Christian in the pew, you can enter into the relationship by listening to and learning about what psychological science has to teach and by enjoying the wonders of the findings. If you are primarily a psychologist, then entering into a personal relationship with God (if you haven't already) and entering into interactions with theologians and theology as a discipline can increase your investment and satisfaction with the discipline. It also can promote a more committed relationship. The deep engagement affects our relationship to both disciplines' subject matters and it affects our love of the relationship between the disciplines.

The Marriage

Psychological science and Christian theology are already in relationship, a long-term marriage. There are good marriages and bad ones. Some are intimate. Others are stone cold or battlefield hot. But most marriages have periods marked by different interactions.

Over the years many have suggested general models for the science-religion relationship. Ian Barbour, for example, suggested four ways that science and religion relate to each other—conflict, independence, dialogue and integration.[7] We looked at similar though distinctive models for psychology and Christianity in chapter two. These models characterize the relationship between science and religion as conflict, independence, dialogue or integration. I am proposing that science and religion are in a marriage-like relationship that has gone through and will go through periods of conflict and of intimacy.

Conflict. There are local conflicts and differences that Kirby and I have had to resolve. Since Kirby has been going through menopause— about ten years now—her internal thermostat has changed. She has hot flashes several times a day. I seem to be getting more cold natured. When I get in the car in the winter, I want to crank up the heater. Kirby wants to open the windows. Both of us can be a bit cranky about the temperature, I suppose. We have little conflicts over who controls the crank (and who might be the crankiest at the moment). Yet we usually resolve these differences with good humor and a sense of mutual submission to each other. So, there are times of conflict in our marriage, yet there are far more times of intimacy and sharing than of conflict and differences.

Independence. There are areas of specialization, as in all marriages. I do the taxes. Kirby keeps the checkbook. I care for the yard and car. Kirby cares for the kitchen. I cook breakfast and make my lunch. Kirby cooks dinner and makes her lunch. So there are definite times when we move on parallel tracks and don't interact with each other.

Dialogue. There are times when we have great dialogue about mutual interests. Kirby shares her perspective. I share mine. We influence each other. Both benefit from the dialogue.

Integration. There are also times when we submerge our interests within the other's expertise and interest area. Kirby is more knowledgeable about child rearing than I. So, throughout our parenting years I often took cues from and deferred to her. I had my own opinions and certainly felt that I knew more about being a father to our four children. But I was eager to learn more from her about being a parent. I could be secure in my own strengths and be integrated into her specialty as well.

So I'm proposing a bit of a different slant on the science-religion relationship. Previously, writers suggested categories to describe the whole relationship—like Barbour's conflict, independence, dialogue and integration models—and people thought of themselves as endorsing one category or another. Yet it has seemed to me, during my thirty-plus years trying to relate psychological science to Christianity, that a more fluid relationship model is needed. For example, the conflict model does not fit perfectly. I do not always want to feel that there are conflicts between science and my Christian faith. But there certainly are times when I have to draw a line in the sand and fight over an issue. Nor does the independence model fit snugly. I do not always want to walk away from dialogues with theologians. But I confess that there are some people with whom I try to adopt an independence model. I like the dialogue model, but it isn't perfect either. I sometimes thrive on dialogue—the give and take of sharing with someone who approaches human behavior and faith with a different methodology and set of data. It is stimulating to have such dialogues. Yet sometimes I just don't want to exert the needed effort. I am not sure whether it is mental laziness, simple mental exhaustion at work or has more to do with the rhythm of life. Life is meant to be exciting, stimulating and absolutely riveting. Yet even the writer of Hebrews speaks of entering God's rest (Heb 3:16–4:5). The writer speaks of the periods of creative activity by God, but also the period of the sabbath rest.

Finally, in many ways, I have been always in the integration camp. Indeed, there are times when I think integration is appropriate. But I must admit that there are many areas that theologians address that psychological science cannot. I cannot study eschatology by conducting psychological experiments. I cannot address history scientifically but have to rely on people's memory of history. Theology uses different tools, data, models and experiences, and there are times when I must simply subordinate my psychological expertise to theology. Similarly, there are times when I think psychological science can speak with a firmer voice than theology. Theology can tell us that we must forgive. But God doesn't share in Scripture *how* we are to forgive. Psychology has a lot to say about that. On areas where Scripture is silent—both psychological science and clinical psychology—can often speak.

How Does This Relational (Marriage) Model Benefit Us?

A relational model of science and religion might help us not to put ourselves in boxes quite as often. Instead of labeling myself as an integrationist or as an adherent to the conflict (or warfare) model, I can recognize that—as with any relationship—there are times when we integrate and other times when we fight. Those times are subject to change and do not mark us—or others—as forever enemies or as wimpy doormats. Perhaps an ebb-and-flow relational model can build a tolerance that will sustain contact and deepen dialogue. I believe it can promote better discussions.

But all is not rosy. Even with a relational model we still see God (and the other discipline) through a mirror darkly (1 Cor 13:12). My goal is to help us clear the vision as much as possible so we can learn more about God through looking at the natural world, and so we can actually know God better. There are reasons—in each discipline—for the mirror's inaccuracies. Perhaps if we examine those reasons we can move to a place where our vision is clearer.

SUMMARY

As I reflect on the deepest, most intimate human relationship I have known—with my wife—I marvel at how varied the sources of knowledge are. I see those same sources in my relationship with God. What seem to be unlikely sources of knowledge about Kirby (e.g., cards she writes to others or notes she leaves as reminders to herself) turn out to stir affection and love in my heart because they inform me of her personality and character.

Our relationship with God is like a marriage. The marriage-like relationship between psychological science and Christian theology tell me more about that marriage of people with God—the bride of Christ with the bridegroom—and deepen its love. In addition, viewing the relationship of psychological science and theology as part of a marriage may smooth out some of the rough times in the future of that relationship. We may thus stay engaged in the relationship through a wide range of emotional ups and downs. Let's look closer at this marriage.

UNDERSTANDING THE
RELATIONAL PARTNERS

LET'S GET TO KNOW A BIT about the partners in the relationship between psychological science and Christian theology. My thesis is that psychological science can help us know more about God. Thus it can affect our formal and informal theology. Also psychological science can inform, inspire feelings and stimulate our reactions in a way that actually helps us see, know and love God more.

SCIENCE AND MATERIALISTIC EXPLANATIONS

Let's begin by being sure we are on the same page in understanding what science is and does. Linguist S. I. Hayakawa[1] argues that in language the map is not the territory. The same is true in science. Scientific data, models and theories are maps of people's experience, but they should not be confused with actual experience. If I gave you a map of Richmond, you wouldn't confuse it with the real city of Richmond. That would be true whether it was an aerial photograph or a line drawing. Both maps would tell you important information about the real city of Richmond. Both would be "true" or "accurate." But both would be maps. Sometimes nonscientists (and scientists too) mistake the map of a scientific theory for the territory of the experience. When they do, misconceptions occur.

For example, sometimes people think that because science measures materialistic cause and effect, but does not admit the movement of the Holy Spirit or the direct acts of God, then science adheres to a materialistic conception of reality. Even though some scientists (and nonscientists) are materialists, materialism is not inherent to science. Scientists can believe in many nonmaterial causes within reality but simply exclude them from the "map" of a particular science. They do so because, by convention, that science aims to explain materialistic relationships among variables. By analogy, an aerial photograph will not reveal the presence of an underground river or a fault deep within the earth's crust even though the photographer knows that both exist.

As for science and religion, I believe in divine and human free will. Yet I cannot directly measure free will. Nor can I measure the direct interaction with God, Jesus or the Holy Spirit. I can, however, often infer God's action based on indirect evidence. Similarly, I don't think we can measure the effects of prayer. I believe that prayer has real effects in our lives. But those effects are not materialistic causes. Therefore, they do not fit with science.

All scientific disciplines attempt to relate materialistic variables in cause-and-effect relationships and in correlations (which describe the strength of relationship to each other). That is, science is focused on what it can observe directly or indirectly and what it can measure. And things need to be material if we are to measure them. Measurement can include observing things that cannot be seen with the naked eye, of course—like wind or subatomic particles (or strings). But we have to be able to use some tool to transduce (i.e., convert) the weak—undetectable with the naked eye—signal into the movement of a needle on a measurement tool.

We obviously cannot measure many important unseen spiritual experiences in life. For instance, no one has yet found a satisfactory way to measure love directly. Nor can we measure the feeling of wonder we experience when we see Rembrandt's *The Return of the Prodigal Son*. Like measuring the effects of wind or the tracks left by subatomic particles in bubble chambers, we can infer the existence of love and of wonder from self-reports and from other measurements. But our inferences might be mistaken. Therefore, science can never be more than a good map of people's experience. Different models and theories will illuminate different aspects of human experience, just as a map can be an aerial photograph or a line drawing. Which map is best depends on the need of the person using the map.

PSYCHOLOGY

The Subdisciplines of Psychological Science

Psychological science is composed of several subdisciplines that further localize the measurement of experiences. Psychological science tries to make coherent models and theories about the data that come from the measurements. These subdisciplines include biopsychology (which studies how the body, especially the brain, affects behavior), developmental psychology (which studies expected changes throughout the life cycle), social psychology (which studies how people affect each others' behavior), personality (which studies why people act the way they do across time and situations), health psychology, disordered behavior and helping behavior. There is also a subdiscipline of the psychology of religion, but that subdiscipline seeks to describe how people experience religion rather than what I am trying to do with this book—to let all of psychological science speak to us and (we hope) help us know God better. The common denominator in all of these subdisciplines is adherence to an empirical epistemology and an empirical method of discovering God's truth.

How the Science of Psychology Works

Empirical means learning through observation (with all of its shortcomings). There are several empirical methods, including observational, correlational and experimental methods.

Psychological methods. Observational methods are aimed at describing phenomena. Usually, observational methods are employed early in the study of a phenomenon. This was true in the psychoanalytic method. Freud began writing about psychoanalysis by describing famous cases— Anna O, the girl who couldn't breathe, Little Hans and others. The study of most new psychological phenomena usually starts with careful observation and description of cases. Today, sophisticated qualitative analysis methods are also used. Typically, those methods are aimed at discovery and hypothesis generation instead of hypothesis testing.

Correlational methods observe several variables at the same time and translate their co-occurrence into numerical expressions—correlation coefficients or regression coefficients. Correlations range from +1 to -1. The plus sign indicates that both variables increase together. The negative sign indicates that when one variable increases the other decreases. A correlation of 1 indicates perfect prediction. A correlation of zero represents complete random occurrence—no relationship between the two variables. For example, number of social workers per city block is positively correlated with number of pregnant teens per city block. Note that with correlations we cannot infer that either variable causes the other.

Experimental methods seek to determine causes. They do so by equating or experimentally controlling all variables except the one the experimenter seeks to manipulate, called the independent variable. Then the effect of the manipulation can be seen on the dependent variable.

Here is an example. Suppose an experimenter wants to study the effect of praying on people's personal peace. There are many ways to test this relationship. The experimenter could observe people praying and describe whether they seemed peaceful (using an observational method). Or perhaps the experimenter could ask many adults how much they pray and how peaceful they feel. That experimenter could then calculate the strength of the correlation between amount of prayer and degree of peacefulness (using a correlational method). Using correlation, it might be that people pray when they feel at peace, people pray and then feel at peace, or people experience God's grace and both pray and feel peace as a result. With correlation, we cannot tell what is causing what. But suppose the experimenter has a hypothesis that prayer could *cause* people to be peaceful. The experimenter would use an experiment. People might be assigned to pray a specified amount (say one hour per day above what the person usually prays). Others would be assigned to pray as usual. The experimenter would assess whether a sense of peace increased for those who prayed more than usual. That would show that praying caused people to feel increased personal peace.

How the empirical method works. Studies work by *sampling.* When we take a sample, we investigate a portion of all possible situations. There are three primary dimensions on which sampling most regularly occurs.

Some studies sample adults from the entire population of the United States. Others sample only members of a local congregation. The experimenter would attempt to draw a *valid* sample—that is one that really represents fairly all the people in the population that the experimenter wishes to generalize about. In this case the national sample would be a more valid sample for making statements about how people in the United States are affected by prayer.

The experimenter could sample among the many experimental treatments of the subjects. What is the best way to get a person to pray and to ensure that the person really does pray? The person might simply be told to pray. On the other hand, the experimenter might require that the person complete a prayer log over the week, or get up an hour early each morning to pray, or say a particular prayer aloud into a voice recorder a thousand times—such as the Lord's Prayer (Mt 6:9-13) or the Jesus prayer (a prayer uttered in concordance with breathing in and out as a spiritual discipline). Each would sample a different treatment of praying.

Finally, the experimenter would sample measures of peace. That is, there might be twenty or two thousand ways for a psychologist to measure peace. People could fill out a peace inventory (PI), which could be scored and compared to national norms on the PI. People could fill out the "Personal Experience of Affective Calm for Everyone" (PEACE) scale. That would sample peace a different way even though both the PI and PEACE were questionnaires. The experimenter could also measure brain waves (percent alpha waves for an hour after praying relative to sitting and relaxing, but not praying). Brain scans could be used. Peripheral physiological indexes—like heart rate, blood pressure or skin conductance—could also indicate peacefulness or lack of it. Or hormonal measures (i.e., the stress hormone cortisol in the blood) could be used. Finally, behavioral measures could be used. The person could be subjected to harassment from an aggravating confederate of the experimenter and the person's behavior recorded to detect how peaceful or agitated the person becomes. The person could be followed surreptitiously by an experimenter, who could record instances of loss of temper or seeming frustration. How scientists measure the outcomes, called the dependent variable, is again a matter of sampling. In modern psychological science the best studies use self-report instruments plus at least one other kind of measure.

How scientists act. I skipped over some very interesting aspects of science—the acts by which scientists conduct their crafts. Hendrika Vande Kemp[2] wrote about the parallels between science and religious methods. For example, she observed that scientists rely on the testimony of past witnesses. They use hypothetico-deductive reasoning. They appeal to authorities. They find things serendipitously. They use intuition to decide what to study, how to study it, how to analyze the data and how to make sense of the findings. In short, scientists behave much like theologians. Both behave like people in the pews who employ "theological" and "psychological" methods (although laypeople do so less rigorously than professional theologians or psychologists do).

Sampling at the higher level of studies. It isn't just the nuts and bolts of studies that depends on sampling though. Sampling is at the heart of science. Any individual study to test the relationship between two variables is one of thousands that could have been performed. Furthermore, because a particular study is always a sample of one study from a universe of possible studies, I caution consumers of science to never fully trust a study. Good as it might seem at first, every study is quite subjective. Each is composed of thousands of subjective choices in trying to measure a phenomenon and yield data. Scientific data sound objective, but data have meaning only within a system that says that such studies will actually yield usable information that apply to some scientific model of a phenomenon. Models must be supported by many studies (using different methods and done by different researchers) before we can have any confidence in them. Models, when closely related to other models and when elaborated in sufficient detail, can become theories. Unlike a layperson's use of the word *theory*, which is often contrasted universally with *fact* (as in, "It's not true; it's just a theory"), a scientist's use of the word *theory* suggests something that is quite comprehensive and supported by much evidence. Theories can hold together with other theories. If a network of theories is sufficiently supported, it can become a scientific paradigm.

Basically, science is a set of procedures that aims at uncovering an understanding of nature that is as true as possible. Remember, the map can be accurate or true, but not be fully coincident with the territory. A street map of Richmond could be completely accurate in listing streets, locations and names, and yet not tell where a single tennis court, super-market or Starbucks is.

Science depends on scientists subjecting themselves to nature as an arbiter of truth. Scientists must be willing to let findings correct the accuracy of their models, theories and even paradigms. Philosophers like Michael Polanyi[3] convinced scientists that science is loaded with subjective choices and cannot be treated as completely objective. Karl Popper[4] proposed that nothing could in fact be *proved* by science. How-ever, Popper believed that science could actually *falsify* theories by find-ing results that did not fit with the theory.

Critiques of ideal scientific methods from historians of science. But it isn't as simple as it sounds. Historians of science who are also philosophers of science, like Thomas Kuhn,[5] have criticized science that is built on an ideal scientific method. They have shown that real scientists rarely be-have like most early philosophers said ideal scientists ought to behave. When results falsify standing theories, ideal science prescribes that sci-entists abandon those theories. Real scientists don't. Something isn't happening in real science that was expected from the ideal version.

Scientists simply don't rely on data from nature as the final arbiter of truth. Imre Lakatos[6] took seriously the historians' critiques but contin-ued in a more positive tradition of philosophers of science. Between the level of theory and paradigm, Lakatos described what he called the "research program," which is a set of theories and a body of data. Typi-cally, there is one central theory at the center of the research program, which Lakatos calls the "hard core." Surrounding the hard-core theory are auxiliary hypotheses, other theories and data that are directly re-lated to the theory. For example, the auxiliary hypotheses might in-clude a theory about how to measure the phenomena of interest, an understanding of which evidence is considered to support the hypoth-esis and which doesn't, and other hypotheses that have not been tested but would be expected to be confirmed. Those auxiliary hypotheses provide a firewall around the hard-core theory. The idea that nature is an arbiter of truth seems to imply that falsification of the central hypothesis of a theory ought to result in the abandonment of the theory. Yet Lakatos showed that scientists allowed the firewall to shield the hard core of the program. When a scientific test of a hypothesis failed, scientists questioned their methods. They abandoned auxiliary hypotheses. But they held onto the core unless it was soundly and repeatedly found to be inadequate or just plain wrong.

Lakatos pointed out that instead of successive paradigms, as proposed by Thomas Kuhn, the history of science was better explained in terms of competing programs of research. He calls some "progressive programs" and others "degenerating programs." In response to challenges from studies that don't work out, progressive programs revise the core theory plus alternatives (called simply the theory) to (1) preserve the unchallenged portions of the theory and (2) widen its scope by making modifications that predict new novel results successfully. The applicability of the new, modified theory progressively advances. Degenerating programs rescue the core theory as a whole by modifying the firewall but restricting the applicability or usefulness of the theory. Thus the applicability of the theory contracts or degenerates.

Summary regarding psychological science. Like any other science, psychological science is an admittedly imperfect picture of psychological reality. It consists of broad, general beliefs about psychological truth, which are like the center of a bull's-eye. It also consists of less-central beliefs, which are supported by less research, are less central to the entire structure, and are less resistant to modification by contradictory research findings. To the nonscientist this structure might sound like a house of cards, insecurely attached to reality and ready to tumble. As we shall see, however, it bears a striking resemblance to theology.

THEOLOGY

The Subdisciplines of Theology

Primary subdisciplines. Theology can be seen as a series of related subdisciplines.[7] *Exegetical theology* seeks the author's intended meaning of scriptural texts. It includes etymology, grammar, context and so on. *Biblical theology* builds on exegetical theology and seeks to describe books or themes, which are conceptually integrated into metathemes. *Systematic theology* seeks to organize scriptural understanding according to topics (such as justification) for the purpose of answering questions about how we should believe and act. The subdisciplines of exegetical, biblical and systematic theology are primary theologies in that they deal directly with the meaning of the primary data of theology—Scripture texts.

They are also primary in their similarities to Lakatos's core theories in science. Systems of theology, like Reformed theology within Christian theology, are hard-core theological "theories." They are resistant to modification by new data. In theology, new data might come from new texts (such as the discovery of the Dead Sea Scrolls), new tools (such as literary criticism), new scholarship (such as E. P. Sanders's[8] scholarship on Second Temple Judaism) and new ideas (such as those continually proposed by theologians).

Exegetical theology deals directly with the data of the words of Scripture. It is parallel to interpreting a particular scientific experiment or study. Biblical theology is aimed at constructing accurate local models of, say, a particular book or a particular doctrine. It parallels science's attempt to construct scientific models that seek to explain accurately a circumscribed portion surrounding a phenomenon. Systematic theology puts theology together in a complex, interrelated but self-consistent way. It is similar to theory construction in science.

Primary theology—which depends heavily on the study of texts—is aided by study of Greek and Hebrew. Language or linguistic studies inform translators how to interpret passages of texts compiled from copies of the original autographs. One might compare this to the scientific method of collecting or analyzing data.

Secondary or supportive subdisciplines of theology. Behind these primary subdisciplines, which deal most directly with biblical texts, theology is informed by secondary subdisciplines. These support the primary subdisciplines by providing contextual understanding for properly interpreting scriptural texts. These include subdisciplines such as historical theology, anthropological theology and philosophical theology. These parallel Lakatos's auxiliary hypotheses.

Historical theology studies historical evidence, using the methods of historical research. It analyzes Scripture's historical context as well as the contexts of theological debates and how controversies were (or were not) resolved.

Anthropological theology uses the methods of anthropology, cultural studies, sociology, psychology and perhaps other human sciences and humanities to help scholars understand the people and culture to which the Scriptures were addressed. In a related but slightly different way, theological anthropology also seeks to understand what people are like through using the discipline of theology—including all of its subdisciplines. It attempts to create an understanding of humans, primarily in their relationship to God, secondarily in their relationship to other humans, and less centrally in their relationship to animals and the environment.

Philosophical theology studies the philosophy of historical times. Knowledge of the secular philosophy of the time helps theologians understand some of the arguments that Scripture's authors were making.

Practical theology applies all the disciplines and subdisciplines of theology to help people within the church work and live with each other. Practical theology describes life in the body, Christian education, pastoral care and pastoral counseling. It also can reach out to those outside of the church, minister to those inside the church, and help Christians evangelize and disciple others. Clinical practice, clinical science and community psychology can inform practical theology, as can the humanities, the arts, the sciences and other social sciences.

We can see that psychological science and theology have similar but different methods. In each, fallible humans work with what each discipline considers to be relevant data and provide interpretations. The two disciplines share more in common methodologically than is usually thought to be the case.

THE RELATIONSHIP BETWEEN PSYCHOLOGY AND THE THEOLOGIES

Faith and Science, and Theology and Psychology

At their root there is no conflict between God's truths as revealed in Scripture and in nature. I believe that we must clearly adhere to faith rather than science if they were to ever come into serious conflict. But this does not mean that I adhere to a filter model in which I measure every psychological finding against an inviolable understanding of Christianity that derives from my particular theology. I have drawn an admittedly oversimplified model of this in figure 7.1.

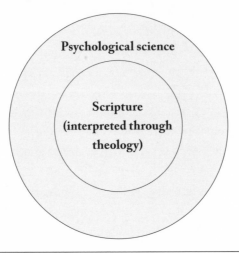

Figure 7.1. Oversimplified filter model
Oversimplified (and caricatured) filter model in which Scripture, as perceived through a particular theology, is seen as dominant and more central to truth than psychological science, which must be measured against the theological interpretation of Scripture to filter the wrong, bad or inconsistent truths.

To correct this oversimplified model, we must take into account that we never deal directly with the data of Scripture, namely with the original autographs that God intended to be Scripture. In fact, no original autographs exist. At best we have early copies of some autographs. Those copies (although some can be shown to be quite accurate) do have some transcription errors, and even early manuscripts may omit or add sections that are not in other early manuscripts. In effect, humans who are sinful contaminate the most basic data. There is, in effect, a layer between pure Scripture (i.e., the autographs) and the human understanding of God's Word, involving potential human errors (see fig. 7.2). These include errors the transcribers made while copying the original autographs (which no longer exist); errors of translations to more modern language (the originals were in Hebrew and Greek); councils who selected books that were considered the canon (which depended on church traditions and potential errors introduced there); errors of theologians (who have personal agendas) in translating. Translators are influenced by systematic theologians, biblical theologians and exegetical theologians, who in turn are influenced by historical, anthropological, philosophical and practical theologians. All of these theologies may have errors. There are also contextual pressures (political, historical, social and cultural) that influence translations and interpretations of Scripture.

Of course, I am not minimizing the many potential errors that can occur in the process of arriving at a scientific conclusion. But I am observing that because of the potential for errors in *both* my theological and scientific interpretations, I cannot support a filter model that *always* prioritizes theology over psychology. There are obvious areas where, despite the potential errors and distortions in applying Scripture, we can have great confidence in applying a filter model. These involve such areas as the basic truths in Christianity. For example, a psychological finding suggesting Jesus is not divine—although it would be unlikely that psychological science could ever make such a claim—would be rejected.

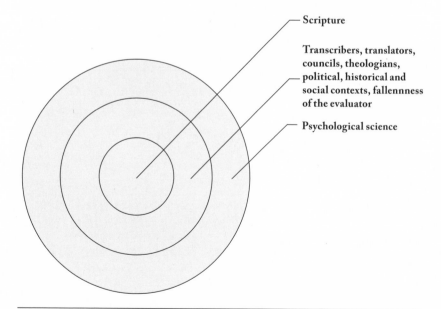

Figure 7.2. Corrected filter model
A corrected filter model suggests many potential sources of human error in formulating and applying theological critiques of psychological science.

When we speak of psychological science and theology—not allegiance to science and faith—we are referring to maps, not to the actual territory (i.e., truth) or to our values. The maps of psychological science and theology are drawn based on explorations of different aspects of the one territory of God's truth. Thus the maps (i.e., psychological science and theology) will use different data, models of the data and theories that connect the data. While we might hope that we could harmonize the scientific and theological maps, and perhaps this can be done, chances are there will be some areas of conflict. I have represented this state of affairs in figure 7.3.

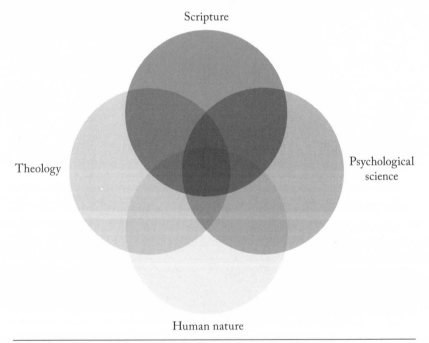

Figure 7.3. A relational model of theology and psychological science
Each area samples incompletely and, occasionally, incorrectly from the full available data. Sometimes they address the same issues, but more often they do not. Sometimes they come into conflict with each other. Each has different realms of relative expertise.

Let's call the sources of data in each discipline of "Scripture" and "nature"—both of which are not perfectly perceivable by humans due to different human distortions and limitations. Theology is the map of scriptural data. Theology provides an interpretation of the data, and thus much of theology overlaps with Scripture. Some theology, through human error, falls outside of Scripture. Theologians (like all imperfect, fallen people) usually do not recognize which aspects of their theology lie outside of the data of Scripture. The theological system seems internally consistent to them and to many laypeople. Similarly, nature includes the natural data. (Here we are looking at human nature in particular.) Psychological science is the map of human nature. Like theology, it generally is a correct description of the territory of human nature, but also like theology, it has areas that fall outside of the truth of human nature. And, like theologians, psychological scientists are not sure which areas are incorrect.

Just as Scripture and human nature overlap (see fig. 7.3), theology and psychological science overlap. They agree about most things. But some things involve statements about different truths that the other does not typically address. Each discipline is expert in different areas, though sometimes each addresses a topic about which the other discipline has more expertise. There are a few areas of conflict, and the best strategy for these relational partners is humility and giving more analysis to the issue rather than haughtily dismissing the other discipline.

The solution to any conflict between psychological science and theology lies in having the two sides enter into conversation with each other. By discussing their assumptions, methods of gathering data and inferences, they can piece together a shared story—one in which each might interpenetrate the other's story. Perhaps even better, theologians could do science and scientists could do theology. The two would thus explore both disciplines. But because professional time is limited, a close relationship is perhaps the best practical relationship. As in a marriage, the two disciplines dance with each other.

Which Discipline Leads the Dance?

The question of disciplinary priority has been debated since Thomas Aquinas. The debate typically ends like this: theology leads, but psychology can make a creative contribution. In many cases, theologians have tried to show that there is no final conflict. For example, in his 1898 Stone Lectures at Princeton, Abraham Kuyper found no conflict between true faith and science, only between misinformed faith or science.

And now I approach my last point, viz., the assertion that the emancipation of Science must inevitably lead to a sharp conflict of principles. . . .

Notice that I do not speak of a conflict between faith and science. Such a conflict does not exist. Every science in a certain degree starts from faith, and, on the contrary, faith, which does not lead to science, is mistaken faith or superstition, but real, genuine faith it is not. . . . Hence it follows that the conflict is not between faith and science, but between the assertion that the cosmos, as it exists today, is either in a normal or abnormal condition.[9]

Kuyper then argued that the real conflict is between those who see the world as always and only natural (materialist state) versus those who think the world is now not in its natural state but is fallen and requires a supernatural in-breaking from God to redeem it. Theology, if done properly, should begin with a supernatural God and end with God, but the natural world, as it exists, calls out for a scientific, observation-and-fact-based explanation. Both science and true religion do this, according to Kuyper.

Malcolm Jeeves, in *Human Nature at the Millennium*,[10] also argues that there should be no final conflict. Jeeves observed that the Bible, and indeed all of God's revelation, is not aimed at helping people understand each other better. Rather, it is aimed at helping people live in right relationship with God. Jeeves does not believe creation is *anthropocentric* (e.g., with humans as the apex and center of creation). Rather, creation is *theocentric*, meant to reveal God so that people can know God better. Jeeves thus implies that if—and it is a big if—both theology and science are aimed at the right end, knowing God better, whichever reveals God is useful and no reason for conflict exists.

The Red Herring: Which Discipline Has Priority?

The dance. In a way, then, any dispute over which discipline has leadership is a red herring. It involves human power politics. When a couple ballroom dances, the man is the designated leader. The man does not drag the woman around the dance floor like a shiny-shoed Neanderthal, and the woman does not follow like a little puppy. Rather, both man and woman assume their individual dance frame. As the man begins a move, he slightly shifts the body, indicating that he is going to step forward, for example, with his left foot. The woman can see the slight sway. She can also feel it because she has a firm dance frame. So, when the man actually steps forward, the woman follows, responding to the slight pressure of hand to hand. The audience does not have the impression that the man is leading at all. The impression is that the couple is moving as one. And in fact, they are.

Male leadership in dance becomes even more ambiguous as the dancers become more advanced. The male knows perhaps four moves that can take place with a particular indication—such as raising his left arm in a particular way. He has in mind which of those moves he intends to lead. But because there are multiple moves that could actually occur, the woman might make a different move. The wise male will not stop dancing, look askance at his partner and mutter about her not being able to follow. Instead, the wise male will admire the beauty and flair with which the partner executed the move and will flow into his next indication.

Psychology and theology. The relationship between psychological science and theology is in fact a cooperative venture in which either partner can give an indication to the other. The other has the option of what kind of response will be made.

A psychologist might read a theological paper—say about God's balance of justice and mercy toward Israel—and get an idea for a study about a manager's balance of justice and mercy in leading a work group. A theologian might read a psychological study—say about a victim's need to punish wrongdoers even if the punishment is also costly to the victim—and suddenly see how the justice motive is built within humans, reflecting light on God's just character. Each discipline can follow the indication of the other. Yet each will do what seems appropriate to its discipline and will use its discipline's methods.

Summary. God is the prototypical dance instructor in the dance of eternal life. Humans are to discern God's instruction and follow. God's instructions, like a good dance teacher's, are usually subtle, not gross. God has the ultimate teaching technique, open and inviting. If we put ourselves in God's hands, and if we maintain a strong dance frame ourselves—as we, in our discipline dance with the other disciplines—with our prime directive to be sensitive to God's movement, then surprisingly both the psychological scientist and the theologian can move together to the beautiful music.

There is no final conflict between God and human nature. However, the disciplines of psychological science and theology can come into conflict due to human sinfulness. Conflict can be minimized in several ways, though. When we pursue the end of knowing God better, both psychological science and theology can contribute. If we follow each other's lead while maintaining a firm disciplinary frame, we can learn from each other. Even when we seem to be at odds on an issue, if we stay in close relationship we can usually work it out.

IN-GROUPS AND OUT-GROUPS

Psychology tells us that the natural tendency is to see many subdivisions in our in-group, but to make few distinctions among an out-group. As a Christian, I see the many varieties of Christianity, and I make many distinctions. I might say, "I'm not a premillennial, postrapture, dispensational, evangelical Christian who believes in free will. I'm far different. I'm a premillennial, postrapture, free-will, evangelical Christian, but I'm definitely not a dispensationalist." But, my Jewish friend persists in talking about what "you Christians" believe about Israel, as if there are no distinctions.

If you are a psychologist, a theologian or just an interested layperson, then you might not have thought about the subdisciplines in one or the other discipline. Yet each subdiscipline approaches questions of faith and living in a specialized way (even though they share many similarities at root). And it is difficult for me to break free of my own subgroup.

Yet God wants me to love all people—my family, my neighbors and even my enemies. God wants me to be just to all, not only to a select group of insiders who share my way of thinking. By seeing the differences in psychological science and theology, I have come to appreciate even more the radical nature of this call. Yet I also see how Jesus died for everyone. And I am ashamed that I cannot even transcend my disciplinary boundaries. But God is a God of mercy and grace. If I bring to God my shortcomings, God will enable me by grace to lead a life worthy of being called a Christian.

SUMMARY

In the present chapter, I have continued to try to build both mutual respect and understanding of the two disciplines—psychological science and theology—which exist in their marriage-like relationship. Most notably I explained the processes of each and found them to be remarkably similar. I also showed that each had various subdivisions. I suggested that both disciplines had ample human errors; therefore, it is not a wise decision to privilege one discipline over the other as a general policy. Instead, each must act in humility, subjugating itself to the Great Instructor, the triune God.

For many people, accustomed to thinking of theology as queen of the sciences, this will be a difficult position to accept. They will likely offer some challenges. I will try to deal with those in the following chapter.

DEALING WITH
SOME CHALLENGES

THREE OF MY IDEAS FOR PSYCHOLOGICAL SCIENCE and Christian theology will be especially difficult for many people to put aside. First, many believe that to formulate a Christian understanding of human nature requires the integration of the insights of *clinical* psychology and Christian theology. I will suggest that this isn't the best strategy, and we should use psychological science as our basis of a human anthropology, not clinical psychology. Second, many espouse a filter model as superior to a relational model. I will critique the filter model and will plead for a humble approach that treats the two disciplines as relational partners. Finally, despite Romans 1:18-21, in which Paul argues that general revelation is available to even the darkest mind, some theologians (e.g., Karl Barth) and psychologists (e.g., Eric Johnson) have argued that there is no way to know God through nature. But I believe that, despite the distortions of sin and its effects and that special revelation is necessary and sufficient for salvation, humans can receive meaningful communication from God through psychological science. I suggest that through God's general revelation we can enrich believers' and nonbelievers' relationships with God.

THE VALUE OF APPLIED CLINICAL PSYCHOLOGY
AND PRACTICAL THEOLOGY

Clinical psychology is a part of psychological science. Both clinical psychology and the rest of psychological science are useful to living in the world of personal relationships. But each is useful for a different purpose. Clinical psychology is more helpful in pastoral care or Christian helping. Psychological science is better for revealing truth about people in general and perhaps in revealing God's character to us.

Although I am a counseling psychologist whose roots are deep in the helping side of psychology rather than basic research, I also do basic research in social psychology, personality psychology, developmental psychology, health psychology and biopsychology. Over the years my studies have grown in both directions. I have not abandoned my clinical roots. Nor am I abandoning my belief in the value of lay counseling. In fact, when we care for suffering people, that too reveals the way to heaven. Clinical psychology offers us daily opportunities to walk in the steps of Jesus—who healed, talked with the suffering and gave himself for a world that was lost and needy. When we approach counseling as an opportunity for compassion instead of as a job, clinical psychology can help us know God.

However, I believe that clinical psychology is not the best base to approach integration of psychological science and theology. Psychological science is broader, more scientifically controlled and just as connected to human experience as clinical psychology. I believe that, in most incidences relevant to the present book, psychological science is a more apt relational partner to theology than is clinical psychology. Most integration of clinical psychology and theology has been applicable to practical theology. Psychological science is far broader than clinical psychology. It is more useful for telling us about people's lives both apart from and within their suffering, and therefore telling us more about God.

Clinical Psychology's Method Is Not Objective

When I practice clinical psychology, I come into direct contact with people. I can observe their behavior in an intimate, helping situation. But when I use my clinical observations to generalize about human nature, I am not doing clinical psychology but clinical *science*. I am generalizing from the data supplied by my subjectively filtered observations about people. When I am counseling, I collect data unsystematically using ill-specified methods. My purpose is to alleviate a client's psychological pain, not to collect the data at all. Yet I am using those clinical data to generalize. Also, my sample consists of those seeking my help, and they usually do not agree to be research participants.

Clinical Psychology, Human Experience and Psychological Science

Generalizations from clinical samples are no more human or humane than are generalizations from psychological science. Psychological scientists can study hurricane victims, trauma survivors, 9/11 helpers or earthquake refugees. Psychological scientists, like clinicians, feel the pain, see the dreams, hear the yearning and empathize with the disappointments of those they study. But someone once quipped, "Statistics are human suffering with the tears wiped dry." When making generalizations about human nature using clinical science and psychological science, clinical science doesn't measure up.

Weaknesses of the Integration Done by Clinician-Theologians

There are several weaknesses in the ways clinician-theologians attempt to integrate psychology and theology. First, most clinician-theologians are weaker in theology than in clinical practice. Second, there are limitations on what can be derived about human nature and, by extension, God's nature, from clinical psychology.

Weak on theology. First, probably since the beginning of the movement to integrate Christian values into the helping professions, the movement has been criticized for being stronger on clinical practice than on theology.[1] We can easily see how this might be true. Clinical training requires a curriculum of five or six years to meet licensing requirements in most states. Usually, these counselors don't have nearly enough time to receive a comparable training in theology. It is not surprising that theological depth is often weak. Even in clinical programs that explicitly promote integration of theology into clinical practice, far more time is spent in the curriculum on counseling than on theology. Many Christian clinical psychologists have never systematically studied theology.

However, at times the criticism has also applied to trained pastoral counselors. (I am differentiating pastoral counselors from pastors who counsel.) Pastoral counselors have often relied on clinical psychology for deriving much of their counseling theory. There are important reasons for this. Pastoral counselors want to be acceptable as mental health providers. After receiving (usually) a master's of divinity degree (which typically is not as extensive in training in theology as the master's of theology degree), the typical pastoral counselor trades in the currency of clinical psychological theory and technique. Pastoral counselors see clients for much of their work week. They spend much less time monitoring and teaching doctrine than they do helping alleviate human suffering. Thus, their expertise in theology is usually much weaker than theologians.

Another reason for the weaknesses in the integration by clinician-theologians is that clinicians, looking for ways to harmonize their psychological theory and theological presuppositions, sometimes adopt theories of therapy that are not current. Presuppositions may trump data on the effectiveness of the theory. Some pastoral counselors, who value love and acceptance, favor Carl Rogers's person-centered approach, which they see as consistent with their values. Evangelicals, who value truth and right thinking, often gravitate toward the cognitive and cognitive-behavioral approaches. Some, whose theology emphasizes the stain of sin and the unconscious control it has on behavior, are drawn to psychodynamically informed approaches. Even lay counseling approaches, such as the theophostic approach,[2] draw heavily on psychoanalytic assumptions of early childhood influences needing to be emotionally worked through.

Meanwhile, the field of psychotherapy has moved increasingly beyond general theories of psychotherapy—like behavioral, person-centered, cognitive, cognitive-behavioral or even psychodynamic approaches. The current emphasis is toward evidence-based practice or empirically supported treatments. Most practitioners use a variety of methods from various theories. These methods have been shown repeatedly to be effective with particular human problems. For instance, in a single day of therapy, a therapist might use dialectical behavior therapy with a person who has a borderline personality disorder, Hans Kohut's psychoanalytically informed self psychology with a person who has a narcissistic personality disorder, David Barlow's cognitive-behavioral therapy with someone who has a social phobia, Aaron Beck's cognitive therapy for a depressed client, and in the evening use emotionally focused couple therapy with a troubled couple.

A Critique of the Field on Informing an Anthropological Theology

I have been affiliated with the field of the integration of clinical psychology and Christianity since beginning graduate studies in 1974, and I have written much about integration from this viewpoint.[3] I value the field of Christian counseling and will continue to pursue integration in the field. I am not abandoning the field of integration of clinical psychology and Christian theology. Yet I think it is important that we, as a field, recognize some of our weaknesses and limitations.

I believe that integration of psychology and Christianity by therapists *based on clinical information* generally is *not* a good basis for understanding human nature. General integrative attempts based on the clinic assume that counseling theories provide true information about individuals. That *can be* the case. But usually the counselor's database is too narrow and too distorted.

Database is too narrow. The database is too narrow because even a good psychotherapist's experience is too limited. Even if the therapist has twenty clients active at all times, and perhaps fifty to one hundred clients every year over a thirty-year career, that therapist is, in a lifetime, seeing only fifteen hundred to three thousand clients. Typically, though, clinicians solidify their theories of counseling far before they have seen thousands of clients. In fact, their theories of counseling are often formulated within their first year or so of seeing clients as a counseling trainee. Larry Crabb's[4] first book was *released* within five years of his graduation (and was written earlier than that). So was mine.[5] Thus, in reality, the counseling theory, and any view of human nature derived from it or used in forming it, is often based on a limited and nonsystematic accumulation of data. (Some therapists have articulated theories after many years of experience and clinical research, but I believe that this is the exception, not the rule. Even in the best case, the database may involve only 3,000 clients.)

Database is distorted. There are three sources of distortions that can arise from using counseling experience to inform us of human nature. (1) Distortions can occur because counseling provides limited samples of behavior from clients. (2) People overgeneralize from counseling theories because they don't understand how counseling works. (3) Distortions can come from the counselor. We will look at each of these in turn.

1. Counseling does not tell us about how people behave, think or feel in general. Rather, clients come to a counselor only when they are stuck and under stress. Thus, at best counseling theories reveal how people behave when aroused with troublesome emotion. Counseling theories do not consider how clients might behave normally. Emotional decision making is different than non-emotional decision making. Clients are usually making emotional decisions. That slice of life seen by therapists is limited.

There are other limitations. Even in the United States, where psychotherapy is often sought, only 10 to 15 percent of the people have psychological problems that are serious enough to see a counselor, and not nearly all of those seek counseling. Far fewer people seek counseling in other countries. Thus, counseling theories are based on a small sample of people who are (inherent in the fact that they are in counseling for help) not in their normal frame of mind.

2. Counseling theories do not inform us how people normally behave, think and experience. They are about *helping people think, feel and experience **differently*** than they did at the outset of counseling. Furthermore, counseling seeks to promote particular kinds of ***different*** experiences. The different experiences stimulated by counseling presumably help clients feel better about their lives. Counseling then creates a powerful situation that sweeps the client along to follow the thinking of the counselor. Both the client and the counselor hope that the strong situation will result in positive changes.

In counseling, the psychotherapist's goal is to develop a method that can lead *every* client to 100 percent positive change. Deviation from that goal is considered a therapeutic failure. That is, the therapist tries to create a powerful situation in which everyone behaves in the same way (i.e., reports low distress, eliminates or ameliorates the problem behavior) regardless of their personal characteristics, quirks or problems. In a way, then, counseling theories do not tell us how people really behave. They tell us more about how *a counselor behaves* in order to get a person to have experiences that the counselor and the client believe will lead to positive change.

Counseling theories are based on assumptions. Usually, these assumptions are limited and are based on the uncontrolled experience of a counseling theorist. The counseling theorist decides what he or she believes to be important about human nature and how to lead a person into changing that portion of his or her life. Those assumptions of the counselor strongly influence the behavior of the client. For instance, a cognitive therapist believes that if he or she can help the client change thoughts, the client will think better, feel better and get better. The therapist focuses the session on the client's thoughts. After years of doing cognitive therapy, it is not surprising that the therapist believes that humans are most influenced by their cognition. If the therapist does not have mounds of data that changing cognition will change experience, then the therapist must not have been very effective as a therapist. But notice that the data are very limited (e.g., data supporting the idea that changing thoughts will help clients get better) and are collected in such a limited way, because the therapist *began* with a cognitive theory and looked only for confirming data.

Psychological science tells us that people perceive the world in self-serving ways[6] as we reviewed in chapter 3. The counseling theorist (like all of us) is subject to the self-serving bias. He or she selectively confirms an already-existing worldview and counseling theory by paying attention primarily to supporting data. Thus, we are told by psychological science that, like all of us, the counseling theorist makes up his or her mind and *then* seeks evidence that supports his or her beliefs. The beliefs about the person, put forth by a counseling theorist as universal, often come from a single, unsystematic (and biased) source, the psychotherapist.

3. The counselor's background and personality will also strongly affect what he or she thinks is important in promoting change. Therefore a counselor's theory says a lot about the counselor's background. Counseling theorists usually claim that all (or most) of their clients fit their

theory. I doubt Freud ever said, "Dang, this patient does not fit my theory. She has no unconscious conflicts. I must refer her to a behavior therapist." Counselors find similarities in the way that many of their clients behave because the counselors, due to their personality and background, *evoke similar responses* in their clients. Behavior that looks like a pattern in different clients turns out to occur because the same counselor is counseling the different clients.

Counseling is specifically *not* designed to be an *objective* window into human behavior. Rather it is designed to be *subjective*. It deals with how individuals perceive the world. Those perceptions are based on the interactions between the therapist and the client. The view of human nature derived from counseling interactions is, then, heavily distorted.

The result. Earlier I reviewed the research program of George Bonanno (see chapter 3, pp. 49-52). I showed that the theory on dealing with trauma that arose from clinical practice described many of the experiences of patients. However, it revealed (see fig. 3.1) that most people either are completely resilient (35 to 55 percent of all people) to potential traumas or recover within a brief time (15 to 35 percent). If we don't pay attention to the full range of human experience because we are generalizing from patients, then we might develop a distorted view of human nature.

Strengths in the Integration Done by Clinician-Theologians

I have pointed out many reasons why clinical psychology is not a strong basis for a Christian view of human nature. That does not mean that clinical psychology is not valuable. It has great value. In clinical practice we see the personal and relational qualities of humans at their peak. We also see these in practical theology and pastoral care. We observe loving and caring behavior. Love is forced to operate in some of the most difficult and conflict-ridden human situations. Sympathy and empathy motivate most helping behavior. We see in the clinical integration, more than in any other field (except practical theology and pastoral care), the loving heart of people, which reveals the loving heart of God. Therapists are among the most self-sacrificing group of people called to a profession.

Furthermore, psychotherapy is difficult. With most individual problems, but with substance abuse and marital or couple problems particularly, a real sense of humility is evident in most therapists. Humility arises because it doesn't take long to see how little able we counselors are to influence a person's life. More than any experience I've had, except dealing with death and disease in loved ones, psychotherapy teaches that without God I can do nothing. Counseling practice quickly throws us at the feet of Jesus if we hope to help others.

Overall Evaluation

I have been hard on clinical psychology. However, there are some exceptional strengths that allow us to know God through that discipline of Christian counseling in ways that other disciplines do not permit. We Christian counselors work with people directly and during the times of their greatest vulnerabilities. We see how a helper relates compassionately to those in need. We can extrapolate from that to how God must love and care for us. We also see how we must at times frustrate him. Through clinical integration we see the love of God. Though fallen humans may not always manifest it well, we can certainly see that God cares for us and wants to redeem our lives from the pit.

A RELATIONAL MODEL IS BETTER THAN A FILTER MODEL

Must we filter the findings of psychology through theology? I will begin with a critique of the filter model, and then plead for a more humble relational model.

Critique of the Filter Model

While theology and psychology are not completely equal partners in determining truth, theology is not an infallible ruler against which psychological science is judged.

Main critique. My main critique of the filter model is that theologies are not infallible. We often hear that Scripture is a better source of truth than science (which I firmly believe is true). But to refine this, permit me to interact with an extended quote from Eric Johnson's *Foundations for Soul Care.*[7]

The major problem with labeling psychology "general revelation" is it implies that the texts of psychology and the Bible are *both* products of the direct activity of God (perhaps leading to the conclusion that psychology texts have a validity and authority equal to that of the Bible).[8]

This is a misreading of the claim that general and special revelation are two methods God uses to instruct us about who God is, how to know God and how to live in relationship to God. No serious proponent of psychology as general revelation has claimed that general revelation is *equal* to special revelation. Nor do conservative theologians. Special revelation is always more specific and more privileged. Yet general revelation is still true revelation of God to humans.

But God's activity with respect to psychology is not directly causal; he does not inspire psychology or psychology texts. The latter are more socially constructed attempts to describe human nature based on research and a set of worldview assumptions, and as we all know, the assumptions may be flawed, the research more or less faulty, and the texts may contain some falsehoods.[9]

Everything Johnson says here is correct. But arguing that science may be in error does not mean that God did not intend nature to reveal aspects of the divine character and personality through science. Johnson goes a bit off the path when he says,

In contrast, the Christian faith understands the Bible to consist of human writings that are simultaneously divinely authored. This dual authorship renders the Bible unique, gives it an authority over human life that no other text has and also guarantees that it is free from deception and error; therefore, its assertions and worldview assumptions are uniformly and permanently correct, something that cannot be said of any set of scientific texts.[10]

There are a number of questionable statements in this excerpt. First, Johnson suggests that "the Christian faith" understands Scripture in a particular way. Yet clearly different Protestant denominations, Roman Catholics and the Orthodox do not all understand the inerrancy of Scripture in the same way. Are we prepared to say that the Holy Spirit preserved a particular theological approach from error but allowed error in the other approaches? Not with any humility.

Second, Johnson refers throughout to the Bible as if people's understanding of Scripture was the same thing as the Bible. But we must make a critical and careful approach. As I pointed out in chapter 7 (pp. 113-19), there is a thick layer of human involvement between the original autographs and an individual's understanding of Scripture. So Johnson is optimistic (and I would say incorrect) in claiming that the Bible (as he understands it) is uniformly and permanently correct. This statement can only be made of (1) the original autographs in (2) the books that God intended as God's written Word. We do not have infallible access to either the autographs or God's intentions.

Third, I accept with Johnson that Scripture is dually authored and thereby authoritative in ways that other writing (including theology) is not. Scripture is God's verbal revelation, and on areas pertaining to salvation it is inerrant in the original autographs. I also believe our present Bibles have been sufficiently superintended by the Holy Spirit that even the presence of transcribers, translators, church traditions and theologians has not changed the essential meaning. But unlike Johnson, I would not claim to know the exact permanent and uniformly correct meaning of the Scripture. We must, I believe, remain humble about the ways that humans might have contaminated our translations over the centuries and the ways we interpret meanings.

But I believe we can guarantee the authenticity and authority of the salvation message of the Scriptures. But in humility I know that my view of the salvation message has not been always shared by Orthodoxy, Roman Catholicism and the many variants of Protestantism. Thus, I believe that the Holy Spirit has superintended the essentials of the Christian Scriptures to give us necessary and sufficient information for our faith and practice of life under the lordship of Jesus.

We have many reasons to doubt psychological science. First, it does not claim to yield ultimate truth, only temporal truth, so we cannot take it as authoritative. Second, it is often revised through (1) future findings, (2) radical scientific revolutions or (3) scientific evolution (e.g., the findings of Imre Lakatos). So I am not claiming any authority for science except as it uncovers what God reveals in nature. I can never have certainty about scientific findings, but I can be certain of the essential salvation message we learn in Scripture—that God redeems sinful, needy humans.

Discernment When Words Are Not Sung in Harmony

Sources of knowing. Relying on God's Word is neither simple nor easy. Discerning the truth of a scientific finding, model or theory is not as easy as merely reading Scripture, which is done through a particular theological lens, and knowing whether the scientific finding, model or theory is consonant with God's truth. We need a consistent epistemology (way of knowing). There are many ways of knowing, including

- Scripture (special revelation)
- the witness of the Holy Spirit (revelation)
- theologies
- God's Word through preaching, teaching, ritual, liturgy (which do not have the authority of Scripture itself but are legitimate ways of knowing God's will)
- church or faith traditions
- reason (induction, deduction, formal or practical)
- community consensus (which could involve historical consensus of the church or the agreement of people within a local community of faith)
- historical understanding
- confessions or creeds (which embody the consensual beliefs of the confessing church)
- science via nature
- feelings
- authorities

Epistemology is best when based on *consensus* among the ways of knowing. We can be most confident in the truth when we hear voices singing in unison, or at least in harmony. In navigation, when entering a harbor, the captain does not rely on a single harbor light. Instead, the captain lines up several lights, which allows accurate steering.

Need for humility. Where there are disagreements among sources of knowing, it might come down to Scripture having the last word. After all, Scripture is our final rule for faith and practice. Yet we must remain tentative and humble rather than dogmatic, especially in matters of disagreement among sources. Not only do we not have access to pure and uncorrupted scriptural data, but also *we* are fallen instruments of discernment. We have unconscious motives that all too often empower our fallen lives.

Therefore, we should look for consensus where possible. Strength of numbers should take precedence. If several nonbiblical sources point to a common-sense interpretation of a situation, yet we discern that Scripture teaches something else (e.g., the harbor lights do not line up), then that indicates we should be humble, not dogmatic.

Our attitude toward nature. Science is the study of nature, and psychological science is the part of science that studies humans, animals and humanlike machines (i.e., artificial intelligence). Our attitude toward nature will condition how we approach psychology. At one extreme, people venerate nature. This can include orthodox Christians who treat nature as a sacred part of creation and evolutionists who treat nature as the mother who bore, nurtures and rules us. At the other extreme, people view nature as profane. But nature is neither mother nor slave. The golden mean between those extremes is, as G. K. Chesterton argued in *Orthodoxy*, to see nature as a sister we have been asked to care for until our parent (the Creator) returns.

> The essence of all pantheism, evolutionism, and modern cosmic religion is really in this proposition: that Nature is our mother. . . . [For Christians], Nature is not our mother: nature is our sister. We can be proud of her beauty, since we have the same father, but she has not authority over us. . . . To St. Francis, nature is a sister, even a younger sister; a little dancing sister, to be laughed at as well as to be loved.[11]

Science honors nature by studying it. This includes psychological science, which observes humans and sees the image of God within, but also the stain of sin. The tentacles of sin can strangle our hearts if they are not redeemed. We do not abandon humans or create a theology that consigns sin-fouled humanity to the city dump. Instead, we study and honor nature, and try to understand and appreciate the virtuous qualities within even the seemingly most nonredeemable. We counsel and give pastoral care to each person because each is valuable. We reach out in love to those who reject us personally, and we embrace Christianity as a way of living under Jesus' lordship. We try to help the needy repair the flaws, we redeem the fallen as Christ's body, and we witness to the kingdom of God—as Jesus said we should.

Psychological science is part of the human participation in God's redemption of nature. Psychological science can be part of our noble calling by God to participate in God's redemption, and I believe it is as valid as is preaching, discipleship, teaching, being an elder or deacon, articulating theology, witnessing, or doing any other work for the glory of God (e.g., art, music, engineering, plumbing, trash collecting and scholarly research).

My argument is twofold. A relational model treats psychological science and theology as respectful members of a mutual conversation. This model is more humble than a filter model that might claim too much for the authority of theology. A relational model doesn't presume that one particular theology is the only one or the best one. Second, rather than promoting judgment of one discipline by the other, this model fosters an open mind and encourages dialogue in the event of a disagreement.

SIN AND SCIENCE

We are created in God's image, but we are thoroughly tainted by the Fall. When we look at nature today, we can never be sure whether it is revealing the nature of God or fallen nature. The noetic effects of sin (i.e., the effects of sin on the human mind and understanding) have led many to doubt whether anything of God can be known at all through nature. There are several lines of support for this claim.

Arguments for the Noetic Effects of Sin

Paul said, "Nothing good lives in me, that is, in my sinful nature" (Rom 7:18). The early church leaders from Tertullian to Augustine drew sharp distinctions between the life and thought of Christians and non-

Christians (2 Cor 6:14-18; Eph 2:1-3; 1 Jn 2:15). Dutch theologian Abraham Kuyper termed this the antithesis. The Dutch Reformed tradition emphasizes the radical differences between those who are redeemed and those who are not. As Johnson presents it, for the unredeemed,

> the so-called noetic effects of sin . . . lead to misunderstandings regarding reality so serious that they obscure our interpretations and warp our descriptions of important aspects of God and his creation. . . . These distortions can only be undone by the illuminating work of the Holy Spirit (1 Cor 2), yet because of indwelling sin, Christians can never assume that the noetic effects of sin have been completely eliminated from their own minds.[12]

In Paul's passage dealing with self-control, he asserts that the old (sinful) human nature is hostile to God (Rom 8:7). The noetic effects of sin are not merely due to limitations or to innocent misunderstandings, but to a hostility to God that sets people against God.

Response

Because I believe that we can indeed know things about God and even know God better by observing nature through science, I must address this challenge: that the pervasive noetic effects of sin spoil the possibility of a general revelation. I will make five points in response: (1) Scripture argues for general revelation; (2) there are ways to know God when people didn't or don't have Scripture; (3) virtues were present before Christ's redemption; (4) two analogies support this view (sin as a cloud that cannot completely blot out the sun and knowing a painter from seeing the painting); and (5) the study of nature creates awe.

Biblical Claims Support General Revelation

Romans 2:14-15 says that people have God's laws written on their hearts. In Acts 14:15, Paul appeals to God's creation to persuade the people of Lystra not to worship nature as God but to come to the true God. Psalm 19 begins with the well-known verse, "The heavens tell the glory of God." And Romans 1:18-21 says,

> The wrath of God is being revealed from heaven against all the godlessness

and wickedness of men who suppress the truth by their wickedness, since what may be known about God is plain to them, because God has made it plain to them. For since the creation of the world God's invisible qualities—his eternal power and divine nature—have been clearly seen, being understood from what has been made, so that men are without excuse.

For although they knew God, they neither glorified him as God nor gave thanks to him, but their thinking became futile and their foolish hearts were darkened.

Despite how dark and confused their minds became, Paul still claims that people have knowledge sufficient to make them morally responsible for knowing God.

The point from Paul that there is nothing good within the flesh does not mean that there is nothing good within humans. Regarding self-salvation through following the law, which is the context of the passage in Romans, the flesh offers nothing. The flesh is corrupt. Our only hope for salvation is in the triune God. But Paul is not arguing that absolutely nothing good can be found in human nature, which would argue against his earlier point in Romans 1:18-21.

People Can Know God When They Don't Have Scripture

God's special revelation includes both the person of Jesus and the Scriptures (i.e., the living Word and the written Word). People have known God in times when no written Scripture existed, yet people knew God. God made a way through the sovereign operation of the Holy Spirit to bring people into a knowledge of God. Presumably, in these situations, general revelation played a part in salvation.

Virtues Are Present Before Redemption

We retain the human limitations and the physical and psychological scars we had before accepting Christ as our Savior. Still, Christian virtues were present before redemption. We could forgive, love, act justly, be creative and think before we were redeemed. These virtues did not come from the flesh. The image of God must have shone through. The noetic effects of sin did not prohibit the exhibition of virtue. Similarly, in general revelation—despite human sin—God can and does reveal the divine character.

Two Arguments from Analogy

Sin is like a cloud, but we can still know about the sun. If we think of God's image as the sun and the general revelation as seeing that image reflected in human nature, then sin is a cloud. How big and thick is the cloud? Can it blot out all light, making darkness the sum total of our existence? If we admit to any light getting through the cloud of sin, which I think we must if Romans 1:20 is to be believed, then we must begin to ask how pervasive the cloud is. What can we observe, through the cloud, of the image of God borne by humans? Pessimists suggest we can learn nothing. Optimists say that the cloud essentially is a light fog and doesn't distort any but the grossest human motives. Reason tells us that Aristotle's golden mean is the place we should come down.

First, we know that it is light out, not dark. We are drawn to God. The world can see the effects of God, we have no excuse for denying God's existence (Rom 3:19-21). Second, there are holes in the cloud. Jesus Christ came down directly and is the sun in human form. Also God's written Word describes human actions and is the story of God reaching to humans, who do see and respond even though they are sinful beings. Third, even though it's cloudy, we can see (1) the beauty of the world in sunsets, mountains, hills, valleys (Psalms)—which reflect the glory of God—and (2) the things people do that reflect the image of God.

If we do not respond to God (as God calls us), we can spend our whole life dwelling in darkness. If we look up and see the light and allow it to enter into us, however, we reflect his glory. We shine. This is beauty to those also in the light, and it can draw others to the light.

Knowing the artist by seeing the work of art. Can we know God by knowing God's creation? If we see a painting, can we learn about the painter? If we read a book, can we know about the author? We can know some things regardless of whether the author is trying to tell us something about him or her. We can know more if the author is trying to communicate his or her character through the author's creation.

The Study of Nature Creates Awe

A psychological experiment. Remember the Gosling et al. study that I described in chapter one (see pp. 23-27)? Strangers went into a person's room and, by looking around at the artifacts of the living space, the strangers could know the personality of the person better than the person's friends.

If strangers can know each other through such a limited amount of interaction, then how can people see the Rocky Mountains, observe the Pacific Ocean, listen to Tchaikovsky's *1812 Overture,* read Victor Hugo's *Les Miserables* or gaze at Michelangelo's David in Florence and not see and know God.

And is it possible to study the marvels of the brain and the way it interacts with hormones and the peripheral nervous system and not marvel at a Creator of massive complexity? Can we read of Jean Piaget's studies of the development of thought and not see how God works to develop children's and adults' brains? Can we study the marvels of intelligence and the way the mind works and not see a greater mind at work in creation? Can we study the interactions among people in families, groups, communities and nations and not see that we have a social God?

Earlier, in chapters five and six, I described ways that either a stranger or a loved one might enter our family's home and look around, coming to know Kirby better than before. And this is true even though the person who enters our home is fundamentally flawed and sinful. Is there any reason to believe that people who look carefully at the works of creation cannot see the character of the loving, Creator God shining out—regardless of how flawed and fallen they are?

I believe God has revealed the divine character within the creation. Of course, we know more about God when we accept the lordship of Jesus described in Scripture.

Limits of General Revelation

General revelation is not sufficient. Looking around our home is certainly not sufficient for establishing a good, intimate relationship. In fact, it probably is not really the beginning of the relationship. No woman is going to enter a single man's house, fall in love with him on the basis of what is seen, and agree to marry him sight unseen. But it might set the stage for the relationship.

We should not glorify nature. Nature and Scripture reveal God—one generally and one in the very specific sense of how the Son of God became a man. Yes, nature is good and even revelatory. However, we should not glorify nature. Even though we should appreciate a beautiful sky with the sun peeking through silver-bordered clouds, only God is worthy of our worship and praise.

Special Revelation Is Necessary and Sufficient for Salvation

The argument is often advanced that the Bible is sufficient for us. Indeed, the written Word of God is sufficient for salvation just as the Holy Spirit may sovereignly reveal Jesus through or apart from Scripture. Scripture delivers the gospel, the good news, and Scripture is useful for teaching, correction, reproof and training in righteousness (2 Tim 3:16). God's Holy Spirit brings us into connection with the living Christ. Through listening to the Holy Spirit, who works through Scripture, circumstances, other believers and situations, people grow in their relationship with the triune God. Nevertheless, my contention is that psychological science can provide other opportunities to grow in knowledge of God.

In chapters one, three and four we discussed many interesting psychological studies. We looked at John Gottman's amazing study that can predict marital satisfaction four years in the future (pp. 17-19). We examined Malcolm Gladwell's thin slicing (pp. 19-23) and rogue general Paul Van Riper's defeat of the U.S. military's advanced technology (pp. 19-22). I summarized Sheena Iyengar's studies that showed that increasing choices resulted in less buying of her jams (p. 23). I described in detail (and had you predict) the results of Samuel Gosling and colleagues' dorm-room study (pp. 23-27). Barry Staw and Ha Hoang's NBA draft number study reveals the power of initial expectations (pp. 30, 56-58). And George Bonanno's work on resiliency in the face of trauma showed how our clinical experience can often lead us astray in predicting the responses of regular people to potentially traumatic events (pp. 49-52). We looked at Dov Cohen and Richard Nisbett's culture-of-honor "chicken" game with Northern and Southern college men (pp. 59-63), and we looked at Robert

Cialdini's studies of the prevention of theft in the Petrified Forest and littering (pp. 63-65) to see hidden factors in shaping human behavior. Through Daniel Gilbert's studies we saw that we can't predict our preferences in the future as well as a randomly selected observer who has already been measured in the situation (pp. 66-71).

I chose these particular studies to show that in spite of our knowledge of lay psychology (or even professional psychological science) and in spite of our knowledge of theology, we still cannot always correctly predict the outcome of human behavior. Psychological science uncovers many of the mysteries of human nature. While it is neither necessary nor sufficient for salvation, psychological science can certainly reveal much about humans and God's creation that is not otherwise available to us.

Reducing What We Experience Without Being Reductionistic

Through the practice of mindfulness we can reduce the data of nature. If I am mindful of the experiences God has arranged—like a beautiful sky, for example—then I reduce my experience. I turn off the radio and attend to the sky. I reduce my experience by focusing or concentrating on nature. A poet could focus on a spectacular sunset and put it to verse. A songwriter could be riveted by a storm and turn the experience into a melody. Someone might observe a grove of redwoods and decide to depict it on canvas. The same thing is happening in each case. The pure experience is being reduced by taking in part of it and conveying that part to others. I am continually reducing my experience so I can attend to a specific area.

Science similarly reduces nature. (I am not recommending scientific *reductionism*, which reduces nature to *mere* matter and twitching neurons.) Psychological science poses a question and applies the scientific method to describe the one aspect of nature that is being understood so that it can be conveyed to others in a meaningful way. Just as a Christian poet, songwriter or painter conveys the reduced version of the experience to people with the hope of enlarging and informing the recipient's world and experience, scientists do the same.

SUMMARY

In this chapter I identified three challenges I anticipate to the relational model of psychological science and theology that I am advocating. For example, some people might argue that clinical psychology is a better way to learn about people than is psychological science. Others might say that a filter model is better for describing the way psychological science and theology should relate than is the relational model. Still others might suggest that God cannot really reveal the divine nature through psychological science because human sin distorts the revelation so much that people cannot see the revelation. I tried to deal persuasively with each belief. I know how hard it is to modify these beliefs. It takes courage to substantially modify ideas we hold firmly.

The main points of part one are:

1. I take seriously Scripture, the Bible and Christian tradition.

2. I see great value in both psychological science and in clinical psychology. However, I believe that psychological science has an advantage in building a Christian view of human nature.

3. The disciplines of psychological science and Christian theology should be involved in interdisciplinary communication, although the areas they talk about differ in emphasis. The Scriptures emphasize the Christian worldview. Psychological science emphasizes life's how-tos.

4. Both disciplines are flawed and imperfect. While psychological science is further from the data and scientific data are more general and less specifically directed to the lordship of Jesus, our interpretation of Scripture cannot be naively taken as authoritative in any conflict.

5. When conflict arises between the disciplines, instead of using theology to filter psychological science, psychological science and theology should engage in respectful conversation, which must be understood in relational context.

6. Psychological science can learn from theology. Scientists could choose to study, for example, topics like the psychology of religion and positive psychology (like forgiveness, gratitude and humility). This is not the purpose of this book, however.

7. Christians can learn things that are valuable to them from psychological science despite the noetic effects of sin.

In the first part of this book I have developed a way that Christian theology and psychological science can humbly relate to each other. Neither discipline is better than the other, but each is better at handling particular data than the other. I have likened this relational model to a marriage. Though this analogy breaks down if pushed too hard, the marriage analogy tries to promote a relationship of mutual respect, if not love, between the disciplines. Each contributes unique parts to the marriage relationship. In part two, I will examine what psychological science can offer to the relationship, or marriage, between Christian theology and psychological science. If Christians come to peace with psychological science, what benefits will accrue? That is our mandate for the following chapters.

PART TWO

WHAT PSYCHOLOGICAL SCIENCE
HAS TO OFFER THEOLOGY

PSYCHOLOGICAL SCIENCE
PROVIDES A NEW TOOL

THROUGH USING DIFFERENT TOOLS psychological science can extend the human senses in different dimensions than can physics, biology, theology and even psychotherapy. This suggests two central uses of tools. Psychological science is itself a tool to interpret Scripture, physical creation, spiritual development and spiritual behavior. It has not traditionally been used to aid spiritual life—at least not often until recent decades. It is often through developing or using new tools that progress comes. Psychological science has developed specialized tools, and it continues to add new ones. These new tools and methods can not only help psychology progress but also advance our knowledge about God.

In this chapter, I will discuss the role of tools in scientific progress. Then, I will consider psychology itself as a tool. Finally, I'll look at the psychological toolbox, with the new tools that can extend our senses to better measure how people behave.

THE ROLE OF TOOLS IN SCIENTIFIC PROGRESS

All sciences derive from both philosophy and the crafts. As a derivative of philosophy, psychological science attempts to conceptualize the nature of reality by observing, measuring and quantifying life experiences. As a derivative of the crafts, psychological science invents, makes and employs tools to extend the senses.

Sciences have always used tools to extend the senses. Physicists extended the vision of the naked eye through inventing the telescope and the electron microscope. The physician extended the senses by using tools such as the stethoscope, EKG and MRI.

Scientific progress occurs when people conceptualize differently or when new tools are developed to measure phenomena that previously could not be measured. In this chapter I hope to reveal how psychological science as a new theological tool can help people understand God better. To do so, I will survey the role of tool development in the history of science.

Historically, science has consisted mostly of long periods of normal science in which theories slowly evolve. Those long stretches of conceptual evolution are punctuated by upheavals or revolutions. There are two leading explanations for scientific revolutions, which have been described by Thomas Kuhn[1] in the 1970s and Peter Galison[2] in the 1990s.

PROGRESS THROUGH CHANGED CONCEPTUAL PARADIGMS

Thomas Kuhn

Thomas Kuhn, a physicist who turned to the philosophy of science, rocked the philosophy of science in 1970. Instead of describing the way science was "supposed to" work, Kuhn looked historically at the way science actually worked.[3]

Kuhn maintained that during the normal science of slow evolution, a scientific field agreed how to conceptualize the field (a *paradigm*) and how to investigate it *(shared exemplars)*. This is what Kuhn calls the "disciplinary matrix." In any science—but let's take physics as an example—a variety of theories are contained within the conceptual paradigm. In what Kuhn called "normal science," scientists discover increasingly more about a field. Scientists propose hypotheses that they think should work according to existing theory. They test the hypotheses by collecting data. Most of the time, the hypotheses are supported. Occasionally they aren't. Failures to find what was expected are the little problems of normal science.

When a problem occurs, one of three things happens. The scientist modifies the hypothesis or the method of testing it, and an expected result materializes, saving the theory. Or perhaps the scientist moves to a different study and simply ignores the problem, hoping that someone in the future will find the solution. Occasionally, the scientist declares the hypothesis falsified and modifies the theory. With each of the three ways (solving the problem, ignoring it or modifying the theory), science creeps ahead—evolving new extensions of knowledge, new methods of measuring, new twists on old hypotheses and occasionally new directions of the theory.

Kuhn's analysis suggests that revolutions occur when the entire way of looking at a science—the accepted paradigm—goes through a crisis, like the problems of normal science but on a big scale. The classic example is Einstein's new look at Newtonian physics. Newtonian physics was the reigning paradigm that governed physics. But problems had arisen involving the speed of light that Newtonian physics could not explain. Scientists tried to unravel the knots in the paradigm for decades, to no avail. Tension built until physics was in crisis. The crisis could be resolved in one of three ways—the same ways that individual scientists solve the little problems of normal science. Scientists might solve the problem within Newton's framework, and normal science would resume. Or scientists might tire of the crisis, decide to let future generations solve the problem and return to normal science. Or perhaps someone would solve the problem by coming up with a new framework.

Albert Einstein (1879-1955), in a series of thought experiments, realized that time and space were intimately connected, making them relative to each other and describing the time-space continuum. He proposed a new theory—the special theory of relativity—that explained the problems in Newtonian physics, but to use the solution, scientists would have to reject Newtonian physics.

The essential tension. This created a problem for the progress of science, which Kuhn calls the essential tension.[4] Newtonian physics was supported by 150 years of experimental data. But the theory of special relativity was supported by a single thought experiment unsubstantiated by actual data. Physics was ostensibly an empirical science, which valued empirical observation and data. Yet scientists, frustrated with the problems in Newtonian physics were considering whether to defect to a completely unsupported theory. Eventually, some did, usually the younger scientists, but others didn't because they had too much invested in Newtonian physics.

Application to the personal. We can apply this process in a way that Kuhn never intended. We see the same effect at work in personal transformation and in the healing of psychological problems. Imagine this. A person experiences a psychological problem. Let's say a man is rejected by his girlfriend. He worries about whether he is acceptable to women. He tries to get a date but is turned down. Another try, another rejection. And he focuses more intently on the problem: *Am I acceptable to women?* The unsolvable problem becomes for him a crisis.

Like normal science prior to a scientific revolution, he can resolve the crisis in one of three ways. He can solve the psychological problem without changing his worldview. He can tire of the problem and just put it aside. Or perhaps a friend, trusted confidant or counselor will suggest a new way of looking at life. "It's not that you are unacceptable to women," says the counselor. "You are just depressed, and as long as you stay depressed, it is difficult for people to deal with you if they don't already know you. As soon as you get over the depression, you'll have plenty of dates." This paradigm shift settles the man. Or perhaps the paradigm shift is a religious conversion experience. Perhaps it is a shift in philosophy or life goals. Perhaps it is a career change or a change in relationships. Whatever form it takes, the major change results in a different worldview.

Peter Galison

Peter Galison[5] spins the story of scientific revolutions differently. He suggests that the invention or application of new tools, not the intellectual crisis from an unsolved problem, has historically stimulated major scientific changes. New tools can dump massive amounts of new data into a disciplinary matrix in short order. The explanations simply can't keep up. Galison argues that the worldview shifts that Kuhn noticed come later, not as cause of revolution but as effect of it. New tools allow new data to enter the disciplinary matrix. Those new data *then* must be explained. Thus new worldviews and theories are born.

The classic example is the invention of the telescope. It allowed scientists to observe celestial events they could not see with the naked eye. Massive amounts of new data from observation of the skies accumulated. As data accumulated, they needed to be explained. Eventually, a new understanding of physics emerged in which the earth was not seen as the center of creation but as part of a much larger creation. The old paradigm was overthrown, not caused by the shift in thought from science's philosophical roots but from the invention and application of new tools, from science's roots in the crafts.

Application to the personal. Just as we might apply Kuhn's understanding of paradigm shifts to changes in people's worldviews, the tool theory might also be applied to psychological life. For example, suppose that Shannon, a young woman with a settled worldview, goes to college. She learns a new way of accumulating knowledge, a new way of thinking. She has new intellectual tools. She can analyze, synthesize and understand in ways that were not possible before. After applying these new tools, Shannon realizes that she has thoroughly transformed her worldview.

In this age of the social sciences, Galison's analysis suggests that perhaps psychological science is itself a new tool that might be used by theologians. In the past, theologians rarely referred to psychological science. If psychology were referenced at all, it was usually clinical psychology, which was employed in service of practical theology. We can no longer afford to ignore psychological science. Largely, that has resulted from psychology's own tool revolution. New tools in psychological science have already produced new theologically relevant data.

PSYCHOLOGY AS A TOOL TO INTERPRET SCRIPTURE, CREATION AND SPIRITUAL BEHAVIOR

Psychological science is a *new* theological tool. If findings about people and their interrelationships can inform us of God and human-God relationships, as I have argued in the first part of this book, then psychological science can aid theology. It is far from the only tool to help us know God better. Psychological science fits with other tools—historical methods, hermeneutics, anthropological and sociological studies, and linguistics—to interpret theology. Tools are used to help us apprehend God's work, ways, person and relationships.

Survey of Tools to Know God Better

Through the ages people have employed a variety of tools to help them know God better. God, of course, is the initiator. God reveals the divine character and relationships. Yet we are not passive. In fact, we are counseled in Scripture to seek to know and trust God. We are to act in faith—not as a blind leap but through steps of faith. How do we narrow the knowledge gap? How do we see more of God and experience God more palpably? We experience God through both general and special revelations.

Evangelism. The tools of mission work today are far better than those used of the past. For a start, missions are more culturally sensitive than in past centuries. Methods of teaching and writing are different. Psychological science tells us more about culture, learning, sharing and receptiveness to new and old ideas presented in different ways.

Private devotion. In private devotion we use many tools. We can employ different kinds of prayer, meditate on God or Scripture, and contemplate God's essence and will. We can have personal conversations with God through prayer. We can employ many of the spiritual disciplines, originally developed by Ignatius. We can worship, sing praise to God, or write psalms, poems or journal entries. We can read and study the Bible or other Christian literature. We can even study ancient culture and history. Private devotion can be enriched by applying findings from psychological science regarding effects of focused attention, flow and mindfulness.

Public worship. Worship in the catacombs in the first century was not a charismatic praise service complete with worship band, large screen video and decked-out choir. Nor were "seeker services" separated from mid-week growth groups for core church members. Cluster and home groups probably did not include guitar accompaniment. Sermons were not ten-minute homilies or two-hour Bible expositions. In short, the tools of modern worship have evolved to meet each age's needs. Psychological science has told us much about group dynamics and persuasion, and those findings have been applied by Christians designing worship services and experiences.

Life in the church. Church life has changed radically as well. As population centers grew in size and more people became Christians, the center of church life evolved. Originally, church life centered on the city church. Then, people lived in communities and walked or rode horses to the local parish church. With the automobile and technology, we have moved to distant suburban churches and even worship services on television. Life in the church has changed. The one-room rural church has given way to Sunday schools, choirs, administrative structures, electronic copies of sermons, webpages and tailor-made programs for all ages and interest groups. All of these are tools to promote Christian growth. Psychological science has much to say about learning and technology.

Summary. In this brief section, I made three points. First, there are many classical ways of knowing God. Second, they have evolved and incorporated new methods as the culture has changed. Third, even in this brief survey, we can see that psychological science has been used to reshape classical ways of religious knowing.

Theological Tools

Of course, the tools to enhance the study of theology are legion. Theologians study languages, church history, systematic theology, biblical theology in New and Old Testament studies, anthropological theology, philosophical theology, and historical theology. Obviously, theologians also study people. Social psychology tells us about the effects of people on each other in groups and communities. Educational psychology tells about how people learn, remember and store information. Emotion and motivation are important aspects of being involved in a religion, and psychological science tells us much about those. Culture and perception are also important bodies of knowledge that can enrich theology.

Tools in Service of Knowing God Better

Through tools, we extend our senses. We do not wait passively for God to speak to us. We also follow God's initiation and seek to apprehend what God has revealed in Scripture and nature. Each subfield of psychology has different methods, and each new source looks at people through a different lens. It reveals new information that complements, reinforces and occasionally challenges our theological models. At those moments of conflict, we tend to pit psychological and theological models against each other. We must ask whether we need to modify our theological model or our scientific model.

Psychological science, as it is applied by professional theologians or by laypeople, is a theological tool. In a wider sense it is a tool that can help us understand, know and trust God better. It is a tool that goes beyond what is normally available to the theologian because psychological science has developed its own new tools to extend the senses so we can understand people better, and therefore, we hope, make better inferences about God.

PSYCHOLOGICAL SCIENCE EMPLOYS
NEW TOOLS TO EXTEND THE SENSES

Scientists attempt to look into the "black box" of nature. In the case of psychology, we hope to look beneath the human skin. We can draw conclusions from employing disciplinary observation—as playwrights, novelists and poets have done for centuries. But we also have employed the craft of psychology to develop tools (and use some that have been developed by other scientists and technologists) to look at persons and the situations they find themselves in.

Looking Inside of People and Situations

Psychological scientists have developed tools for looking into the human head. *Brain scanning* equipment includes the electroencephalograph (EEG), computerized axial tomography (CAT), positron emission tomography (PET), functional magnetic resonance imaging (fMRI), and magnetoencephalography (MEG). Facial muscle tension also can be measured using the electromyograph (EMG) or facial coding systems.

Cognitive neuroscientific methods attempt to determine the operation of the mind rather than the physical operation of the brain. Most cognitive methods assume that when people are spending lots of time thinking about something or emotionally reacting to it, their reaction time can reveal what they are or aren't thinking about. *Computer modeling of biological processes and behavior* involves simulating mental processes or simulating behavior through artificial intelligence.

Psychological scientists have developed tools for looking into the heart as well. The *peripheral nervous system* (as distinct from the central nervous system of the brain and spinal cord) measures include blood pressure, heart rate and skin conductance. Often the peripheral nervous system is activated under stress and is calmed when the person's stress lessens. *Heart rate variability* (HRV) refers to the beat-to-beat alterations in heart rate, which can reveal stress. Higher HRV is healthier. It indicates less stress.

Genetics are at the heart of much of people's behavior. Biochemically, we can map the human genome. We can identify the genes responsible for physical and behavioral characteristics. Astounding research is underway on protein synthesis, signaling proteins, RNA and how mitochondria work. We hear almost daily of scientific breakthroughs. *Behavioral genetics* is not aimed at the biochemistry of genetic proclivity or gene expression, but with how genes interact with the environment to result in behavior. Two basic methods of behavioral genetics are the twin study and the adoption study. By looking at twins raised together or separated at birth, behavioral geneticists can disentangle much of the variability attributable to environment and genes. *Biochemical techniques* such as hormonal analyses (including cortisol, oxytocin and brain neurohormones) and analyses of other chemical aspects of the body have advanced in the age of the life sciences.

Psychological scientists have developed tools for examining how people behave as well. For a long time we have been able to record behavior with very high resolution cameras. Minute fluctuations in movement or even facial muscle twitches can be observed. Coding systems for behavior help people analyze the data in ways that are comparable across studies. Verbal behavior—whether spoken or written—is important. Linguistic text analysis programs have been developed for analyses of narratives.

Psychological scientists have developed tools for looking into situations instead of looking inside the person. Situations are extremely powerful in influencing our behavior—more powerful than we might have anticipated. In *game theory*, which has led to people winning the Nobel Prize, games seek to simulate behavior. For example, scientists have thoroughly examined a game called the prisoner's dilemma. In the prisoner's dilemma two people are apprehended for a crime and questioned separately. Each one knows he or she can rat on the other and, if he or she is not ratted out by the partner, get away scot-free. But the other person will take all the blame and will be hurt badly. If both partners rat on each other, though, both will suffer—but not as much as if he or she had all the blame pinned on him or her. If neither one rats on the other, then they both might get off with only a little punishment. This creates a real dilemma. If I rat out my partner, I can either get off free or, if he or she also rats me out, I might suffer. Or I can hold firm and be faithful. But if I do, I'll suffer a little if my partner also remains faithful, but I'll experience severe consequences if my partner rats me out and leaves me hanging. Because prisoner's dilemma uses a betrayal scenario, its application is legion. It can provide insight into office politics, international cooperation, friendships, sibling interactions and hundreds of other situations.

Interdisciplinary triangulation uses methods in psychological science that derive from other disciplines. National probability surveys are the specialty of sociology, but they have been used in psychology as well. Cultural anthropology has developed methods that are applied in cross-cultural psychology and in multicultural psychology.

New Tools for Designing Research and Analyzing the Findings

Research design methods. Research designs have paralleled the way psychologists think about behavior. The idea of giving a person a set of questionnaires and reporting correlations among the scores is a thing of the past. Behavior is seen as being influenced by thought, emotion, motivation, learning, memory, behavioral repertoires and situational variables. Each of those variables changes quickly with time. It thus is almost de rigueur for psychological scientists to measure behavior using different types of measurements of different variables over several times.

Developmental psychologists, for example, try to explain how people change as they mature. To do so, they must separate the effects of being different ages, which could be easily detected through a *cross-sectional research design,* which measures all ages at the same time. But people aged sixty have different life experiences than will twenty-year-olds who will be sixty in forty years. Sixty-year-olds have lived their adult lives under the experience of Vietnam while twenty-year-olds will live theirs under the shadow of 9/11. Cross-sectional designs cannot take account of the effects of experiencing different cultural events at different points in the life cycle. *Longitudinal research designs* sought to take care of this problem by measuring the same group of people year after year. But the story of maturation that followed the baby boomers won't necessarily describe the Gen-Xers. So *cross-lag sequential research designs* followed separate cohorts, each measured longitudinally. Psychological scientists could then separate the effects of cohort from those of maturation.

Statistical methods. As theory has changed and become more sophisticated, and as computing capabilities have increased, the statistical and analytical methods used to make sense of the data have also increased in complexity. In the 1970s most statistical tests had to be computed by hand or using a desk calculator. By the early 1980s new statistical techniques could be used to determine the interrelationships among many variables, because mainframe computers were available. Nevertheless, computer runs were slow on the mainframe, so statistics could not be very complicated. By the late 1980s, almost every psychological scientist had a personal desktop computer and sophisticated statistics could be computed many times each hour. Within the last ten years, structural equation modeling has allowed scientists to test whether a whole data set fit a theoretical model. Now, statisticians have developed methods for multigroup hierarchical time-series modeling. That is a real mouthful. Let's just say that those statistical methods reflect exactly the way we think about reality. At least today. Statistics are complicated, and they change with time just like other scientific tools.

THE NEW TOOLS OF PSYCHOLOGICAL SCIENCE
MIGHT HELP US SEE GOD MORE CLEARLY

Psychological science studies people. It can reveal the complexities, joys, frustrations and love in *complex relationships*, both within individuals and between and among people. God is triune and relates to the physical and interpersonal world, a world of intricate balance that ebbs and flows unpredictably. The biological, psychological, social and spiritual come together in psychological science. The triune God is by nature relational. Each of the persons of the Godhead relates to people and the creation differently.

We might intuit that the study of people might provide an ideal way to understand God. In psychological science we see things as *objectively* as possible, but we are looking at intensely *personal* processes and relationships. Thus we are able to see connections between people and the nonpersonal aspects of animals and the rest of nature (recall fig. 5.1, p. 80). And we are able to see the *personal* connections between people and God. Psychologists also use methods that are sometimes *impersonal* (such as naturalistic observation and tightly controlled experimental studies, and the use of equipment to measure brain and body functioning). Yet at other times, their methods are intensely *personal*— as with interviews and qualitative and phenomenological studies.

SCIENTIFIC STUDIES ARE NOT FULLY OBJECTIVE (AND IMPERSONAL)

Psychological science is a science. Because science is caricatured to be coldly objective, psychological science is often thought to be too objective to be personal and reveal a personal God. However, we will find that the human aspect of psychological science can redeem its objectivity. On the other hand, science is not necessarily as rigorous and coldly rational as it is often thought to be.

The idea that science is strictly objective started in the eighteenth century. David Hume (1711-1776) put forth a philosophy in which ideas (i.e., truths of rational logic and mathematics) were opposed to empirical data (i.e., observations through the sense organs). From that beginning, positivism was developed by Auguste Comte (1798-1857) and culminated in Percy Bridgman (1882-1961), who suggested that science depends on *operational definitions.* Namely, a definition is no more or less than the operations used to measure it. Positivism was an attempt to make science completely objective. That attempt failed. Positivism was discredited as a scientific philosophy by philosophers such as Michael Polanyi (1891-1976) and Karl Popper (1902-1994). They observed that many *subjective* decisions are made in the conduct of scientific studies. Scientists *subjectively* decide which problems to investigate. They *subjectively* decide which theories to test, how to test them, which instruments to use, how to interpret the results, how to analyze the results and how to put the results into context. In short, *subjectivity permeates science.* A person reading such critiques of science might naively conclude that science is no more objective than is counseling.

EXPERIMENTAL STUDIES, THOUGH FLAWED, ARE USEFUL

We learn things about people through the experimental study of people and relationships that it is not possible to learn through other sciences or through humanities (including religion). As far as the sciences are concerned, psychological science studies people using a disciplinary methodology. As far as the humanities are concerned, psychology addresses the how-to questions from a different disciplinary perspective. Each discipline contributes to our knowledge of people. Let's look at some ways that psychological science can contribute.

Developmental Change

None of these disciplines, except psychological science, tells us how people develop and change as a consequence of their biological maturation coupled with the situations they normally and irregularly face. As strange as it might seem to us now, in an age when the findings of developmental psychology have been disseminated through the media and books, people used to think about children as if they were miniature adults. Sure, people have always known that a three-year-old is not the same as a thirty-year-old professor. But the differences were seen as quantitative. The child just didn't have enough reasoning, morality, experience or common sense. The biggest finding from developmental psychology is that the changes are often qualitative as well as quantitative.

A two-year-old or younger senses and manipulates the world. A five-year-old has started to see that the dimensions of the world are related to each other. A nine-year-old can reason by visualizing things in the mind's eye, and a twelve-year-old can reason abstractly. Furthermore, the neurons of the brain have not finished maturing by adolescence. They continue to be coated in a myelin sheath—a protective coating that allows high fidelity neural transmission and prevents the pathways from being mixed up as often. So, even twenty-year-olds are still changing. We also know that aging continues to affect brain functioning throughout life—though most change is through winnowing out unused pathways and strengthening well-used ones.

Personality, Cognitive Science, Abnormal Psychology and Positive Psychology

From psychological science, we learn how people think, feel and act. In the early part of the 1900s, personality psychology was aimed at uncovering the normal traits and personal characteristics that made people both similar to each other and unique. By the 1970s, though, evidence from social psychology and cognitive neuroscience revealed that the situations people found themselves in seemed to be almost more formative than personality. However, since the mid-to-late 1970s, the focus of personality psychology has been on the match of personal dispositions to situations. Certain situations do call for common responses, yet no situation is so strong that it makes everyone behave the same way. Other situations are so weak that personality almost completely governs the person's behavior, thoughts and feelings.

In the 1970s computers were beginning to be used widely, and psychologists began to make computer models of behavior. Strangely, computer models—which were the height of a machine model of human thought, emotion and behavior—broke the stranglehold that behaviorism had on psychological theorizing at that time. It freed scientists to begin to look at hidden mental processes again.

In about 2000, Martin Seligman[6] began to lead a movement of psychologists who thought that psychology had, for too long, focused on negative behavior. Seligman observed that most behavior was not problematic or abnormal. But because clinical psychologists focus their attention mostly on helping people deal with problematic behavior, thoughts or emotions, and because healing its citizens is important to the government, the field of psychology had become obsessed with clinical treatment of abnormal behavior. Seligman called for a readjustment of priorities. He didn't want to divert psychology from helping people with problems, but he called for more attention to the conditions under which people flourish and grow. With this agenda, we might think that positive psychology would be the resurrection of Pollyanna feel-good psychology. Not so. The defining characteristic of positive psychology is a strong commitment to using psychological scientific methods.

For some, positive psychology has become a study of happiness. For others, it studies human strengths. I think of positive psychology as the study of virtue for self and others, reminiscent of Aristotle's concept of *eudaemonia*. And as a study of eudaemonia, theology can inform the agenda of this large and growing branch of psychology. Furthermore, through positive psychology, we know a lot about Christian virtues—forgiveness, altruism, compassion, love, gratitude, modesty, humility and hope.

Social Psychology, Cultural Psychology and the Psychology of Religion

Social psychology studies the effect of people on individuals and the behavior of individuals in larger groups. Social psychology seeks to find general truths about people. It reveals how the groups that give us our identity affect us—such as families, work units, churches, civic organizations, communities, ethnic identity groups, states or nations, and religious groups. It examines the development of our beliefs and can show us the amazing coercive power of a simple social norm.

Cultural psychology is a branch of social psychology that focuses on how ethnicity and political-group membership affect people's lives in society. It tends to use sociological methods and surveys besides social psychological experiments. By concentrating on large societal groups, cultural psychology tries to separate out the effects due to ethnic-group membership and influence of people in that group.

The psychology of religion studies individuals' experience of spirituality and religion. It also examines individual behavior within a religious organization, and the behavior of the organization and its effects on the individual. The psychology of religion and spirituality seeks the most direct study of religion, and can tell us much about the things that affect us as religious people.

Clinical Psychology

Clinical psychology studies how to help people who are having problems. Sometimes those people want help and seek psychotherapy. Sometimes people don't want help but are court-mandated to some treatment. Sometimes people have mixed feelings and motives for seeking help. By examining how to help people change, especially people who want to change but find that they are not able to, we can learn much about (1) free will, (2) balanced influence of many cultural, personal, family and situational pressures, (3) God's grace at bringing about change, and (4) ways that helpers can act to promote change within a therapeutic setting.

Do the Fingerprints of God Found in Psychological
Science Reveal God?

From these subdisciplines of psychological science, we see many things clearly. We see that people do what they want to do. This testifies to the existence of free will. We see—probably to a large degree as a result of their free will—that humanity gets itself in trouble, suffers and is often looking for redemption, help and hope. Whether we study developmental psychology, personality psychology, positive psychology, social psychology, cultural psychology or the psychology of religion and spirituality, it is clear that hope is a central aim of people. When we reflect on God becoming incarnate in Jesus, and Jesus' willingness to take on not only the limitations of humanity but also the suffering of humanity to provide us with hope, we see how much he loves humanity.

People are relational. It is in relationships that identity is formed, happiness is felt, pain is experienced, and suffering not only is felt but seems to multiply. In relationships people are often healed and experience hope and redemption. Our positive emotions seem most commonly manifested in relationships. Caring wouldn't exist without people to care for. Nor would loving, empathizing and sympathizing. We also learn that we do not have to do everything. For better or worse, in relationships we divide workloads, power and influence, but we multiply satisfactions.

DO WE REALLY NEED PSYCHOLOGICAL SCIENCE?

Through viewing surgical procedures I have been enthralled with the wonder of the complexity of the interconnected systems of the body and the ingenuity of the precisely designed surgical tools. As I look back at this chapter, I have the same sense of wonder. Psychological science is itself a tool. Within the discipline, the subdisciplines each have toolboxes full of specialized tools. Those tools are all used to reveal more about humans and God. As a tool, disciplinary psychological science reveals people's suffering, joy and hope. As tool users, we use psychological science as a whole and all the subdisciplinary tools to aid us in our private worship, devotion, public worship and theological knowledge.

The cardiovascular surgeon knows that heart replacement is a new tool to extend life and its quality. Psychological science is a tool that can help people get ready to seek a new heart from the Lord. We marvel at the complexity of the human body and wonder of a new heart. Likewise, we should wonder even more at the new heart offered by the loving God to a flawed yet marvelous humanity. If we tremble at the surgeon's skillful hand, we should quake at God's hand as God uses tools to bring life to humans dead in their sin.

The heart transplant is a marvelous tool. But the surgeon also uses other tools to conduct the actual operation. The surgeon does not hold contempt for the scalpel that merely cuts through the skin. Nor does the surgeon derogate the curved needles to suture the wound at the operation's end. And the surgeon doesn't refuse to pull a blood vessel from the patient's leg merely because the surgeon's focus is on the heart. He or she knows that other tools, regardless of how humble, are needed if the heart and body are to be restored to health.

Similar to the heart surgeon, I marvel at the intricate connections among God's various tools. Psychological science is interconnected with tools to aid our private devotion, public worship and theological understanding. All form a web to help us know God better. God initiates. People respond. God wants us to know the divine personality in its triune form just as God knows us. So, God put in each of us a drive to know the Sacred by using our ingenuity, cleverness and God-given intelligence. Furthermore, God does not form us and stand passively by, but activates in us the motive to know God.

People have created all sorts of devotional, theological and scientific tools in service of that drive to know God. Sometimes, however, we do not realize we are seeking God. We have, in psychological science, nurtured the drive to discover things about people. We have spent less time reflecting about the meaning of our discoveries. Yet our hearts are challenged as we look at the tools of psychology. A tool has no use apart from a tool user who knows the tool's purpose. Unfortunately, we do not often refer back to the purposes of psychological science—to think the thoughts of God, to know the Creator by learning about the creation. We have let psychology all too often become autonomous— doing its own thing, building a tower of Babel as a monument to its own cleverness.

If our hearts are hardened by pride, we can lose heart muscle, which damages our hearts. We need to come with open hearts to the great heart surgeon to receive the new heart prepared for us.

SUMMARY

In this chapter I have argued that psychological science as a discipline is a tool that can help people understand human nature. Because human nature is formed in God's image, that disciplinary tool, and all the subdisciplinary tools within the science, can reveal God. This is true even though sin can, at times, seriously distort the revelation.

Throughout history, people have developed new tools that they have employed to know God better—new devotional practices, new worship methods and new theological understandings. When psychological science began at the end of the nineteenth century, its promise for revealing human nature and God was just a whisper. As psychological science has progressed, progressively more of the human and divine nature has been revealed. Yet, as strong a tool as psychological science is, it is not unlimited. Furthermore, any tool can be misused to harm instead of help people. So we need to carefully consider how psychological science is limited and how its use should be limited.

PSYCHOLOGICAL SCIENCE
IS LIMITED

PSYCHOLOGICAL SCIENCE IS A POWERFUL but limited tool. In this chapter, we look at the factors that limit psychological science and keep psychologists humble.

In over one hundred years, psychological science has evolved to include neuroscience and cognitive science. Testing—one of the core parts of psychological science—has evolved into sophisticated assessments using multiple types of measures within all of the social sciences, including sociology, political science and economics. Psychological science has made great strides in the history of the science. What we do in the lab and what we know from psychological science looks vastly different today from what it did in 1890.

However, curiously, in those years the practice of counseling and psychotherapy has changed little. Treatment for psychological disorders has evolved. We now have powerful psychoactive medications, and clinical research has documented which treatments are effective with particular disorders, which can be better diagnosed than previously. But when it comes down to what goes on between counselor and client, things look about the same as they did in 1890.

WHY THE DIFFERENCE?

This difference in rate of progress between psychological science and counseling is because most of psychological science is just that, science. It strives to be an objective enterprise. It is aimed at seeking general truth about people. Counseling, however, is a *private, subjective matter* between counselor and client. Its inner working is not subjected to external review. True, some clinical research looks at the clinical process—what goes on in the counseling room—but this is an intrusion into a private experience. And we cannot be sure how much the presence of observers changes the process of counseling. Counseling, after all, is not meant to discover general truths about people but to help a single individual, couple, family or group.

Psychological science, on the other hand, is meant to reveal general truths about people. People live most of their lives in an environment full of observers—at work, with friends, at school, in churches, in community groups, with family. So scientific observers tend to be less obtrusive than in a private therapeutic setting. The methods of psychological science have been crafted to eliminate as much subjective bias as possible. Clearly, though, it has not been completely successful.

PSYCHOLOGICAL SCIENCE IS PUBLIC

The explicit values of science advocate objectivity and skepticism about the interpretation of results. And experimental studies are subjected to external review. Nevertheless, the people doing each study and employing the scientific method cannot be completely objective (as demonstrated by Polanyi and Popper). But the subjectivity of psychological science is limited by the variety of people who critically evaluate the result before it becomes part of the canon of science. These include the collaborators within the project, each of whom have different points of view. In addition, even before publication, the research results are often presented at colloquia and conventions. Respondents critically evaluate the procedures and the outcomes as well as the interpretation of the findings. These criticisms are presented to the authors, who try to deal with the publicly raised critiques before they submit their study to a scientific journal.

Once a research article is submitted to a journal for publication, further objectivity is sought through many reviewers, each of whom brings a different perspective to the study. When scientific articles are submitted for possible publication, editors invite experts with a multitude of viewpoints to review the article on its scientific merits. The reviewers critique the study, and the editors evaluate the reviewers' comments and recommendations. Editors also provide an independent evaluation of the scientific study.

After the publication, other scientists review the study, and if it is thought to be generative, it might stimulate a follow-up study or citation. Researchers critique published studies as they are designing their own studies. And additional researchers critique the study by testing its results in the field or lab. Thus the merit of an article is judged by how much it influences the work of other scientists. Science does not depend on a single study. Rather, the meaning of the results is evaluated as psychological scientists write reviews that analyze the study's methods. The analysis might be quantitative (in a meta-analysis) or qualitative (in a narrative review). Reviewers tie the single study to other studies.

Scientific studies are not completely objective. But they are subjected to so many different points of view that a triangulation on truth occurs. Many scientists use viewpoints from different places to look at the same study. That method allows us to locate truth—as seen through a scientific lens—more accurately than one viewpoint (e.g., a counselor) looking at a single client.

Science seeks to uncover applicable truths. It does not presume to discover eternal verities. It maps out general understandings of the how-tos of life as understood within a particular scientific framework. It is understood that the framework will eventually change.

However, because some things change slowly and others virtually (or actually) never change, psychological science can uncover things of eternal significance even though that is not the intent of science. Only through theology can we speculate about the eternal *significance* of scientific discoveries. Theology is about eternal truth, and it can fit the fruits of scientific research into a framework that helps us understand any eternal significance it might have.

Psychological science, like theology, can reveal the marvels of the mind: emotions, motivations, memories, perceptions and consciousness. It can reveal specifics that theology can't address, like the intricacy and elegance of how brain and mind coordinate activities with the endocrine system. Psychological science, like theology, can inspire awe at the beauty of people's relationships. But it can go beyond theology in examining the dynamics of those relationships. And psychological science can observe the cruelty and the evil people are capable of. I believe that psychological science is particularly well suited to the task of stimulating emotions in us as we learn about humans. We are empathic creatures, and it is easy to relate with the human experiences revealed in good experimental studies. In them we see ourselves.

Paul often wrote about the seen and unseen world. Ultimately we will see the glory of God face to face (1 Cor 13:12; 2 Cor 6:16). Until then, though, we walk by faith, not sight (2 Cor 5:7). We see through a mirror darkly. Although darkness is a matter of degree, we do *see* through the mirror. We are limited to that dim sight. We can know God better through the blessing of psychological science, in the same way that we can know God better through Scripture, the Holy Spirit and the church. But we can never know God fully until the resurrection to new life.

What does psychological science say about the mirror's darkness? Can we obtain clarity of vision? Will psychology help our vision or hurt it?

THE LOGIC OF MODERN PSYCHOLOGY

Modern psychological studies are based on isolating an effect relative to a comparison condition in which other potentially influential factors (called variables) are *controlled*. The size of the effect is measured and expressed *numerically*. The measurement of variables, usually in terms of numbers, is the hallmark of modern science.

Early science was based on simple studies that compared the effects of few variables, but modern science has become more (1) multivariate, (2) time conscious and (3) tolerant of indeterminacy. That is, the tools of science have become more sophisticated.

Multivariate

Multivariate methods have increased through computer technology. We have the computing power to crunch huge arrays of numbers that measure many variables simultaneously. Thus, research designs are usually multivariate. We are no longer content to measure a main independent variable (i.e., hypothesized causal variables) and one or two dependent variables (i.e., hypothesized effects). Instead, we try to account for the effects of a vast array of variables at the same time.

Time Conscious

Just as Einstein-based physics developed its understanding of the relationship between space and time, psychologists now examine how psychological and relationship variables change with time. Today, scientists are more interested in change than in static descriptions. Many of the experimental designs and statistical methods of psychology are meant to reveal the extent of change as it occurs at many interlocking but different levels of measurement.

Tolerant of Indeterminacy

From its beginning, psychology has taken into account that humans are somewhat unpredictable. The logic of inferential statistical analyses assumes this. Experiments do not ever *prove* that changing an independent variable will result in the change in a dependent variable. Rather, statistics examine how large differences in measurements are. Are the differences so big that, relative to chance alone, in random drawings, such a difference could occur only one in twenty times? Or one in a hundred? One in a thousand? Experimenters choose how big a difference they wish to require before they are willing to infer that the differences are "significant," which means they are *probably* not due to chance alone. Nevertheless, free will, individual differences, and various forces and variables affect most psychological inferential statistics methods.

LIMITATIONS OF PSYCHOLOGICAL SCIENCE
EXTRAPOLATED FROM PHYSICS

While physics and psychological science don't have a lot in common, let's think about some shared limitations.[1] Quantum mechanics has been elaborated throughout the twentieth century. At its base it is probabilistic. The behavior of a bunch of particles can be predicted through the Schrödinger equation, one of the fundamental equations of quantum mechanics. It predicts analytically and precisely the probability of events or outcomes. The detailed outcome is not strictly determined—such as the behavior of a single particle or even an inter-twined pair of particles—but given a large number of events, the Schrödinger equation will predict the distribution of results.

We can make one of those "duh" conclusions here. If the behavior of lifeless particles is not always measurable, then perhaps behaviors, per-sonalities and relationships—which seem more complex than basic subatomic particles—might also not be determined precisely.

Even using the most powerful computers and the most powerful statistics, we cannot precisely predict behavior, much less control it. Perhaps, something like the Heisenberg Uncertainty Principle might apply in psychology. Heisenberg noted that when measuring the speed and position of microscopic or nanoscopic particles, the physicist must bounce a photon (i.e., light wave) off of the particle and then detect the photon in an electron microscope. But the photon takes time to travel from the electron to the microscope and then to the eye (or computer). In that time the electron has moved somewhere else and at a different speed because it was measured. Thus the position of the electron that our eye sees in not, in fact, where the electron is.

Measurement disturbs the object measured. It doesn't take a particle physicist to validate this in daily life. People who know they are being measured might change their behavior. So what an experiment measures might not necessarily reflect the way people would act if they weren't be-ing measured. Of course, the measurement could be ham-fisted: "Why don't you complete these questionnaires because we are measuring your answers to see whether you get the coveted job?" Or the measurement could be subtle—watching unobtrusively how people behave when they do not know they are in a study. Regardless, we could never be sure that the measurement is not affecting behavior. We thus are destined to see through a mirror darkly using experimental methods.

SELF-SERVING BIAS LIMITS INTERPRETATION

Theologians, psychologists and other scientists base many of their un-derstandings of truth on reasoning. For years psychological scientists have examined how people reason.[2]

Perhaps some of the most interesting studies have shown how people solve problems and make decisions, inferences and judgments. It often has been more instructive to examine errors in reasoning and judgment than correct reasoning. If we have a problem to solve that has a limited number of possible solutions, we can choose a response based on an *algorithm*. An algorithm is a step-by-step procedure that examines all possible outcomes and selects the best solution. For example, at the first move of a checkers match, there are only four possible moves. Once the opponent responds, though, the possibilities soon become unmanageable if we try to consider every possible move. We thus defer to *heuristics* for complex decision making. A heuristic is a rule of thumb that considers only the solutions that are most likely to be successful. Most decision making, by necessity, cannot use algorithms to help make a decision or solve problems. There are just too many possible options. Heuristics make problem-solving quicker than considering hundreds of possible actions, but heuristics do result in errors.

The *availability heuristic* predisposes us to select a solution that is readily available in our consciousness, even if a better solution exists. I once testified before some committees in the Virginia General Assembly. I reported on research involving over ten thousand participants who described their emotional decisions about parental consent in adolescent abortion decision making. I summarized the research as impartially as I could and drew a conclusion that parents—for the most part—could help adolescents make better decisions about whether to seek an abortion than allowing the adolescent to decide independently. The other side had a woman tell an emotion-charged story of how her life was deeply affected by meddling parents. I distilled in numbers thousands of experiences of many people culled from research, but she reported only her own experience. Which do you think was the most likely to influence the legislators?

Her emotional experience probably had more immediate impact on the legislators. But I know about the availability heuristic. So I said, "My research data represents ten thousand human experiences. Don't be misled. The numbers have wiped the tears dry. But there were many tears here. Imagine the amount of suffering that was soaked up by this towel of numbers."

Confirmation Bias in Solving Problems

Similar mental errors happen in solving problems. Suppose I ask you to guess the general rule that governs a set of numbers. You can test your hypothesis before you guess by asking whether any number is in the set. Here are some of the numbers in the set: 2, 4, 6 and 8. What is the rule? What would you ask me to check your guess?

You might ask, "Is 10 in the set?"

"Yes."

"Is 12?"

"Yes."

"Is the rule the set of even numbers?"

"No."

You might ask, "Is 5 in the set?"

"Yes."

You might be tempted to guess the set of positive whole numbers, but you'd better explore further.

"Is minus 1?"

"Yes."

"Minus 100?"

"Yes."

"Zero?"

"Yes."

Should you guess all whole numbers?

You now realize that you could ask about whole numbers forever and it would not help solve your problem of determining the rule governing the set. You must guess something you think is *not* in the set.

"Is minus one-half?"

"Yes."

"How about pi, 3.14159265 . . . ?"

"No."

"How about the square root of 2, 1.41414 . . . ?"

"No."

Now you are getting somewhere.

"The set is all positive and negative rational numbers and zero."

The important point is not to see how people eventually get to the correct answer, but to see how people make mistakes. They quickly develop a hypothesis (2, 4, 6, 8 = even whole numbers). Then they try to *confirm* their hypothesis. That led to an error: "Is the rule the set of even numbers?"

Confirming what we already believe can never solve the problem. Instead, we must disconfirm a hypothesis. Even an incorrect attempt to disconfirm one's hypothesis, "Is minus one-half in the set?" yielded new information. The point is this: People naturally want to confirm their hypotheses and will sometimes resist trying to disconfirm them.

Confirmation Bias in Perception
The same error shows up in people's perception. We have a confirmation bias in what we perceive. When we listen to a presidential debate, we almost always think our preferred candidate won the debate. We think our children are brighter than average—like Garrison Keillor's Lake Wobegon, where all the children are smarter than average.

Overestimation Bias
After an exam, most people overestimate their test score. In married couples, if asked to estimate the amount they contribute to the marriage, the sum of the contributions almost always adds up to more than 100 percent.

Self-Esteem Maintenance
A person with a healthy, stable sense of self-esteem can read ninety-seven evaluations supporting the excellence of his or her speech and three critical evaluations and conclude that he or she did well. A person with poor self-esteem can read the same one hundred evaluations and conclude that he or she is a failure. We look selectively to find the data that confirm our beliefs about ourselves.

Functional Fixedness in Solving Problems
One big obstacle in problem solving is called *functional fixedness*. MacGyver was a television protagonist who thought outside the box. He always rigged novel ways of using common objects to rescue himself from seemingly impossible predicaments. Most of us are not Mac-

Gyvers. We have a hard time seeing any but the common use for everyday objects. Our thinking is fixed by an object's usual functions.

A Big Truth About People

We are zeroing in on a big truth here, called the *self-serving bias*. We base our lives on perceiving things in the way that already fits our beliefs. We choose evidence so that it serves our preexisting beliefs. (Recall chapter 4, "Why You Might Not Believe What You Don't Already Believe.")

Scripture tells us the same thing. "Everyone who has will be given more, and he will have an abundance. Whoever does not have, even what he has will be taken from him" (Mt 25:29). Paul argues in 2 Corinthians 2:15-16 that "we are to God the aroma of Christ among those who are being saved and those who are perishing. To the one we are the smell of death; to the other, the fragrance of life." Believers thus accepted Paul's teaching, but those who began as hostile to God just could not accept them. On one hand, Christian believers can rejoice because their faith helps them discern Jesus' other faith-building works (Mt 13:11-13). The other side of this double-edged sword is not heeded as often. If we are in doctrinal error, we will tend to assume that our (erroneous) thinking is correct. We will selectively perceive evidence to support our position. Our "faith," when it is in error, will blind us, not make us see—as it did the Pharisees and Sadducees in Jesus' day and still does to atheists today.

We focus on our own position, and the self-serving bias has its way. And we are absolutely certain that we are correct. We see here how theology tells us a truth, but psychological science fills in many of the details about how that truth shows up in life. Like good marriage partners psychological science and theology work together to make the relationship run smoothly.

MEMORY LIMITS PSYCHOLOGICAL SCIENCE

Even our memory at times seems to work against our perception of the truth. Research on long-term memory shows that we literally rewrite history in our minds to show we are correct. In a series of classic studies, Elizabeth Loftus[3] showed people a movie of a car crash. Afterward, ostensibly to check on their perception, people answered a few simple questions. All questions were identical except one. The critical question for half the group read, "How fast would you estimate the blue car was going when it smashed into the green car?" The other half had the same wording except that it read "when it hit the green car?"

A week later, people returned to the lab for a memory test. People who had read "smashed into" estimated more damage and more presence of broken glass than did people who read "hit." Sometimes, the smallest things can cause us unconsciously to rewrite history to create a consistent story.

After the September 11, 2001, attack on the World Trade Center in New York, emotional memories could be studied. Most U.S. citizens reacted emotionally to those attacks. Some people reacted more emotionally than others because they knew people who were injured or killed. The attack provided a good way to evaluate the accuracy of the memories. People had access to the same limited television footage, and the accuracy of the facts could be checked easily.

The findings were clear. Emotional involvement did *not* make people more (or less) accurate in their memories of the attack footage. But higher emotional involvement made them *more certain* that their memories were accurate—even though the memories were not really more accurate.[4] Prior research has shown clearly that emotion potentiates long-term memory.[5] That is, when people are emotional, they are hardwired to remember better *what they pay attention to*. But this is a two-way sword working both for and against long-term memory. By paying attention to one detail, emotionally aroused people don't pay attention to other details. Thus, their memories are inaccurate for those details.

What lessons should we draw from this? We need to remain humble about whatever we think we remember clearly. (Is humility beginning to sound like a theme?) Second, we are liable to make errors in directions that justify our beliefs and perceptions. Third, the more emotionally involved we are, the more adamant we are likely to be that we are correct and that the evidence supports our position—even when it doesn't.

This can be especially true with theology. Witness the history of Protestant Christianity. Each faction or denomination believes it is correct on divisive issues. New denominations multiply. Each tries to support its theological stance through selective use of evidence. It doesn't seem selective as we present the evidence, but we usually ignore the things that the other side considers persuasive evidence.

I am not singling out theology. Despite the commitment of science to truth and to allowing the data to speak, I have been a scientist long enough to see the same self-serving biases occurring in psychology. Both theologians and psychological scientists are human. We get wrapped up in seeing things a particular way, and when challenged, we emotionally defend our way of perceiving the world. Even when it isn't correct.

LEVEL OF DEVELOPMENT LIMITS WHAT
CAN BE LEARNED FROM PSYCHOLOGICAL SCIENCE

Developmental psychologists have described a fundamental truth. People at different stages of life experience life differently. At age one, I spit out Brussels sprouts. At age five, I had learned to eat them. At age fifteen, I tried to have urgent business elsewhere when it was Brussels-sprouts night in our house. At age twenty-five, we rarely purchased them. At age sixty, with knees aching, skin cancers, muscle strains experienced mysteriously while sleeping and a general health consciousness, if I found out that Brussels sprouts would help me score three more points per tennis match, I'd be all over them like gravy on mashed potatoes.

Cognitive, moral, emotional and social abilities change as we age. It would be a convenient fiction to believe that as we move from stage to stage, we simply get better, building on the things we learned in earlier stages, never forgetting and growing in wisdom. Sadly, that does not seem to be the whole picture. We do seem to get a bit wiser with age. But progress is herky-jerky, and frankly we often regress.

Like a drama stage, our developmental stage allows freedom of action within the stage. But our behavior does not roam free. Our development limits our understanding of science and its relationship to religion. It limits what we can find out about God from psychological studies. And it also limits what we can experience of God directly by familiarizing ourselves with psychological science and its findings.

BIOLOGY LIMITS WHAT WE CAN LEARN
FROM PSYCHOLOGICAL SCIENCE

Our bodies and brains, the physical parts of our being, are incredibly complex.[6] To experience life as a human, we must have a body. If it were not essential, we would not expect there to be a resurrection of the body described in Scripture and affirmed in the creeds. If we already believe, studying the brain-mind connection can reveal more of God. If our presupposition is that God cannot exist because material is all that exists, then life seems to obscure God.

C. S. Lewis attacked the idea that the material world was real but not the spiritual world. In his essay "Transposition," he argued that the spiritual world is complex and multidimensional, and the physical will never adequately represent it.[7] Drawing from the classic book *Flatland*,[8] he made the following analogy. If a person were a dot living on a two-dimensional piece of paper, the person would explain his or her entire world in two dimensions, speaking only of points, lines and spaces. The person could have no clear concept about what three-dimensional objects were except by imperfect imagination. From a two-dimensional worldview, waterfalls, rainbows and sunsets are incomprehensible.

C. S. Lewis used this analogy to combat arguments that opponents to Christianity might make, such as "God is nothing but your fantasy of a most wonderful father, only grander" or "Heaven is just a glorified earth." These were beautifully illustrated in his Narnia book *The Silver Chair*.[9] In "Transposition" he argued against a one-to-one correspondence between physical and subjective states, suggesting that the subjective was richer than the physical. He said that the same small number of notes on a piano can create thousands of melodies and evoke many complex emotions. Thus, he argued, we can never reduce the spiritual or emotional experiences to mere notes on a piano. Or we can never reduce spiritual experiences rich in emotion, thought and meaning to mere physical processes, like chemical reactions.

Finally, Lewis argued that for the dot to come to know the three-dimensional world, it would be most helpful if a three-dimensional creature became a dot and communicated three-dimensional concepts within the two-dimensional world. That, of course, is what Jesus did.

He who was in the form of God became human so we could see God face to face—in human form. And Jesus established the church as his body so others could catch a glimpse, though imperfect, of God.

SUMMARY

There are a lot of limitations on what we can know about God from the study of psychological science. There are even more limitations on how well we can know God more personally.

The limits we discussed in this chapter involve our memory and our developmental status, which we experience because we are finite creatures. The more disturbing limitations we face are our moral and cognitive shortcomings. The ubiquitous presence of the self-serving bias, in its many forms, is perhaps our most worrisome limitation.

Our limitations corral us. Awareness of our limitations keep us from building monuments to our egos, which is illustrated in the Bible's account of Babel. If we are ever to break out of our prideful lives, we need to turn humbly to God. Our little victories will only come at God's instigation and for God's purposes.

Though the moral problem is of great concern, we will not deal with this problem until chapters fourteen and fifteen. We now see how psychological science has developed tools to extend our senses to measure things that people used to not realize existed. But we also have a healthy skepticism that makes us aware of the limits of those tools. Let us now, in humility, ask what psychological science might contribute to theology. That will be our discussion in chapters eleven, twelve and thirteen.

PSYCHOLOGICAL SCIENCE STRENGTHENS THEOLOGICAL CLAIMS

PSYCHOLOGICAL SCIENCE CAN HELP US know God better by providing evidence that strengthens theological claims. In this chapter, I take five basic theological truths and examine whether psychological experiments do or do not support those theological propositions. The five theological truths are:

- Humans are created in God's image.

- Humans are fallen and sinful.

- God is relational and (because we are created in God's image) so are humans.

- Humans are meaning makers.

- Humans need the holy.

HUMANS ARE CREATED IN GOD'S IMAGE

Does experimental research support the theological proposition that humans bear the image of God? The image of God can be interpreted structurally (ontologically) or relationally. I will first address the structural image and deal with the relational image in later sections of this chapter.

Structural Image

Theologians tell us that God is just, merciful, gracious and altruistically loving. (God has many other attributes, but for our purposes of showing that psychological science can strengthen theological claims, these are sufficient.) If humans are created in God's image, we should expect to see these qualities appear in psychological studies of humans.

Justice. First, people have a justice motive. Melvin Lerner,[1] through twenty-five years of experimental research, describes this justice motive as intuitive and not tied to the content of people's moral beliefs. Lerner identifies four situations that trigger the intuitive justice motive. People feel an urge for justice when (1) emotional trigger events occur, such as strong injustices, (2) normative constraints are violated, which provokes a pause for thoughtfulness, (3) people's "flow"[2] is interrupted, and (4) a violation of the sacred occurs, which stimulates the "heroic motive" where a person feels as if he or she needs to rectify a desecration.

Princeton psychologist John Darley[3] has conducted experimental research about how people think about justice. People can understand justice as (1) rehabilitation therapy, (2) punishing wrongdoers, and (3) fairness. Based on experimental studies, Darley concludes that in the general population, at least in the United States, we usually think of justice in terms of punishing wrongdoers. Darley's research thus supports Immanuel Kant's philosophical theory, which saw injustices as violations of an inherent categorical imperative. Traditions of understanding justice advocated by Jeremy Bentham (fairness, the greatest good for the greatest number) or John Locke were not supported.

People have an exceptionally strong justice motive. This was revealed recently in studies by Swiss researchers headed by Ernst Fehr who employed game theory to determine what happens when people are unjust.[4] Game theory uses games, like the prisoners' dilemma (which we talked about in a previous chapter), to model what takes place over time as people interact with each other. In Fehr's game, two players, let's say Alan and Bob, are given the same amount of money. From their stash they draw out ten coins to play the game. (They will have to play five other times before going home.) Alan can elect to give his ten coins to Bob in hopes that both he and Bob will end up with more. Or Alan can elect not to give anything to Bob, and they can both go home with ten. (Parables about burying one's talents in the ground might come to mind here.) If Alan trusts Bob and gives his ten to Bob, the experimenters add twenty coins to Bob's stash. Alan is now broke but Bob has forty coins instead of the ten he started the game with.

Then it's Bob's move. On move two, Bob can give half to Alan—both would then have twenty coins—and both would have benefited by mutual trust. Or Bob can take advantage of the situation, keeping all forty coins, leaving Alan broke. So, at the end of two moves, there were three possible results. Either they both had ten or Bob had forty but Alan had zero, or both had twenty coins.

Move three. If Bob had betrayed Alan's trust, though, the experimenters allowed Alan to have the last word. He could punish Bob by telling Bob how angry he was with Bob. Bob had to sit there and take it on the chin. But as a second option, Alan could punish Bob by making him surrender ten coins. However, to do so Alan had to forfeit ten coins himself from his stash that would be used in other games. Would Alan pay money to punish a wrongdoer?

In a surprising number of participants the Alan-person indeed forfeited his own money to force Bob to forfeit ten coins. So Alan ended ten coins in the red and Bob ended with thirty coins, but Bob really knew that Alan was angry—angry enough to pay to punish him.

This experiment was made more interesting because the participants were being PET scanned during play. PET scans reveal brain activity. Animals (and humans) have a portion of the brain that is active as they anticipate reward. Curiously, it is more active when anticipating than actually experiencing reward. For example, in humans, the reward pathway is activated when gambling, making a risky decision or anticipating kissing a romantic partner.

In the Fehr et al. study, electing merely to tell the other person of one's anger at being betrayed did not greatly stimulate the reward pathway. But deciding actually to punish the wrongdoer by making him or her cough up some loot gave a big shot to the reward pathway. There were, of course, differences across players. Each player estimated how likely he or she was to actually punish "Bob." Those who rated themselves as most likely were the ones whose reward pathways were most actively stimulated.

The justice motive, expressed as a desire to punish wrongdoers, is especially strong. We might ask whether this reflects God's character (i.e., the image of God) or is part of the Fall? Or perhaps it's both. Perhaps the need to see wrongdoing punished is a human reflection of the character of God. In this view, justice, which is understood as punishment of wrongdoers, is important to God. Theologians and biblical scholars may judge differently the ultimate cause of the need to punish wrongdoers. But the fact is that people seem to have a *biological* need to punish wrongdoing. Theologians should acknowledge this human need.

Mercy and grace. A recent article suggests that people have a mercy motive (the motive to restrain harsh justice or vengeance) and a grace motive (the motive to bless people—even one's enemies).[5] The research addressing these motives has been done mostly in the study of altruism.[6] There are various theories of altruism. One important body of research is Daniel Batson's empathy-altruism hypothesis.[7] Evolutionary psychology, which I will touch on briefly, has had a particularly difficult time with what might be called the "problem of good," which is as troublesome for evolutionary theories as the "problem of evil" is for Christianity.[8] One finding is clear. If people can feel empathy for a needy person, they are highly likely to help, even at great cost to themselves. But, empathy is fragile, and we are easily distracted from it, which we see in the following study of whether bystanders will give help to a needy person.

Altruism. Most people think of altruism as a characteristic of a person. However, although there are clearly different personal qualities that make a person more likely to help others, psychological scientists have found that situations can easily sidetrack the basic altruistic motive. In social psychology a body of research on bystander intervention has shown how situational factors, such as not noticing whether an emergency really exists, not understanding that the emergency requires *my* action, the presence of other potential helpers, the ambiguity of whether help is needed and whether a bystander is actually able to provide it, and other factors can convince people to put aside their altruistic motives.[9]

Robert Cialdini,[10] who has studied altruism and was aware of the research of others, was hit by a car—at least so the story goes. Lying in the street he saw people walking by him, uncertain whether something needed to be done and whether they should be doing it. So Cialdini picked out a pedestrian, called loudly to him, "Hey, you." The man looked. "Yes, I'm talking to you," Cialdini made eye contact. "I'm hurt. I need for you to help me. Please call an ambulance."

"Sure thing," said the man, and hurried off to find a phone.

People want to help, but situations can divert us from actually following through. It isn't just unclear situations that divert us. Situations that heighten our focus on ourselves rather than on others can short-circuit empathy. In a clever study, psychologists John Darley and Daniel Batson[11] recruited students at Princeton Theological Seminary who were studying for the ministry to give a speech on either the good Samaritan (Lk 10:30-35) or on career opportunities for seminary students. At the experimental site they were told that their audience was waiting for them, but were told that they either (1) had plenty of time, (2) were on time if they left now, or (3) were late and needed to hurry. On the way to give the talk they passed a man slumped in a doorway, coughing and wheezing, and in obvious need. The outcome measure was whether the students would stop to help.

The results were surprising. The topic of the speech didn't make any difference. Those who had the good Samaritan on their mind weren't any more likely to give help than were those who were thinking about career opportunities. But the amount of available time made a big difference. Students with "plenty of time" were six times as likely to help as were those who "needed to hurry." Thus, research on altruism shows a clear altruistic motive if we really take the time to understand others.

HUMANS ARE FALLEN AND SINFUL

People pervert the image of God that they bear. We demonstrate daily that we are fallen creatures, as theology tells us we are. In his book *On Aggression*,[12] ethologist Konrad Lorenz showed evolutionary evidence that suggests that violence, aggression and evil are built into the human species. And in *People of the Lie*, M. Scott Peck[13] reveals that evil is built into individual personalities. Robert Hare[14] has spent a career studying psychopaths—those people who seem to do evil with little tinge of conscience and who seem to lack the capacity for empathic concern.

Each of these approaches tends to locate imperfection, aggression, violence and evil within humans.

Some people are downright evil, and all of us seem to do things that violate our own moral codes each day. Demonstrating people's fallenness is such a truism that we hardly need psychological science to know that people are fallen. But psychological science can give us ideas about the factors related to evil or bad behavior.

Psychologist Roy Baumeister[15] has written a book summarizing the psychological evidence for evil. Instead of looking to people's interior for evil, he shows how easily people are provoked to evil, aggression and violence using a variety of social psychological studies. Baumeister emphasizes the situational influences that trigger violent, cruel and downright evil behavior in people who are bent toward violence. This tends to be what psychological science can add to the conversation about fallen humanity. Personality factors interact with situational factors to produce evil behavior. Theology looks more toward the personality side of things. But Scripture and theology tell us that the effects of sin have spread to all of creation. It is not a stretch to conclude that situations— which are created by fallen humans—can also be evil. In support of this, I will review three areas from recent research—rejection of God, forgiveness of self and pride.

Rejection of God

We often reject God. Julie Exline has shown this in research that examines disappointment and anger at God.[16] In particular, she found that about one-quarter of those who feel intense anger at God resolve their anger by rejecting God. Even when we remain believers, we too often turn our backs on God's guidance and love.

Exline has identified a number of factors that provoke people to anger at God. Anger at God is seen most often in people who struggle spiritually rather than in those settled in their faith. But beyond the personal qualities, Exline has found many situational factors, including events that are very severe, unpredictable, do not appear to be deserved, affect loved ones, and have effects that the person must deal with for long periods after the event. But not everyone resolves the anger in the same way. Some people, for example, who are not Christians become Christians. Others give up their faith. Mostly, though, anger at God does not provoke a change in faith but results in a period of unsettled feelings that are eventually resolved.

Forgiveness of Self

We don't always blame God for our problems. Many people blame themselves. Often that self-condemnation is deserved. Sometimes it is the product of an overactive conscience. In both cases, we see evidence of an inbuilt sense of wrong and right, and an awareness that we fall short of the mark. Research into forgiveness of oneself has lagged behind research in forgiving others.[17] However, empirical research into self-forgiveness is now being published. June Price Tangney and her colleagues[18] have shown that people respond to their need for self-forgiveness in different ways. Some struggle with self-condemnation and seem almost unable to get past it. Others glibly let themselves off the hook for virtually any kind of wrongdoing. Some seem to wrestle with self-condemnation but can, in time, forgive themselves. Fincham and his colleagues have written theoretically about forgiveness of self[19] and describe a process by which people might come to responsibly forgive their own wrongdoing. Most important, we note from the accumulating literature that whether people can forgive themselves depends on many situational characteristics.

Pride

Pride also reveals how people have fallen. Pride is thought by many to be one of the seven deadly sins. Terry Cooper[20] argues that two competing strands of writing on self-esteem exist. The Augustinian version says pride—too much and unwarranted self-esteem—is people's fundamental problem. In contrast, Carl Rogers,[21] a champion of the 1960s human potential movement, once said that he had never seen a client with too much self-esteem. What does psychology say about pride and self-esteem?

For years, people assumed that violence was generally caused by low self-esteem—and indeed sometimes this is the case. However, Roy Baumeister and his colleagues[22] reviewed massive amounts of research and showed that, most often, violent individuals seem to think of themselves as better than or superior to others—not inferior wimps who use violence to compensate for their wormlike self-esteem.

Violence probably comes more from wounded pride than from poor self-esteem. Perhaps the earliest demonstration of this comes from Morton Deutsch, who had two participants play a trucking game.[23] Both players could earn money by playing the game, but one player was capable of exploiting the other. One of the players was a confederate of the experimenter, and regularly exploited the true participant. After the exploitation the participant was given the option of getting revenge, but at significant cost to himself or herself. In between, though, observers (other confederates of the experimenter) gave the participant feedback. If the confederates gave encouraging feedback, usually the participant did not seek revenge. But when the feedback included an evaluation that the participant was a "sucker," revenge almost always followed, regardless of the cost to the participant.

Baumeister and Brad Bushman reviewed the literature on aggression and concluded:

> The wounded pride factor has found its way into so much aggression research that it is often scarcely noticed. Most laboratory studies on aggression include some kind of provocation in the form of an insult delivered to the participant by the person toward whom the participant will later be able to aggress. Without such an insult, most studies find hardly any aggression. Essentially, most studies of aggression simply show that other factors can increase or decrease the effect of wounded pride.[24]

You might think back to Richard Nisbett and Dov Cohen's study on the culture of honor (see pp. 59-63).[25] The provocation of the obstructionist confederate in calling the Northern and Southern students an obscene name was made much worse if the student came from a traditionally honor-heavy culture like the South.

We don't need research from psychological scientists to convince us that people are fallen. But that research can support theological claims by identifying more personal and situational factors that makes fallenness more likely to show up.

GOD IS RELATIONAL AND SO ARE HUMANS

People need community. Theologically, this fits well with the Christian doctrine of the Trinity as an eternal relational community. There are, once again, many obvious sources of data from psychology that demonstrate the need for human community and relationships. Social psychology, the study of interpersonal relationships and of group dynamics, consists of entire bodies of collected research on the ways that relationships are crucial. Family studies comprise thousands of studies of family relationships, roles and dynamics. Closely related to family studies, couple dynamics reveal how people act during dating, cohabitation, marriage, child rearing and the empty nest. In *The Case for Marriage*,[26] Linda Waite and Maggie Gallagher have arrayed a huge body of research showing social, health and economic benefits of marriage relative to divorce, cohabitation or single living.

Psychological science tells us that people are social. They need to feel passion, communicate, experience empathy, be intimate with friends, family and lovers, and be committed to others. Three recent sets of studies on love, societal conflict and anger at God show the importance of relationships.

Love

Three elements—passion, intimacy and commitment—make up experiences of love. Psychologist Robert Sternberg[27] has described marriages according to the shapes of triangles made of legs of different lengths (see fig. 11.1). For example, the first panel represents consummate love—high in passion, intimacy and commitment. This is the ultimate love, which most people strive for and which seems to usually be related to the most satisfying relationships. This is not only the type of marriage relationship most of us want, but it is likely the type of relationship God desires with humans—one that is on fire with passion, intimate in its every communication and unreservedly committed. Certainly, the Trinity is characterized by this type of love.

While people might feel satisfied or accept other types of love as the best they can expect from a particular person or at a particular time of life, these often seem to fall short of the ideal. In the second panel of figure 11.1, I have depicted a highly committed love characterized with little passion or intimacy. This might be a comfortable marriage, but it does not raise the partners' blood pressure. Such a relationship with God is probably akin to dead orthodoxy. In the third panel, we see companionate love, which typifies the relationship of long-term couples after their sex drives begin to cool. This might also be the committed and intimately connected Christian who longs for a rebirth of passion in his or her relationship with God. Finally, in panel four, we have passionate love, which happens in the weeks and months just after the wedding. Most couples report high sexual activity during those times. Yet, intimacy and real commitment have not yet begun to grow. This is often the spiritual life experienced by the newly converted Christian. We cannot get enough of God, and the passion is high. But it will take time for intimacy and commitment to grow and prove itself.

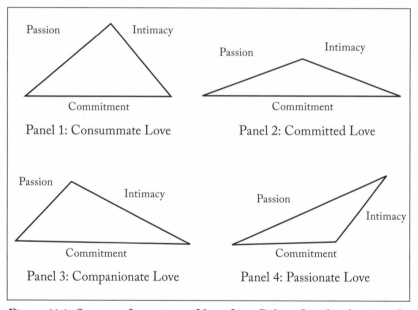

Figure 11.1. Some configurations of love from Robert Sternberg's triangular theory of love

Societal Conflict

Experimental research shows that to restore community, several qualities are necessary. Societal conflict can only be resolved if truth, justice, reconciliation and forgiveness lead to peace. This has been shown in investigations in South Africa,[28] Northern Ireland[29] and Rwanda.[30] In contrast to people who study forgiveness as an individual decision, emotional experience and as a part of ongoing relationships, researchers who study forgiveness within societal contexts strongly emphasized truth, justice, responsibility and accountability, as well as forgiveness, altruism and reconciliation, as leading to legitimate peace—both societally and intrapersonally. Thus peace depends on justice and forgiveness, on fairness and mercy, on accountability and grace. These sets of opposites are like the two ends of a bar magnet. They are united to each other even though they attract and repel materials differently. Together, though, it is almost as if they create a magnetic field that holds society together.

For years, societal peace was thought to be rooted in conflict resolution, problem solving or negotiation. For instance, social psychologist Muzafer Sherif, in a classic field study, helped children at a summer camp resolve conflicts between two groups through working together instead of competing. In his Robbers' Cave study, Muzafer Sherif[31] established "superordinate goals," where the former competitors could work together. Sherif's findings became "received wisdom" in the intergroup conflict literature. I have even applied it with married couples in conflict. By helping partners who seem to be focused on divorce develop positive common goals, sometimes a counselor can derail marital conflict and restore cooperation.

Recent studies in Northern Ireland,[32] however, show that it isn't that simple. When Protestants and Catholics in Ulster worked together on a common project, some got over their prejudices and some became more prejudiced. This should not be surprising, considering the success and lack of it in forced bussing during the civil rights era in the United States as an attempt to end desegregation. People are indeed relational creatures, but it turns out that, as the Northern Ireland studies demonstrated, their identity matters. The people in Northern Ireland who became more prejudiced had the strongest identity as either Protestant or Catholic. The ones who assimilated had the weakest subgroup identity.

People's identity includes their relationships. When we are identified with others, we are an in-group. We tend to focus on differences with out-group members. Because of the strength of group identity, a harm or offense by an out-group member against any in-group member is perceived as against each in-group member. The strength of relationship with other in-group members is related to the strength of identity with that group, and it thus affects how life is perceived.

People's relationships to in-groups and out-groups are not the only factors that strongly affect them. Their religion does too. Yet religion is not merely a set of beliefs or only social interactions with church members. People behave as if they have an important, emotionally charged relationship with God.

Anger at God

Julie Exline[33] of Case Western Reserve University and her colleagues have studied people who get angry at God when misfortune befalls them. People blame God for troubles, but do not as quickly give God credit and gratitude for windfalls. Exline has found that people resolve their anger toward God in different ways. About a quarter of all people express their anger toward God by rejecting God and giving up their faith. This non-scriptural way of dealing with anger at God is a clear result of the Fall. Exline's research shows how relationally we deal with God. We do not act as if religion is mere mental assent to theological propositions. We act emotionally. Even when we reject God, we show that a real relationship exists between us and our Lord. (The imprecatory Psalms establish a rich scriptural tradition of expressing anger at God. Yet the psalmists usually express anger at God within the context of ultimate trust.)

HUMANS ARE MEANING MAKERS

Viktor Frankl[34] was in the Auschwitz and Dachau death camps during World War II. After surviving the war he reflected on his experiences in the moving account *Man's Search for Meaning: An Introduction to Logotherapy. Logotherapy* means "therapy through meaning." Those people who held onto hope and a sense of meaning tended to survive despite the hardships in the death camps. Meaning was discovered by being oriented toward the future—toward a task, person or goal. Those who lost their sense of meaning soon died.

Sense of meaning is often captured in life narratives. Northwestern psychologist Dan P. McAdams[35] has developed a life-story model of adult identity. According to his model, beginning in late adolescence and young adulthood people living in modern societies organize their lives around life narratives. People create life stories that help them understand the past and anticipate the future meaningfully. Their lives are imbued with unity and purpose through the narratives. McAdams argues that personality itself may be viewed as three associated levels—dispositional traits, characteristic adaptations (such as motives, goals, values and schemas) and integrative life stories. Life stories may be analyzed in terms of plots, settings, scenes, characters and themes.

McAdams[36] has studied highly generative people. Generativity is an adult's commitment to helping future generations thrive and therefore pass along one's wisdom to the future. Highly generative adults tend to organize their life narratives around a theme of *redemption*. Usually the person sees a negative event as being followed by a good outcome. The good redeems the bad event. In the United States, perhaps due to religion or the frontier spirit, adults often see their lives in terms of redemption or in the hope of redemption. Sometimes, though, adults organize their lives in terms of *contamination*. They tell stories of being spoiled when negativity intrudes. Unfortunately, contamination narratives are often associated with poor mental and physical health outcomes. Whether redemption or contamination, turning points and life transitions seem often to be organizing themes in people's lives.

We find that meaning is a central theme in people's lives—especially if we draw on McAdams's research. Perhaps not surprising to Christians who believe in the image of God and in the Fall, the central themes of personality usually involve redemption and contamination. People in the United States typically construct their life narratives within a Judeo-Christian framework—even if they do not believe in the concepts themselves. They are likely to pick up the themes of Western Christianity. Though there is no cultural mandate to structure lives according to those themes, people do. Experiments and studies by secular research teams once again reveal a consistency with Christian theological doctrine.

HUMANS NEED THE HOLY

Bearing on God's holiness, Annette Mahoney, Mark Rye and Kenneth Pargament[37] have conducted an experimental research program investigating the consequences of the desecration of the sacred. Not surprisingly people treat religious elements and institutions as sacred (e.g., the church, the Communion elements and the confessional are often seen as sacred). However, more surprising, people also treat nonreligious elements—like marriage, family or country—as sacred. Desecrating the sacred is particularly difficult to forgive. For example, Pargament's colleagues have investigated the motives of people after the 9/11 attack on the United States. People who tended to treat the country as sacred were likely to endorse statements that Osama bin Laden and his followers should be hunted down and killed. The more a person felt that country is sacred, the more they endorsed retributive justice.

I am suggesting that psychological science can and does strengthen the basic theological claims of Christianity. We find abundant psychological evidence supporting the Christian view of human nature. It is helpful to know that God's revelation in nature, as uncovered by psychological scientists (many of whom are not Christians), tells a story similar to Scripture.

THE RELATIONAL NATURE OF EXISTENCE

I contend that a relationship is the best model for the interaction of psychological science and theology. I have used relational metaphors—such as a marriage and a dance—several times. This is intentional because relationships are critical to our human and corporate natures. Relationship reflects the trinitarian concept of God embraced by Christians at least since the Council of Nicaea in 325. The triune God is by nature relational. God created humans to relate personally to the Trinity. And God's pronouncement "It is not good for the man to be alone" (Gen 2:18) suggests humans are fundamentally relational.

Support for Relationality from Brain Processes

Gerald M. Edelman[38] is the winner of the Nobel Prize for his research on biology (namely the structure and diversity of antibodies). Edelman doesn't

leave any room for God in his almost militantly naturalistic and materialistic theory of brain, mind and consciousness summarized in *Wider Than
the Sky: The Phenomenal Gift of Consciousness.* This theory, at least on the
surface, might be one of the least likely candidates to be used in a theological discussion. If we can take a theory that doesn't explicitly address
relationships and also explicitly excludes God and yet find evidence for
relationality and the fingerprints of God, then I believe we have made a
good case that psychological science can strengthen theological claims.
Edelman's theory is, I believe, a much better model of consciousness than
several older models—the computer, the DVD player and the plant. I will
briefly describe each, and then I will explain in simplified terms the essence of Edelman's relational theory of consciousness.

The computer as a model for the brain and mental processes. During the
1960s and 1970s, we thought of consciousness like a computer. It was
said that people had programs to solve problems, make decisions and
make judgments in their brains. This computer model of the brain led
to some great breakthroughs. Yet as powerful as the computer model of
the brain is, it is not a good model of how the human brain actually
works. For example, most neuronal connections in the brain do not
survive throughout life. Also they do not survive in similar ways for any
two people. They die, and others are formed, at different rates and in
different patterns. That is not a good way to make a computer.

The DVD player as a model for the brain and mental processes. Similarly,
memory has been seen as analogous to a multichannel DVD player. As
humans observe, our brains are said to "record" the sights, sounds,
smells, feelings, flow of events and inner body states. We "store" these
memories in something like a mental DVD file. Memory involves re-
trieving the right DVD, placing it in the DVD player of the mind and
playing back the DVD.

Of course, it isn't this simple. First, we make lots of memory errors,
so something must be "demagnetizing" the DVD. Second, as large as
the brain is—a hundred billion neurons—it is not big enough to store
six or seven channels (i.e., sights, sounds, smells, etc.) of information all
day every day—not to mention remembering our dreams.

The plant as a model for the brain and mental processes. Long-term memory has also been said to be recreative. We remember an emotional kernel of a situation and we recreate what we logically think must have happened. Thus, a plant model has superseded the DVD model of long-term memory. Recalling a memory is like "planting" the emotional memory kernel in a "soil" that considers the situation, and our emotions are part of the nutrients in the soil. The new plant that grows with each new recall is a bit different from the one before because the events, thoughts and emotions making up the soil are different, and the kernel of the present memory is also different than previous kernels of memory. This plant model is closer to the way we understand consciousness today. Still, it isn't accurate concerning how the mind works. We don't just remember a "seed" and then recreate the "plant" from a seed each time. The neurons that make up memory do not go away, though some of them fade.

Looking to Neuroscience for Support

Impressionist painting as a model for the brain and mental processes. Imagine an impressionist painter employing pointillism. In pointillism, thousands of dots of paint are arrayed such that when a viewer stands at a distance from the painting, he or she sees an integrated picture. Our perception integrates the individual points into a whole, a Gestalt. Imagine too that the picture is of the young woman–old woman perceptual Gestalt that most people have seen (see figure 11.2). When we concentrate on it, we can see a young woman. But when we look at it differently, we can perceive an old woman. We can shift our attention back and forth between the two images within the same painting. If you are like most people, you perceive one image or the other, flip-flopping back and forth, not a combination of the two images.

Now note that if one-tenth of the points making up the picture were ran-

Figure 11.2. The old woman– young woman perceptual picture

domly turned off, the overall integrity of our perception would not be affected. If those were turned back on and another randomly selected one-tenth were deactivated, again the picture would not be compromised. This quality is known as "degeneracy." *Degeneracy* is the quality of being able to produce a particular mental representation by numerous combinations of underlying dots. The same picture could be perceived even though an exact replication of exactly the same points was never repeated.

The brain produces a flow of consciousness by a complex interaction of neurons stimulated by environment, associations (e.g., in the prefrontal association cortex), memories of the immediate past and present scenes (e.g., in the hippocampus), neurons in the inner-brain areas responsible for emotion (e.g., basal ganglia, cerebellum and thalamus), other brain areas and the body. The relationships among brain areas are crucial to thought and memory, not the firing of individual cells or even patterns of cells or the activation of discrete neural circuits. There is "degeneracy" in the circuits and neurons. Different neurons and circuits can produce the same concepts, mental images or memories—just as different dots could produce the same perception of the impressionist painting—because the different neurons and circuits *have the same relationships to each other.*

The same relationships among neurons form the same memory—or virtually the same. Perhaps different associations, thoughts, feelings or situations shift the relationships, or perhaps attention directs input to different aspects of the impressionist picture. In these cases, the memory shifts and evolves.

Different areas in the brain are integrated into a common integrated perception through "reentrant pathways." These are internal loops from cortex to inner brain to cortex and back again. Reentrant pathways are not like paths taken by NASCAR drivers looping in well-confined paths. Reentrant pathways are more like the paths of bumper-car drivers. Generally they may move counterclockwise but their paths wind helter-skelter and rarely overlap from circuit to circuit.

Edelman's theory of mind, brain and consciousness is called a theory of neuronal group selection because its principles are based on Darwin's ideas that survival fitness drives system change. Edelman's theory describes how some relationships among neurons survive and others do not. Edelman attempts to explain mind and consciousness depending solely on what is known about the structure and function of the brain and what is being discovered by new tools of brain science.

An Experiment by Edelman

An experiment summarized by Edelman shows that (1) different neural firing can produce the same conscious experience, (2) the brain integrates information (represented by related activity in widely separate brain areas), and (3) human conscious experience seems to be unique.

The experiment uses binocular rivalry. Our eyes see slightly different images, because they are separated by three to four inches. They thus project slightly different images on the two retinas. Our brain tries to reconcile the two images into one perceived visual image. Edelman's study enhanced the rivalry between the different images cast on left and right retina by having a person stare at a pattern of right-angle crossed lines. The vertical lines were red, the horizontal ones, blue. The participant wore glasses with one red lens (allowing that retina to see only the blue lines, which were horizontal and seem purple) and one blue lens (allowing that retina to see only the red lines, which were vertical and seem purple). The brain, of course, continually tried to put the images together. Because the rivalry between the retinal images was so keen, the brain could not blend the images. People perceived the vertical lines, and then perhaps a few seconds later they perceived the horizontal lines. This went back and forth, irregularly.

In the study, participants indicated perceiving the vertical lines by pressing a switch with one hand. When they perceived the horizontal lines, they pressed a switch with the other hand. (They never pressed both switches at the same time. This is like most people's experience with the old woman-young woman picture.) I used the word *perceive* to mean that the participant is conscious of seeing. Actually, the light was being seen or sensed continually by both eyes. By this method what the person was conscious of seeing could be separated from what was actually seen.

Magnetoencephalography (MEG) was used to measure brain activity. Mathematical methods showed the portions of the brain operating when the participant reported perceiving horizontal or vertical lines and the portions of the brain operating when the person did not report seeing one or the other lines. Other mathematical methods can detect when brain areas far away from perception or visual sensation sites were activated in coordination with seeing or perceiving.

The results were remarkable. First, when the vertical lines were *reported* to have been perceived, for example, different pathways and areas were stimulated each time perception shifted from vertical to horizontal and back again to vertical. Thus, each instance of perceiving exactly the same vertical lines was produced by completely different underlying neural events. It is the *relationships among the neurons*—like randomly selected points in an impressionist painting—rather than specific neurons, pathways or brain areas that give rise to perception.

Second, different areas in the brain—even at considerable distances apart—were highly correlated with the perception of vertical lines. For instance, some areas of the brain perceive vertical edges. Others perceive horizontal edges. Some perceive brightness; some, color; and others, thickness of lines. In short, the brain is marvelously integrated, and it integrates information from all over the cortex. As with the reports of vertical lines, the relationships among the neurons—not the specific neurons themselves—were important.

Third, not only were pathways within a single participant unique, but also no two participants showed the same brain *activity* patterns when perceiving vertical lines. People truly are unique. Each of us is one of a kind.

Some Speculations

I want tentatively to suggest some provocative (and not warranted by data) theological extensions of this simple yet profound brain-consciousness study. First, each person is unique. Second, relationships within the brain are important. Relationships might be fundamentally as important as the elements that make them up. Third, relationships within the brain are coordinated. That is, while relationships among neurons are important, there are higher levels of relationships between areas of the brain.

We see similar things at the social level as in this study of brain processes. Relationships between people are important. Relationships between people are also coordinated—parent-child, sibling-sibling and husband-wife relationships are coordinated into a family. The church is interconnected across congregations, across cities and around the world. Perhaps even across time. Congregations, individuals, denominations or national churches act independently of each other, yet there is coordination and connection—especially when seen from a higher perspective. These are certainly radical and admittedly unwarranted speculations from a single study. I certainly cannot prove individuality, the relational nature of the church, or the dynamic of human free will and God's sovereignty on this study. That burden is too much even for the whole of science to bear, much less a single study.

Yet I find it illuminating that while Gerald Edelman's theory of neuronal group selection explicitly rejects God's existence, the findings from God's book of nature—using modern brain science tools and theoretical framework—are consistent with what we know of God and the people of God. Nature is relational at its core.

SUMMARY

I have argued that psychological science provides evidence for some basic theological concepts. I illustrated this with research in five areas, just touching on available evidence for each. For instance, we considered evidence from psychological science that (1) people are created in God's image; (2) people are fallen and sinful; (3) God's relational and so are humans; (4) people are meaning makers; and (5) humans need the holy. I closed the chapter by describing Gerald Edelman's theory of consciousness as supporting the thesis I have returned to several times: much of existence is relational. As we see this relational nature of life repeatedly show up, my hope is that we will accept the model I have been suggesting—that psychological science and theology as disciplines are best seen as typically in peaceful relationship with each other, and that each can make valuable contributions to that relationship. In the following chapter, I will suggest another contribution of psychological science to theology—suggesting new ideas for theologians to consider.

PSYCHOLOGICAL SCIENCE ADDS
NEW IDEAS TO THEOLOGY

IN CHAPTER ELEVEN WE SAW that psychological science might provide evidence in support of theological propositions. Can psychological science produce new theological data? And are the data valid? I believe the answer to both questions is yes.

PSYCHOLOGICAL SCIENCE AS A VALID THEOLOGICAL TOOL

Are the Findings of Psychological Science Valid?

As it relates to theology, the problem with psychological science is that it tells how people *recently* acted, thought and felt. Validating scientific truth is restricted to actual observation. We cannot go back in time to conduct experiments on people's minds and behavior in the times when the Scriptures were penned. Can psychology tell about people's behavior in times past? How much of what we discover in laboratories today was true of how people behaved 2,000 years ago and will behave 2,000 years from now (if Christ does not return before then)?

Obviously, scientists can discover true things about the past. Physicists can find evidence today for the big bang. Biologists can test theories about the origin and development of life by making predictions based on presumed early conditions (hypotheses) and testing them today. But psychology poses a unique problem in generalizing about the past. Psychological laws of nature might very well be more changeable than are the physical or biological laws of nature. Which aspects of human behavior are governed by "laws of nature"? Which aspects require a cultural context? Making this distinction is crucial for whether findings of psychological science can be extrapolated backward to biblical contexts (and forward to the future).

Is Theology Any More Valid Than Psychological Science?

The validity of theology is not above suspicion. It roots its understanding of texts to a particular historical context. Effort is made to understand the historical context, word usage and culture at the time the text was written with as much accuracy as possible. Then theology projects forward from that historical text to the present. Biblical interpretations are thus based on our understanding of context and on what can and cannot be generalized to the present. The passages in Paul's letters to the Corinthians on women speaking in church, head coverings, slavery and other issues come to mind. Theologians either must dismiss some advice as irrelevant or try to discern the principle relevant for today. If our understanding of the historical context changes, then our interpretation of Scripture can change. (Witness changes in theology brought about by a more accurate understanding of the climate of Second Temple Judaism from the research of E. P. Sanders[1] and James D. G. Dunn[2] and subsequent interpretations of Paul's letters by N. T. Wright and others.[3]) This, of course, poses virtually the same problem as that faced by psychological science. The more that theology is contextualized to the time and place where Scripture was written, the less likely it is to apply to today. Theology and psychology both require generalization across time, location and culture.

Psychological Science Might Help Theology

I believe psychological science can balance the historical contextualization in theology. Psychological science tells how things are today. We can thus better see which biblical truths may have been heavily cultural and which may be clearly universal. Both disciplines' validity is challenged, but like a teeter-totter, together they can balance each other (see fig. 12.1).

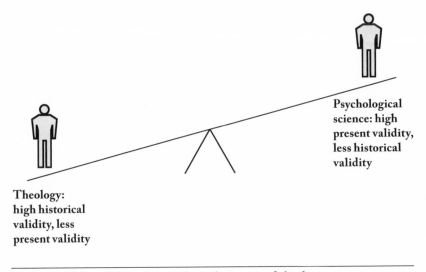

Psychological
science: high
present validity,
less historical
validity

Theology:
high historical
validity, less
present validity

Figure 12.1. The validity of psychological science and theology

BENEFITS OF PSYCHOLOGICAL SCIENCE AS A THEOLOGICAL TOOL

Psychological science can add information beyond most theological methods.

New Theological Hypotheses Can Be Proposed and Tested Against Scripture

Let's examine how scientific research on forgiveness can inform theological understandings of forgiveness. What is the nature of forgiveness? Theologians disagree. They define it in terms of individual self-benefit,[4] of relationships,[5] of the church as a body[6] or of societal transgressions.[7]

We could seek an understanding of forgiveness by analyzing the words used in Scripture. There are four Hebrew synonyms commonly translated "forgiveness," and there are two Greek synonyms commonly translated "forgiveness." The words are used more as synonyms than as ways to consistently differentiate subtleties in concepts. This is like saying, "He runs quickly," "He runs fast," or "He runs rapidly." There is no reason to make a conceptual differentiation merely because I might select any particular adverb. Most linguistic analyses of the Greek and Hebrew words suggest the same regarding the words used to indicate forgiveness. There might be fine shades of meaning, but Scripture seems not to use one word consistently to indicate one experience and another word to indicate a distinct experience. Therefore, all four Hebrew and both Greek words are usually translated "forgive." So linguistic analyses don't help us understand what *forgiveness* is.

We could search the context of Scripture to determine what forgiveness means. In Matthew 6:12, 14-15, Jesus posits that God's forgiveness is contingent on people's own forgiveness of those who have sinned against them. In Jesus' command to Peter to forgive seventy-seven times (Mt 18:21-22; cf. Gen 4:24; see also Lk 17:3-5), we can see how very difficult human forgiveness is. Is it possible to forgive a person who offended us seventy-seven times? What would it mean to "forgive" such repetitive offenses? Is such human forgiveness similar to God's divine forgiveness, in which he separates the sin from people as far as the east is from the west (Psalm 103:12)? Does human forgiveness require a complete emotional transformation in the forgiver? God does not remember our sins against us after he has forgiven our sins. Is this true of humans too? If we did not remember an offense against our transgressor, would this involve a complete emotional clean slate with every transgression?

Some recent studies in psychology can help us reconcile the difficulty of obeying Jesus' command to be forgiving (Mt 6:12, 14-15) with the ebullient forgiveness of the forgiving father in the parable of the lost son (Lk 15:11-32). The father forgave enthusiastically while the son was yet a long way off.

Psychological studies show that forgiveness may actually be of two distinct types.[8] One is more decisional; the other speaks to emotional experience. Sometimes they are in harmony. Sometimes, they are not.

From a psychological viewpoint we can distinguish two types of forgiveness. In an article by me and Fred DiBlasio,[9] we suggest that forgiveness might be a *decision*, and DiBlasio[10] has written often about decision-based forgiveness. Nathaniel Wade and I[11] suggested in 1999 that emotional forgiveness involves the *emotional* replacement of negative with positive emotions toward the offender. My colleagues and I[12] have formalized this distinction into decisional and emotional forgiveness, respectively. In a book for psychotherapists in 2006, I arrayed substantial scientific evidence for the differences between the two.[13] Our research team also completed a series of studies that revealed additional differences.[14] For example, in one study people recalled a transgression against them. In one condition people recalled a completely unforgiven offense—no decision to forgive and no emotional forgiveness. In a second condition people recalled an offense they had decided to forgive but felt no peace about. In the third condition, people recalled an offense they had forgiven both decisionally and emotionally. Then the people wrote positive things about the offender in each condition. The number of positive descriptions people wrote matched the condition. Unforgiving people had the hardest time writing positively. Those with only decisional forgiveness wrote the next most. Those with both decisional and emotional forgiveness wrote the most positive words.

In a different study within the same article, we used an implicit associations test to assess people's inner attitudes toward a target person they had forgiven either decisionally but not emotionally or both decisionally and emotionally for a past offense. The implicit associations test measures reaction time when people have to pair negative and positive descriptors with the target person. We hypothesized that if a person had forgiven someone, the person would react more quickly to positive associations and less quickly to negative associations. We found support that the inner attitudes reflected whether people had decisionally and emotionally forgiven.

Until decisional forgiveness had been distinguished from emotional forgiveness through psychological science, theologians had not made such distinctions. After the scientific differentiation, though, it is evident from Scripture that such a distinction is scripturally sound. Jesus' commands to forgive (Mt 18:21-22; Lk 17:3-5) and his statements that divine forgiveness is dependent on human forgiveness (Mt 6:12, 14-15) apply to decisional forgiveness, not emotional forgiveness. Naturally, Jesus *desires* that all of us experience both decisional and emotional forgiveness, but God *requires* a decision to forgive (but does not require complete emotional change). Psychological science thus uncovered new theological hypotheses, which could be tested against Scripture and thus enrich theological understanding.

Refuting Statements of Universality

A second way that psychological science could add new ideas to theology is to confront a theological statement's supposed universality. If theologians assume that statements made in the Bible apply today and yet psychological science finds that they do not, then such findings cast doubt on whether that statement can be universally applied. There were times when Scripture was used to justify slavery. People have at times used Scripture to argue for ethnic prejudice. Crosscultural studies have often revealed that "superiority" and "favor" of ethnic groups are more often culturally determined than being universal.

Similarly, at other times people have justified gender inequalities on the basis of Scripture. Within post-resurrection Jewish-Gentile Christian congregations, men and women usually fulfilled gender-based roles. Today, even the most theologically conservative people would agree that men and women are treated as equals in Scripture, though they might disagree with more liberal or moderate believers about whether the roles described in Scripture are supposed to be normative or are culturally bound. Most theological conservatives today argue that different gender roles could be carried out without gender inequality. We now take this for granted. Just thirty years ago, men and women were treated as nonequals without much social objection.

Prejudice (and even the Crusades) have been justified biblically. At the time, socially and biblically justified positions supporting prejudice (and the Crusades) were treated as universals. If psychological science can be brought to bear on the claims, though, it might be possible to avoid many of the abuses that have been supported scripturally in the past.

While this is ideal, I hasten to add that psychological science is subject to the same cultural milieu as is theology. So if we were debating slavery in the 1860s, there undoubtedly would be theologians making a case in support of it and psychological scientists trying to show how beneficial it was. So, this balance is not foolproof.

Doubting That Some Truths Are Culturally Bound

A third way that psychological science could add new ideas to theology is to challenge theological assumptions that some biblical phenomenon

is culture-bound. What if—using the new tools of fMRI and PET—
we found out that women who covered their heads during worship actually had more brain activation in the seratonin-rich (so-called) spiritual center of the brain?[15] As far as I know, nobody cares to study this
question, and it is merely a hypothetical statement with no basis in actual psychological science. But hypothetically such a finding could at
least suggest that biblical claims to head coverings may have a spiritual
rather than cultural reason.

Scripture is indeed meant to be universal. However, the universality
of Scripture calls for caution in using it as a source of scientific hypotheses. Science by its nature is meant to be disconfirmed.[16] The progress
of science depends on discovering truths that are successively refined
and made more specific and more accurate. Merely doing a study that
supports a hypothesis does not add much to science, though it gives
some small assurance that a finding is publicly replicable. On the other
hand, God gave us Scripture as a source not of disconfirmable hypotheses but of truth from which all people can benefit, regardless of when
they live. We can learn about human nature in the twenty-first century
by reading about the Fall of humans, sin, love and self-sacrifice. We
can learn about communication with God by reading in Scripture about
the effects of prayer. We can learn about praise and gratitude through
reading the Psalms. While we expect Scripture to be true where it
touches the cosmos, we also realize that the writers of Scripture did not
set out to be scientifically true (at least by modern standards). When
the Bible was written, there was no such thing as modern science, and
the method of science will not move with us into eternity. Rather, the
scientific method is a good way to understand life today. It will itself
someday be supplanted by a more excellent way.

Discovering Truths That Bear on Theological Propositions

A fourth way that psychological science could add ideas to theology is
to discover truths that might bear on accepted theological propositions.
I will discuss in detail one example: the changing understanding of
self-love.

A theology of self-love. Jesus said, "Love your neighbor as yourself"

(Mt 22:39). How we interpret this statement depends on our systematic, biblical and anthropological theology. In the last fifty years this verse has often been used as a Jesus-sanctioned injunction to love ourselves—to maintain a high sense of self-esteem. Often this interpretation has been justified by appealing to God's valuing of humans in general and of individuals in particular. We reason like this: If Jesus consented to die for us, we must be valuable. We thus should maintain a high sense of self-esteem, even if we have fallen far short of the glory of God (Rom 3:23).

Psychotherapy has informed us on self-love. Actually, clinical psychology might have contributed heavily to an interpretation that self-esteem is of crucial importance to people's well-being. Clinical psychologists often see people who have damaged senses of self-esteem. Sometimes clients are beaten down by oppressive circumstances. At other times, they are depressed. Their self-esteem plummets as their emotions become more negative. Other times their personalities are ordered around feelings of their worthlessness. Often the client's poor self-esteem interferes with therapeutic progress. Thus, the clinician will often, even today, help the client improve his or her sense of self-esteem.

The common culture of the 1950s, 1960s and 1970s made self-esteem culturally valued. In the 1950s and 1960s, popular psychotherapists like Carl Rogers and Abraham Maslow gave birth to the human potential movement. It was axiomatic among those in the human potential movement that poor self-esteem was a symptom or perhaps even a cause of human problems. Therefore improved self-esteem was assumed to *cause* positive mental and physical health. As a culture, we bought this. The human potential movement was in full swing during the 1960s. That decade was a time of rebellion against social strictures. Hippies, war protesters, New Agers, drug experimenters and youths from all over the world were throwing off their perceived chains of oppression and glorying in freedom, if not license. Freedom and human potential, which seemed almost unlimited, were of highest value. The absolute right to do what one wanted and to feel good about oneself for doing it were not to be questioned by theology or by psychological research. Culture trumped both.

Psychological science began to study self-esteem. In the 1970s and 1980s, however, psychological researchers began to investigate self-esteem despite cultural pressures. Problems in self-esteem were presumed to be related to almost every type of individual difficulty. Almost always, both social science and the theology of the 1960s and 1970s claimed that poor self-esteem led to problems. People were thought to compensate for poor self-esteem by defensiveness, denial or psychological symptoms. We were admonished to love ourselves *so that* we could love our neighbor.

However, two decades of research by social psychologist Mike Kernis[17] showed that two concepts must be considered to understand the impact of self-esteem—its level and its stability. Thus people may be divided into four types of self-esteem—stable high self-esteem, stable low self-esteem, fragile high self-esteem, and fragile low self-esteem. Mike Kernis and his colleagues had twenty-one male and twenty-four female undergraduates assess their feelings about themselves (how positive or negative) every two hours, which allowed an estimate of how stable or unstable their self-esteem was. At the end of each day, the students reported their overall feelings of self-esteem. The mean level, averaged across the week, determined the level of self-esteem. At the end of a week, the students completed assessments of their anger and hostility. The stability and level of self-esteem were used to predict the students' level of dispositional hostility and anger. Kernis found that the people with the *highest* mean level of self-esteem became most angry and hostile when they received a challenge. (Perhaps people with the lowest self-esteem do not even believe they have the right to get angry and hostile.) However, the *unstable* high self-esteem people appeared to be most reactive to their anger. Those people seemed to have a good opinion of themselves, but that opinion was easily threatened. With shaky high self-esteem, they had the most to lose. They felt that they were precariously balanced and could easily lose their sense of self-worth. They thus responded to any threat very strongly with anger, hostility and aggression.

Ray Baumeister and his colleagues[18] reviewed the research on aggression, crime and violence. Researchers often had initially assumed that high self-esteem would result in less aggression and violence. The data told a different story. The most violent people were those with fragile high self-esteem. They often responded with extreme anger to challenges to their leadership, which in turn, challenged their self-esteem. If they were prone to violence, they became aggressive. People with stable high self-esteem and those with either stable or unstable low self-esteem rarely resorted to violence when threatened.

Thus we learn from psychological science that a theological view of human nature that was prevalent in the 1950s through 1970s, which considers self-esteem to be universally good, was likely to lead to poor interpretations of Scripture. Actual scientific studies—being open to what the data told us—have been able to correct erroneous theology. Self-esteem can be either a positive or negative psychological force. Stable high self-esteem can promote altruism—loving our neighbor self-sacrificially because we are secure within ourselves. But fragile high self-esteem can lead to harming a neighbor.

We thus might view the command to "love your neighbor as yourself" with different eyes. Perhaps Jesus assumed that people are naturally prideful, self-interested, self-serving, fallen creatures. Thus, he knew we would naturally "love" ourselves, twisting and turning things to our own benefit—as indeed the self-serving bias demonstrates. Presuming that kind of self-love, Jesus was urging people to love others as much as we *naturally* would love ourselves.

Applying Biblical Truths in Today's Society

The fifth way psychological science could add new ideas to theology is to stack up psychological theorizing against theological theorizing.

Modernity to postmodernity. Modernity glorifies the individual and embraces the notion of ever-increasing progress. World wars and never-ending conflicts and human rights violations have eroded the optimistic belief that people are getting better. Most people have given up the idea of world peace and harmony. We think of life in encapsulated multicultural forms. The postmodern worldview, which has been adopted by much of today's society, simultaneously unites and divides. Postmodernism is designed for the age of smart phones, texting, the Web and jet travel. Our technological culture encapsulates us within our own little world. We have iPods, iPhones, iTunes and (as a wag recently said) even *we* has two i's in it (i.e., Wii). It seems that the world is shrinking and, as Thomas Friedman[19] has convincingly shown us, the world is flat. People cannot thrive as individuals. We can walk down the street, rubbing shoulders with hundreds of people, and never meet eyes with a stranger. People are so busy texting, talking on their phones, tuning in to their iPods or e-mailing that they can't be bothered with direct human contact. A world of interpersonal intimacy has been exchanged for a world of interpersonal exchange of information.

Postmodernism and the self. Some, like psychologist Kenneth Gergen[20] in *The Saturated Self,* have argued that people's sense of self is fragmented or "saturated." People no longer have a sense of being a unified self, a unique and persisting entity. Rather, they seem to have a sense of multiple selves. This isn't a multiple personality disorder. Rather, people construct their sense of self by their interactions with people: mother, father, brother, teacher, spouse or friend. Though these selves are different, they exist under the same skin. We sense a core self even if we can't tell exactly what it is, and we can't find a situation in which we act authentically according to that core.

Postmodern psychologists argue that perhaps we don't really have a stable core. We are *nothing but* our different subpersonalities. But we aren't our "roles," because we actually change our behavior in different roles. I don't behave the same in my role as a father now as I did twenty years ago. But I seem to have a father persona. I put on my father persona and find that it is different from my professor persona.

This is quite a jump from modernity. In a modern world—as opposed to a postmodern one—the stress was on individualism. We saw ourselves as individuals, and we thought we were consistent across various situations. In a postmodern world we are no longer so enthralled with individualism. Instead, we are aware of our culture. We feel defined by our culture and also by our family or spouse and every other interaction.

Yet we all have an undeniable sense of continuity in our lives. Sometimes we can give in to the notion that there is a big-boss self within our consciousness that unifies the whole. Not likely, say consciousness researchers. To give the sense of unity, we construct narratives to describe our lives. In chapter eleven I described Dan McAdams's[21] research that discovered that people create redemption, grace (luck) or failure narratives—each of which might hold sway in different circumstances. The postmodern worldview has virtually eliminated a belief that individuals can have a unified sense of self.

The response of theologians. Theologians also wrestle with people's sense of self. People like Colin Gunton[22] and Wolfhart Pannenberg[23] have addressed the issue. Gunton particularly has rooted his understanding of self in the triune God—that is, as relational. He suggests that three concepts emerge from a right understanding of the Trinity. *Perichoresis* means that all three persons of the Trinity mutually share in the life of the others, so that none is isolated or detached from the actions of the others. *Substantiality* means that each of the three figures has substantial reality apart from the others. *Relationality* means that there is a relationship of interaction within and between the members of the Trinity. Gunton chides modernity as being a reaction against Christianity. In reaction to theologians' failure to emphasize the truth of the Trinity, modern individualism was born. Modernity resulted in people's disengagement from God, a deemphasis of particulars with a preference for sameness, a loss of a sense of history and time, and an erosion of meaning and truth. Gunton saw postmodernism as the inevitable result.

Gunton reconstitutes the doctrine of the Trinity as a cure for postmodern loss of coherence, overemphasis of individuality within the relational nature of life and loss of meaning. In the end, though, Gunton seems to fall back on a core self. True, he sees self as maintained within relationships. Yet his core self is a rejection of postmodernism.

What is at stake? Of course, theologians cannot be blamed if they find it difficult to accept elements of a postmodern psychology. A lot is at stake. Moral responsibility, for example. If we give up the idea of a single, unified self, we might logically ask, *Is a person to blame for criminal, merely rude or obnoxious behavior? Or is it just one of his or her personas? Why do we have to go to jail for the crime of stealing? It was merely one persona among many.* Besides moral questions, the idea of multiple selves raises ontological questions: If a person is saved and is to spend eternity with God, which of the many selves will spend eternity and what is to become of the others?

Gunton seems on the right track in relating issues of identity in the triune God. He observes the balance, unity, diversity and relationships among the divine persons. But he has not seemed to take seriously enough the findings from psychology that roles, personas and subpersonalities are strongly influential.

SUMMARY

I have examined the possibility that psychological science can provide new theological ideas. I began by considering the validity of both theology (stronger validity in the past) and psychological science (stronger validity in the present). I suggested they could balance each other, and considered two subject areas in this chapter: (1) differentiating two types of forgiveness and (2) examining the self. Theology can be enhanced by the findings of psychological science in these two areas.

In doing so, I proposed several ways psychological science could add ideas to theology. Psychological science could (a) propose new ideas and test them against Scripture, (b) confront theological statements' presumed universality (by testing whether, empirically, the statement holds today), (c) challenge theological statements' presumed cultural boundedness (by testing whether it holds today), (d) discover truths that might bear on accepted theological propositions, and (e) stack up psychological theorizing against theological theorizing.

One of the exciting aspects of both theology and psychological science is a sense of discovery. We mine the data God has provided and find treasure. But we use a progressive set of ever-changing tools as the times change. When Kirby and I were dating and throughout our engagement, my greatest joy and biggest frustration was that I could not know everything about her at once. I was frustrated because I loved her. Having a conversation here, observing her in an interaction with someone else there, seeing a letter she had written in a new light or coming across a sketch she had made was pure torture. I wanted all the information and wanted it right now—preferably yesterday. But it also was a great joy that I couldn't find everything out about her at once. I looked forward to discovering more about her on the next date. I wanted to talk to her. I wanted to phone her ten times a day. (We didn't have cell phones in the late 1960s.) So, not knowing her completely created excitement, adventure and drama in our relationship.

God's revelation has come to us piecemeal and from different directions. It is frustrating, of course, that we don't have a universal, time-resistant systematic theology from on high, but it also is exciting to be able to look forward to God continuing to reveal more about the divine character, human nature and creation.

Theology is our interpretation of this progressive personal revelation of God. As more is revealed and as we dig around in history, the humanities, and the social and physical sciences, we see the drama and adventure unfold. Sometimes on closer examination the mysteries we think we have uncovered turn out to be not so mysterious.

I love the mind of God. God has revealed what is sufficient for us to be in a loving relationship with the Trinity. Yet God has created an absolutely ingenious world that we can negotiate with the hope of finding new buried treasure—new riches of understanding God and knowing God better. Psychological science is one of those treasure-hunting methods.

PSYCHOLOGICAL SCIENCE ADDRESSES THEOLOGICALLY HOT SOCIAL CONTROVERSIES

PSYCHOLOGICAL SCIENCE IS AIMED AT understanding the mind and behavior of humans and animals. Because people spend most of their lives in social situations, psychological science has a lot of say about hot social controversies: biotechnology and cloning, sexual behavior, reproductive issues, abortion, end-of-life decisions, punishment of children, who should be married, educational philosophies, evolution-creation issues, human rights, prejudice, political correctness, decisions by legislatures, wars, access to health care, health disparities among ethnic groups, foreign policy of presidents and Supreme Court decisions. Pick up a newspaper or *Time* magazine, or turn on CNN and it isn't long before we encounter controversial social issues.

Generally, those topics that get the adrenaline pumping have theological implications. About twenty-five years ago, not too long after I had become a college teacher, I was privileged to be appointed to a task force in Henrico County, Virginia, to recommend a curriculum for sex education to the public school board. I entered that political fray naively. I assumed that my relatively conservative Calvinist theology gave me a good understanding of the "correct" theological position on sex education—basically that promoting abstinence was *the* biblical position. I was dismayed to find two ordained ministers on the task force—one Lutheran and the other Unitarian. Both disagreed with my theology (being decidedly more liberal than I). They weren't shy about advancing their views as *the* Christian position. They were armed with ecclesiastical credentials, biblical references and theological sources that supported their views. They were not at all hesitant about using their theological weapons and their authority as clergy to speak for "the Christian church" or "godly people." However, I discovered that professional theology was not irrefutable.

I actually found more agreement on the task force concerning psychological science than theology. When I summarized a body of scientific studies, opponents harrumphed and criticized my sampling or method, but I could address those challenges. Opponents had to scurry for the library to see whether they could discover studies that might lead to different conclusions. Properly understood, psychological science resonated with members of the task force more than theology did. Theology was seen as too airy, floating too high above the data of daily existence, and (surprisingly to me) too disengaged from the data of the Scriptures, which not everyone on the task force accepted as having any authority anyway. We did not all live in the same theological world, but we all lived in the psychological world. We all had to deal with things we could see and touch—and thus things that a psychologist could measure. So, psychological science had an authority in the public square that theology turned out not to have.

I saw that psychological science could speak plainly to social issues that had theological and moral implications. I saw it help to provide a moderating influence on the opinions of people who wanted a libertine program of sex education. It even informed political moderates who listened to and heeded interpretations of psychological scientific data. Perhaps those data even led to a final report that favored modest sex education, discussion of sex within the bounds of marriage and the delay of explicit sexual information, more than mere opinion might have originally dictated. I simply did not go to the scientific literature enough and make multiple cases strongly enough. So the program of sex education was still, I believe, off the mark.

In my first foray into the political arena, I also saw that the decisions made by such a task force could shape the attitudes of a generation of elementary, middle and high school students toward sex, marriage and family. Almost twenty-five years after that experience, I see the children who went through that curriculum, now around age thirty or older. Those adults got an earlier sex education than I thought was optimal. They engaged in talk that sexualized topics that had not been sexualized prior to that curriculum. Those adults now are challenging the cultural understanding of marriage, which likely will have (if it hasn't already) an impact on the theology of marriage. And because marriage is Paul's metaphor for the church, a generation's experiences in early sex education could one day affect the way we understand ecclesiology.

That early experience showed me that psychological science could affect theology by acting through hot social issues. Social controversies occur at three levels—individual, relational and societal issues. I'll briefly sample some topics at each level to try to show that psychological science can inform thinking, which will almost certainly affect personal living and theology.

PERSONAL ISSUES

Self-Forgiveness

We often let ourselves down. We are plagued by guilt—especially, it seems, in the boomer generation and earlier. The younger generations seem to have less moralistic self-judgments in areas like sexual behavior. Self-condemnation in youth or middle years is still rife, but the issues are different. Is a mother who works being a good mother if she puts her child in daycare eight hours each day? Should a husband be a stay-at-home father? Is a person being immoral by not using fair-trade products? Such issues troubled few of us older adults.

What makes this a hot theological topic? In 2005, Michael Scherer and associates compiled a comprehensive bibliography of publications about forgiveness.[1] About 99 percent of those publications considered forgiveness of others. One percent examined self-condemnation and self-forgiveness. Some might argue that this sounds about right, theologically. While Scripture pays lots of attention to divine forgiveness and somewhat less (though still substantial) to forgiving others, the concept of self-forgiveness is not mentioned in Scripture. Based on the paucity of discussion of self-forgiveness in the Bible, theologians, pastors and sometimes people in the pew conclude that self-forgiveness is simply letting ourselves off the hook and does not aid spiritual development but hampers it.

Most people in the United States talk and think about self-forgiveness, especially after they grievously wrong someone. It is important that we do not take a theological position that invalidates people's experience of seeking self-forgiveness. That will drive more people away from Christianity, believing it to be irrelevant to their lives. Instead, we must look to the proper role of self-forgiveness in personal experience. While Christians certainly do not use the term as a replacement for seeking divine forgiveness, it is possible that confusions could accelerate (and could ultimately further erode our understanding of Jesus' propitiation for sin) if psychological science does not investigate what the proper uses of self-forgiveness are and how it can be misused. Psychological science has the potential to strengthen or weaken our understanding of Jesus' death on the cross.

Psychologists Mickie Fisher and Julie Exline[2] studied feelings of self-condemnation. They found that these feelings are associated with more maladjustment. However, they also found that feelings of self-condemnation are associated with higher levels of repentance and with feeling humbled. This is particularly true when individuals accept responsibility for their wrongdoing, experience remorse for it and are willing to put effort into making things right.

Recently, psychologists Judith Hall and Frank Fincham[3] proposed a model in which they take seriously seeking forgiveness from God, as well as forgiving the self. Some people oppose self-forgiveness, because they believe people might not confess their wrongdoing to God if they have forgiven themselves. In a subsequent longitudinal study, Hall and Fincham collected data eight times from people who identified feeling self-condemnation about something they had done.[4] They found continuous linear changes in guilt, self-forgiveness, perception of a reduced severity of the transgression, belief that they had made conciliatory acts toward the person they had harmed, belief that that person had forgiven them, and belief that a higher power had forgiven them for the transgression. Instead of self-forgiveness being associated with seeking and feeling less forgiveness from God, it was associated with more.

In these studies we find concerns that, in self-forgiveness, people will let themselves off the hook and will divert themselves from seeking forgiveness from God (or the wronged party). These concerns are not often borne out. While some people might let themselves off of the hook, this research shows that such behavior is less likely to occur than more God-seeking behavior.

Happiness

Happiness is hardly a controversial social topic these days. But the pursuit of happiness at all costs is. Our society seems increasingly to value temporal happiness. How and where we seek happiness has great theological implications. When Kirby and I travel, we like to stay at hostels and are amazed at the hostel culture. Young adults desperately collect experiences. They almost seem to be operating under the idea that by collecting the largest number of travel, sexual, thrill-seeking, drinking and social experiences, they will be happy. Yet to Kirby and me, these young adults seem far from happy. Many of them wander from bed to bed, pub to pub, ski area to ski area in a haze of unfulfilled good cheer—cheer that only touches the outer layers of the soul. They are desperately searching for happiness.

Some Christians are remarkably hostile to seeking happiness in this life. It is okay, they believe, to seek happiness in heaven. But we should "seek first [God's] kingdom and his righteousness, and all these things will be given to you as well" (Mt 6:33). It is important to have our priorities oriented toward God, but the Bible continually appeals to the human desire for happiness (see the Beatitudes, Mt 5:1-12). It directs us to pursue happiness for the right reasons with the right priorities.

Psychologist David Myers from Hope College has studied happiness for decades.[5] He has found that most people think that improved economic conditions will make them happier. Yet above the level of abject poverty, improved economic well-being is not associated with more happiness. Suffering does make people rate their lives as less happy. Myers has found that some things have been shown to make people happier. Faith, spirituality, a sense of meaning and acting altruistically have all been related to happiness. Psychological science supports what the Scriptures tell us.

Myers's work also suggests that grasping at happiness might almost guarantee it to squirt between our fingers, which is bad news for the youths who travel the world seeking experiences that will make them happy. However, opening our hands in praise to God or to give to others allows our hands to be filled.

Stress

According to biologist Robert Sapolsky,[6] author of *Why Zebras Don't Get Ulcers*, the body is wired to deal with acute stressors. After being stressed, the body must return to normal conditions and rest. But we have created lifestyles that keep us under almost constant stress. Chronic stress keeps the body pumping out adrenaline and the neurohormone cortisol. Elevated levels of these chemicals eventually wear down the body and lead to physical, mental and emotional problems. They affect our cardiovascular system, immune system, digestive tract, reproductive system and brain structure.

Stress is certainly a hot topic. We decry it. We say, like a mantra, we want to reduce our stress. Yet we seek stressful conditions. To compensate, we try to find peace within our leisure moments through television, movies, electronic or other games, and watching or playing sports (almost all of which keep us immersed in conflict). Or we try to find peace chemically—in feel-good downers (like drinking and drugs) or feel-good uppers (like cigarettes or caffeine). Or we try to find our peace through deep breathing, meditating, eating at fine restaurants, getting massages or reading the newspaper. But those activities at best carve out an occasional hour of distraction amid a yearly schedule of stressfulness.

Psychological science has devoted enormous resources to finding how people effectively (and not so effectively) manage their stress. People are often not interested in eliminating stressors, but in *managing* the stress, calming (inevitable) stress reactions, and choosing ways to cope that quickly solve problems and free us to experience the next stressor or manage our feelings so we can tolerate more stressors.

What are the consequences of continuing to make such choices? The physical, emotional and mental consequences are well documented by psychological and biological sciences. But there might be theological consequences as well. On one hand, people often resent the time required to attend church. So, the electronic church has mushroomed. Megachurches have grown, allowing more people to "hide" within the crowd and pursue individualized, consumer-based religion in a church so large that any experience one would like is available. On the other hand, the stress-paced lifestyle has left many seeking a deeper peace than media, chemicals or mindful minutes can provide. Many have recovered Christian meditation, the spiritual disciplines and classic readings in Christian spirituality from church ancestors.

Besides these trends within the church, however, there are some trends in broader society that have been stimulated by our stressful lifestyle. Our interests have gravitated away from religion and toward spirituality. Religion happens within a community. Spirituality can happen alone. Religion makes moral and ethical demands on us to adjust to the community. Spirituality doesn't. Although people can become more spiritual within a religion, the spiritual experience is primarily within each person's skin. Roman Catholic sociologist Michael Casey[7] has said, "Happiness in this account consists of continuing just as you are, but with a new overlay of 'inspiration, myth, and insight' to affirm the supposedly unique and intrepid qualities of a life lived in mediocre selfishness."

In a spiritual worldview faith can become a type of psychotherapy. In surveying U.S. youth, Christian Smith[8] found their religion is deistic, hedonistic and therapeutic. God is seen as a heavenly problem solver who appears magically when summoned for help. Then God conveniently disappears and doesn't hang around (like an unwelcome distant relative) to embarrass the person helped. And God is also seen as a heavenly psychotherapist who is available on demand to maximize our happiness.

Self-Control

It is too easy to say that, if people only had more self-control, they would not engage in such stressful lifestyles or have the problems associated with living in a culture of stress. Dating back to William James[9] in the early 1900s, psychology has long studied self-control. James advocated a simple solution: mental gymnastics. He urged people to modify their thinking in order to control their unwanted appetites and to engage in wanted but difficult-to-perform behaviors. In the 1920s, Freud saw the answer in psychoanalytic exploration of deep and unconscious motives. Only by letting ego rule the id could people control themselves. In the 1970s, behavioral psychologists advocated taking charge of our lives by controlling the environment to set up stimuli that help us act in a self-controlled way, or by programming our rewards and punishments to make us more likely to act as we wish to act.

Now, belief in self-control is shrinking even as waistlines are expanding. Research on genetics has shown that genetic proclivities toward drinking alcohol, overeating and heart problems cannot be ignored. Some people have genes that make self-control a lot of work. We understand that genes and behavior interact. We can have the genes of Arnold Schwarzenegger for muscle building, but if we don't pump iron we won't have muscles. New research even shows that we can change the epigenomes (chemicals called epigenetic marks, which turn on and off the expression of genes) through our behavior (e.g., stress, diet, exercise, etc.).[10] But we also understand that genes are powerful, and if we have the genes that predispose us toward being overweight, it will be a continual battle to keep that gene expression at bay. We also find that the more self-control we must exert, the more our ego strength is depleted.[11] Thus, with our stressful, demanding world, coping with bad genes that predispose us to weight gain, for instance, seems hardly worth the effort we know it will take.

We know that Christian living should be characterized by self-control. Self-control, after all, is one of the fruits of the Spirit. Yet we would like the fruit to fall from the tree into our laps, with no more effort than praying. This certainly resonates with the view of Christianity that Christian Smith[12] uncovered—deistic, hedonistic and therapeutic. But sometimes getting fruit requires a strenuous climb of the fruit tree, not just today but every day. That is not a message we long to hear. Perhaps the unpopularity of that message is one reason that the "health and wealth gospel" became popular in the latter part of the twentieth century.

Emotion

In the 1970s, the Campus Crusade for Christ fact-faith-feeling train became one of the ways Christians looked at faith. That particular evangelistic tool, part of the four spiritual laws,[13] characterized faith as deriving from the facts of Jesus' substitutionary death for people. Feelings were seen as following faith, not as preceding it or even accompanying it. In that model, people made a commitment to Christ without first feeling joy or eager motivation. Once people made a decision to accept the lordship and salvation that attends Jesus' work, good feelings indeed followed in many cases. This evangelistic tool hit Christian culture about the time that the cognitive revolution was hitting psychology. On television, on the lecture circuit and in books, therapists frequently told people that their situations did not cause their negative emotions, their thoughts did. So, they were admonished to change their thoughts and they would change their emotions. Psychological scientists even used computer metaphors to describe people's lives. For that time in history, emotions got a bad rap.

Now, however, behavioral genetics and emotion have become rising stars in psychological science. Emotion, in particular, is seen as increasingly important. Brain science is paying more attention to the entire brain (and its connections with the body) instead of the portions of the brain that govern reasoning. We find that heightened emotion usually can motivate us to act. Sure, by will, we can impose our thinking over our emotions, but that takes a lot of effort and usually won't last because it is so energy intensive. As a result, we hear more and more about the roles emotion plays in motivating behavior.

Attention to emotion by psychological scientists has elevated its importance in the minds of the general public. We see television news and feature stories that describe the importance of emotions, and we begin to pay closer attention to our own emotions. The shift in attention to emotions has affected the church and will inevitably affect theology. The fastest growing denominations throughout the world are the more emotionally expressive Pentecostal forms of Christianity.[14] Pentecostal theology will eventually shape Christian theology in general.

However, there are differences in the way people experience and handle emotions. Psychologists have developed the Affect Intensity Measure[15] (AIM) scale to assess how intensely people feel emotions. People who score high on AIM experience emotions intensely, but people who score low have a controlled emotional life. Which is better? Of course, that depends on the person. For some people high-intensity emotions make them feel out of control. For others, high-intensity emotions give them *joie de vivre*. There are advantages to each. People with high-intensity emotions are passionate, but they also might feel swept away with negative emotion if adverse events occur. People with low emotional intensity are even-keeled and tend not to react to stress, but they also don't react strongly to exciting and pleasurable events. Of course, life circumstances play a big role in what one believes is good at a particular time. When our lives are going great, we want those emotional highs. When our lives are in turmoil, we want to settle the boat lest the storm capsize our emotional lives.

Personality and Self

We know that acceptance of Jesus' lordship translates us into the kingdom of God, and our dwelling in that kingdom begins immediately. We do not wait for heaven to become a citizen of the kingdom. In the United States, as a very individualistic culture, we tend to interpret this individually. We see the self as very isolated—an atom-like individual. However, it is not likely that Jewish Christians saw the self this way. Their culture was more collectivistic, and identity was rooted in being one of the chosen people. They were identified as members of a collective, living under either the old or new covenant.

So, somehow the view of the self has changed dramatically since the apostles. It is reasonable to expect that the cultural view of the self will continue to change, and new theologies of the self must also be formulated. Through most of the twentieth century we have used the personality as an integrating and stable part of the self. The personality is thought to be transformable, but any transformation is thought to be extremely slow. Regardless of the transformation, we do not really expect a makeover. The core personality, shaped by early childhood experiences, is thought to endure with perhaps a few basic tweaks. This is like trying to shape a tree. The tree can be shaped to some degree early in life. But it always grows toward the sun. The recent branches of the adult tree are moldable. They can be lopped off, trimmed or removed so the shape of the tree is changed. However, that change is thought to be mostly cosmetic. The trunk is not changed.

Today, though, this view of personality has come under assault from philosophy, literature, politics and race relations. And by psychology and theology as well. This has not occurred so much in a bloody public war as by assumptions that have been fed to us through popular culture and other opinion leaders.

Situations are far more powerful than we might believe. In Stanley Milgram's obedience studies,[16] we discover that basically decent people are willing to deliver electric shocks to the extent that they believe they might have injured or killed another person. Why will they do this? The situation is inexorably powerful. People, it appears, are defined by the situations they live in. It is easy to move from a belief that personality is not as powerful as we believed to personality doesn't matter. The postmodern, multicultural world that we live in bumps up against the progress-seeking, striving world of modernity. Social critics like Kenneth Gergen[17] argue that situations define us. We thus are social chameleons. Perhaps, like Gergen suggests, we have no personality of our own. We are a product of our culture, a product of our particular time and place. We act differently in our family, at work and on the golf course. The multiple selves are at peace with each other (unlike a person with a multiple personality disorder in which the personalities are at war with each other). We don't even see that we have different personalities.

Theologically, this fragmentation of the self raises some important issues. What is the soul or the human spirit? What is redeemed when we become Christians? What will be with God eternally? What does it mean to say that a new believer is a "new creation; the old has gone, the new has come!" (2 Cor 5:17)? What does it mean when Paul calls us to "be transformed by the renewing of your mind" (Rom 12:2)? If we are situationally defined, then what exactly is transformed?

The implications for our understanding of human nature from theology is always informed not only by Scripture but by the experiences that theologians bring to interpreting Scripture. Theologians are informed by psychological science, so postmodern understandings of the self will inevitably filter into theology and shape the way we understand people and thus the way we interpret the Bible in other areas.

CLOSE INTERPERSONAL RELATIONSHIPS: MARRIAGE

There are many areas in which close interpersonal relationships are hot topics of relevance to theology. Psychological science can inform us in those areas. Let's just concentrate on one issue—marriage. By surveying that one area, we can see how much psychological science has contributed to our understanding, and we'll also see the immense social issues that can be informed by psychological science.

Traditionally, Christianity Has Been Pro-marriage

Rooted in the early chapters of Genesis, Christian belief has favored a one man, one woman marital commitment. This has come increasingly under debate since the early 1970s when the divorce rate hit 50 percent and cohabitation became increasingly more common. The intensity of the debate increased in the 1980s and continues to increase as the gay, lesbian and bisexual minority has become more demanding of equal social and political recognition and rights. The definition of marriage is currently the subject of intense debate. At the most basic level, society is debating the nature of its own building blocks.

The debate can be carried out ideologically—with the opponents screaming at each other, rounding up political allies, cutting deals and coercing cooperation. Both sides of the power struggle enlist scientific evidence on their behalf. While the debate reflects many political and philosophical undertones—freedom versus responsibility, state control versus individual rights, perceived liberty versus oppression, and perceived license versus responsibility—there are some facts that can be brought to bear. Linda Waite and Maggie Gallagher have written an excellent evidence-based book, *The Case for Marriage*, addressing much of the evidence supporting marriage against its competitors.[18] Though we don't have the space to examine the studies, figures and facts of their book, we can look at a few studies from psychological science that suggest the value of marriage.

Divorce Expectancy or Divorce Rate

For the majority of human history, society has been organized around marriage. A great majority of societies throughout history have believed that a lasting commitment of a man and woman to each other, permitting shared labor and opportunities for pregnancy and child rearing, is necessary to the stability of society. In 1860, the divorce expectancy was about 1 percent. By 1900 it had raised to about 8 percent.[19]

Divorce expectancy measures the likelihood that a couple marrying today will divorce before one of them dies. That should trigger some questions? How do we know how long people are going to live, and how do we know that trends won't change between now and when one of the partners dies—perhaps sixty years from now? We can't know these things, so the divorce expectancy rate is an estimate based on the number of people who get divorced this year relative to the number of people who get married this year. If the number divorced is half the number married, then 1/2 = 50 percent divorce rate. If the number divorced is one-third the number who get married, then 1/3=33 percent.

Until the last part of the twentieth century, commitment of married men and women for life was assumed. In 1900, the mean age of first marriage was around seventeen. The life expectancy of someone born in 1900 was about forty-five years. Commitment for life meant, on the average, commitment for less than thirty years. At the beginning of the twenty-first century, however, the mean age of first marriage has increased to around twenty-five. This has occurred for several reasons: (1) More people go to college and graduate school, delaying marriage. (2) Birth control technology and freer sexual mores have lessened the sexual pressure to marry. (3) There is increasing acceptance of single parenting, making the desire to have children achievable without marriage (though actual pregnancy often leads to cohabiting couples deciding to legally marry). (4) Professional opportunities in entry-level positions often require geographical mobility, which mitigates against marriage that ties people to finding two jobs or forces distance relationships. (5) Advances of medical research have led to an enormous lengthening of the life expectancy. Today, it is close to seventy-eight. Thus, the average couple who marries at twenty-five will remain married fifty-three years if one spouse dies at seventy-eight! Making a marital commitment for life seems much more daunting under today's circumstances than it did a mere century ago.

Note how this divorce expectancy rate is affected if people live longer. If longevity doubles, it means there are probably a lot more people getting divorced each year just because people are living much longer.

Change in the Idea of Commitment to Marriage

The marital constraints have been loosened. Marriage has changed correspondingly. Marriage is often seen as a relationship that, statistically speaking, will likely end in divorce. Thus, instead of psychology focusing on ways to strengthen marital commitment so that it will never end, most people have given up on *commitment* as death-do-us-part. The focus is on increasing marital satisfaction, intimacy and sexual happiness. All marriages are seen as fragile and ephemeral. The reason for problems in marriage is not usually seen as a failure in self-control, moral resolve or commitment. Failures are thought to be due to poor communication, intimacy, sexual fulfillment—all of which can change from moment to moment or over short periods. People "drift apart." Lots of attention is devoted to seeking and attracting mates (thus the popularity of sites like eHarmony.com). Correspondingly less attention is given to holding on to a mate for a lifetime.

As a person who has done marital therapy, conducted research on marriage and lived in a happy marriage for over forty years, I sometimes fancifully wonder what would happen if I found the "secret" to lifelong marriage. What if I found that when a couple does X every day, they are *guaranteed* to live happily together with their one partner until one of them dies? Would people do it? What if that secret were as simple as (1) each morning and each night kiss and hug each other, and sincerely say "I love you" at least five times each day; (2) ask yourself each day, *What can I do today to bless my partner?* and then do it; (3) seek forgiveness at the slightest hint that your partner is hurt or offended; (4) grant forgiveness immediately in your spirit if you feel the slightest bit of anger, hurt or disappointment; (5) ask "What can I pray for you today?" and then do it; (6) listen to what your spouse tells you and acknowledge that you hear and take it seriously. Would we carry out such a radical program? Of course, we know those principles now. Do we carry them out? I believe that we don't because we have become less concerned with marital commitment and more concerned with our satisfaction, intimacy and sexual happiness. Still, psychological science suggests that marriage is still valued—in spite of changing views of marriage and a loosening of the idea of commitment. Here are two lines of research that suggest this.

Evidence of the Value of Marriage from Psychological Science

Cohabitation. What are the effects of cohabitation on individuals, the couple, their children, their friends, people in the community or even the national economy? Should cohabiting couples have the same rights and responsibilities as legally married couples? We cannot resolve all of those questions using current research, but there is substantial research on the effects of cohabiting before marriage on subsequent divorce. In general, couples who cohabit prior to a first marriage are about 10 percent more likely to get divorced (i.e., 65 percent) before one of them dies than are those who marry without living together first (i.e., 55 percent).

That statistic hides that there is a bigger difference. First, people who cohabit and then marry tend to marry later than noncohabitors. Second, some people just do not handle living with a partner, and others are not prone to take commitments seriously. Those are risk factors for divorce. When people cohabit, many who would likely divorce end the cohabitation relationship before they ever marry. That makes the sample of cohabitors who eventually decide to marry a selected sample. Namely, many of the noncommitters who cohabit never marry. We are looking only at those who do eventually decide to marry. Also many people poorly fitted for a spousal relationship sometimes don't find that out until early in the marriage (or cohabitation). For cohabitation, those relationships terminate and don't get counted in the divorce statistics, but for marriage, they do get counted in the divorce statistics. Third, because cohabitors marry later than noncohabitors, they have fewer years of marriage before one partner is likely to die. Despite these three reasons that stack the deck against marriage and in favor of cohabitation, still the rate at which marriages after cohabitation fail is greater by 10 percent than for those who do not cohabit. The research also shows that cohabitation before a second or subsequent marriage does not lower the divorce rate.

Why is cohabitation not good for marital stability for many people? Three possible reasons have been studied: (1) Cohabitors tend to take more risks; (2) they seem to be less committed to the idea of marriage, and are thus likely to end marriage; and (3) there are a higher percentage of religious people in the noncohabiting group, and the more religious folks tend to value the stability of marriage and assume marriage will be for life. At the present, reason 3 looks as if it is correct.

Extramarital sex. Research on extramarital sex also points to the value of fidelity in marriage. First, extramarital sex is less frequent than it might seem from the movies. But the amount of true extramarital sex is hard to estimate accurately. For example, if infidelity is defined as sex with some other partner than one's spouse, that would include lots of sex that occurs when couples have separated and are awaiting divorce. If it is defined as sex with a partner one is not maritally committed to, then we run into problems defining what *committed* means. One reliable survey of currently married couples who were, at the time of the survey, living together reported that 75 percent of men and 90 percent of women had been completely faithful over the entire duration of marriage.[20] (Of course, people might use different standards to define *completely faithful.*) Furthermore, only 23 percent of men and 12 percent of all married people report extramarital sex.[21]

Extramarital sex is related to breaking relationships. While not all couples divorce after one partner has an affair, infidelity is a definite risk factor increasing the chances of divorce.[22] This is true even if the couple say they have an "open marriage," meaning they say that it is okay for either or both partners to have sex with someone else. The truth is, when that happens, it is a risk factor for divorce.

Marriage Is Worth Fighting for

Marriage is not only the fundamental building block of society, it is also a major metaphor for our Christian faith. Numerous Christian authors, following Paul's lead, have argued that our relationship with God is like a marriage (Eph 5:32). If we understand marriage as providing a spouse for us to meet our needs for pleasure and happiness, then is it any wonder that sociologist Christian Smith[23] found that we see religion as deistic, hedonistic and therapeutic? But if marriage is seen as a source of meeting our deepest needs, being generative, and finding happiness and fulfillment, then this reflects positively on the Christian faith. The conception of marriage is one of those political issues that seems to be worth the battle.

SOCIETAL AND ORGANIZATIONAL RELATIONS

Hot Societal Issues

Individual and relational issues writ large. Society is beset by hot issues. In fact, many of the same issues that plague individuals and people in close relationships—like marriage—are debated at the societal level as well. Other societal hot buttons include the roles of gays, lesbians and bisexuals; the type and timing of sex education and science education; the societal benefits and obligations when special relationships (like marriage or single parenthood) are recognized by government; and even public policy over biotechnology, cloning and stem-cell research.

Social issues also involve things such as workplace relationships, church conflicts and tensions among people of different ethnicities and countries. Companies or employers can affect the lives of their employees through policy decisions. Relationships within the church also have a societal component. Church policies can affect the lives of people in the pew. Race and ethnic tensions have not disappeared. The acceptance of a multicultural social philosophy and the shift of the distribution of ethnic groups in the last few decades have led to a greater awareness of diversity in the West. Caucasians are no longer a numeric majority within the United States. With psychological science's interest in multiculturalism, psychological science informs much of our daily relations between people of different ethnicities. This ethnic mixing within the United States and the prevalence of electronic communication technologies will likely increase awareness of globalization. This awareness has already affected missions within the church. Most mission organizations now train indigenous workers. Ethnic awareness also will increasingly affect our understanding of different religions throughout the world. How will Christians interact with people committed to religions that bear no animosity to Christianity and to those that are hostile to Christianity?

Ways psychological science contributes understanding. Psychologists have a lot to say about the hot-button issues, workplace relationships, relationships in groups (such as churches), and ethnic and world relations. Psychological expertise involves social psychological effects like conformity, obedience to authority and group dynamics.[24] It can also involve more internal processes like consumer psychology, workplace concerns, personality and psychological reactions to stress.

Terrorism

One issue that is addressed particularly on the societal level is international politics. Many major issues have sprung recently from terrorism. The fear of and the war on terrorism that came after September 11, 2001, led to the United States and coalition wars of Iraq and Afghanistan. The U.S. response to terrorism has resulted in protests within the United States and massive disapproval of American foreign policy abroad. Domestically, it has led to more scrutiny of private citizens' affairs.

Psychology is beginning to unravel some mysteries around terrorism.[25] Because this had not hit home with force in the United States until 9/11, intense research scrutiny had not been focused on terrorism. The roots of terrorism lie in a sense of helplessness against overwhelming odds. Like guerrilla warfare, terrorists use their strengths—small numbers, insulated cells, use of weapons that a single person can detonate, and geographical dispersion—to inflict terror and fear on noncombatants. Finding people who are willing to give their lives in suicidal missions involves (1) a history of perceived oppression, (2) a sense that there is no other way to combat a powerful enemy, (3) an ideology of reward or obligation that motivates self-sacrifice (e.g., the promise to care for a terrorist's family), (4) a mentality that views noncombatants as the enemy, (5) a religious belief system that sees self-sacrificial behavior as a religious duty, a personal calling or an indication of supreme religious dedication, and (6) a numbing of the conscience at taking people's lives.

There have always been terrorists, but the systematic use of terror as a worldwide strategy has not been prevalent until recently. We are not much closer today to knowing how to deal with terrorism than we ever have been. Our population doesn't know how to live with the anxiety that terrorism engenders. Our politicians do not know how to reduce terrorism.

Whereas there have been longstanding theological justifications for avoiding vengeance and pursuing nonviolent responses to terrorism, only in the last twenty-five years has psychological research accumulated to show how beneficial forgiveness is to individuals and to groups. Michael Scherer and his colleagues[26] compiled over 950 references on the psychological study of forgiveness and reconciliation.

SUMMARY

In terms of hot societal issues, we find that the data of psychological science are applicable to every level of human life—individual, relationship and society. Thus, psychological science can support theological propositions. Let's not be naive, however. Psychological science can be easily misused. In the same way, every controversial topic seems to pit Christians with different theologies against each other. So theologies can also be misused. Power and love are continually in tension in a fallen society. We must resist the temptation to treat God's general revelation and God's special revelation as political tools.

The Son of God is acquainted with suffering. He knows how we feel. He empathizes. The self-emptying God cares for the suffering person and doesn't want the sufferer to take matters of justice into his or her own hands through revenge. Instead, God has instructed people to love, even our enemies. Love, not power, will draw people to God.

PSYCHOLOGICAL SCIENCE

HELPS US UNDERSTAND

VIRTUOUS LIVING

IN CHAPTER FIVE I CONSIDERED Paul's dilemma in Romans 7. Paul essentially said, "I try to do what is right, but I can't do it. I try to avoid doing what is wrong, but I do it anyway" (my paraphrase). What was wrong with Paul? Theology tells us. It is serious and fatal. He's fallen and flawed. He has a principle of sin within him. That gives him a moral self-control problem.

For our redemption, we must know that at root we are flawed and must depend on God for all of our needs. God has spelled out the divine story of redemption through Jesus, as we read in the Scriptures, and through the indwelling Holy Spirit. Sometimes I've wished to say to God, "I trust you, but I need more of your help. I don't want the lack of moral self-control to reign in my life. Although you have pronounced me free from the power of sin, I feel under its sway all too often. Please tell me *how* to control myself?"

God *has* told us more—in the book of nature. Psychological science unfolds intriguing stories that help us understand moral self-control (as we will see in the present chapter) and exercise our morality through virtuous living (as we will see in the following chapter).

WHAT PSYCHOLOGICAL SCIENCE REVEALS ABOUT MORALITY

The Footbridge Problem

Scenario 1. Pretend you are standing on a footbridge that extends far above a trolley track. In the distance, five strangers stand on the track. They are unaware that a runaway trolley is bearing down on them. They are not in voice range. A spur off the main track is situated on the tracks just before the place where the five stand. If the trolley is not diverted to the spur, the five people will certainly be killed. A nearby switch will allow you to divert the trolley. However, standing on the spur is another person also unaware of the danger. If you pull the switch, diverting the trolley from its natural course of killing the five people, you will certainly, by your deliberate act, kill one person. You must decide. Will you pull the switch deliberately, killing one person to save five? Princeton's Joshua Greene and his colleagues[1] found that 80 percent of the people who responded to this moral dilemma would pull the switch.

Scenario 2. The setup is similar to scenario one. A runaway trolley is bearing down on five strangers, who will certainly be killed if the trolley is not diverted to the spur. This time, no one is standing on the spur. However, in this scenario the switch is far below. As much as you are tempted, you cannot jump down from the footbridge to successfully trip the switch. But a stranger is balanced precariously on the railing of the footbridge directly above the switch. You realize that you can push the stranger, who will fall on the switch. In doing so, you would save the five from certain death. But the stranger would die. The dilemma is the same. Would you deliberately push the stranger to his death to save the five? If you are like 80 percent of the people who faced this moral dilemma, you would *not.* This completely reversed the findings for the first scenario.

Are these equivalent moral dilemmas? Some people say, "Oh, no. These are not comparable moral dilemmas. In scenario one, I have to manipulate an impersonal piece of metal, and someone at a distance dies. But scenario two is a hands-on experience." This is the argument that Konrad Lorenz[2] made in his book *On Aggression.* He suggested that aggression has become so prevalent over the millennia because it has become impersonal.

Still, I maintain that the dilemmas are essentially the same. Let me change scenario two. Suppose that instead of being close enough to push the stranger, I was quite a distance from him, but I pulled out my .44 Magnum (a powerful handgun) and shot the stranger perched on the railing. Thus, I simply manipulated an impersonal piece of metal at some distance from the stranger, and he died. Does that change things?

A wrinkle in the plot. What made this study more interesting is that people were in functional MRI units when considering these dilemmas. In scenario one, rational reasoning was the dominant mental activity. The left prefrontal cortical and association areas of the brain lit up in the fMRI. People frantically tried to decide what to do. In scenario two, the cortical areas were lit up during the beginning of the scenario. But when the experimenter mentioned pushing the person who sat on the rail, cortical reasoning decreased markedly and the brain centers associated with emotional functioning lit up. Reasoning was dominated by emotions.

Many moral philosophers argue that these two scenarios are morally equivalent despite a few differences in situation. In both cases the subject must act; that intentional act results in a person's death. Without the action, nature takes its course and five people die. Logical, philosophical or theological reasoning cannot reliably differentiate these two scenarios. But psychological research shows a marked difference in response to the scenarios. Logical and emotional reasoning differ.

Phineas Gage

From the footbridge problem, we see that moral decision making is not always as straightforward as it seems. In fact, we often make important decisions emotionally, not logically. Additional evidence comes from the classic case study of Phineas Gage,[3] who was a moral and upright pillar of the community. He worked as foreman whose group blasted rocks to clear the way for building a railroad.

One day Phineas was tamping explosive powder into a hole drilled in a large rock. Tamping involved pouring explosive powder into the hole, placing a cloth over the powder, and using a long metal rod to pound the cloth deep into the rock and seal the powder. Phineas forgot to put the cloth into the hole. Bad mistake. A spark ignited the explosive powder and blew the rod upward. Phineas was leaning over the

hole as he tamped, and the rod was driven completely through Phineas's cheek and out the top of his skull. In most cases, this will ruin
one's entire day.

Phineas sat up after the rod had passed through his head. He was
"stunned." Bystanders were amazed that he seemed virtually unim-
paired. They loaded him onto a wagon and took him to a surgeon. The
surgeon cleaned the wound by passing a cloth through the hole in Phineas's head. Although Phineas did not show much physical damage (of
course, some people might consider having a hole in their head as more
than modest damage), he did suffer brain injury. His behavior was
markedly different.

Phineas had always made sound moral decisions. He looked thought-
fully to the future. He considered other people. He made self-sacrificing
and moral decisions. After the accident he seemed unable to make decisions with the same moral resolution. His decisions were risky, and he
did not consider the moral consequences. He responded to desires immediately. If he was hungry and food was available, he would take it.
When he felt low, he drank alcohol. He moved from job to job, finally
touring with a circus as a "freak" who was able to pass objects through
the hole in his head and yet behave normally, or so it appeared. As he
aged, he continued to drink, gamble, exhibit poor self-control and take
risks. He died destitute and seemingly an immoral reprobate.

Hannah Damasio and Antonio Damasio

What happened to Phineas Gage when the tamping iron blew through
his brain? Hannah Damasio, a physiological psychologist, got access to
Phineas's skull, which had been kept for posterity at Harvard University. She modeled his skull on a computer. Then she graphically placed
the structure of the normal brain within the computer model of Phineas's skull. Hannah found the structures in the brain that were probably
damaged by the tamping iron. People began to call this the moral center of the brain. But was it?

Antonio Damasio, Hannah's husband, is one of the world's leading
researchers in the study of the physiology of emotions. Antonio studied
people whose "center of morality" was damaged by tumors. They acted

like Phineas had. He compared those people with people whose brains were undamaged.

Antonio Damasio wanted to study why people with damage to that section of the brain experienced poor judgment and engaged in risky and often self-injurious behavior. He developed a "gambling" game in the laboratory that posed risky situations. Four piles of cards were turned face down. A participant was given a fixed amount of "play money" to begin the game. At the end of the game the person could trade their play money for real prizes. Each pile of cards had different outcomes. Two of the piles were high-risk, high-gain piles. They contained cards that said things like "Win $1,000," "Lose $2,000" or "Win $2,500." The cards were randomly shuffled. The person was never told that those two stacks of cards were high-risk, high-gain packs. If the person played consistently from those piles, though, he or she would almost certainly lose money. The other two randomly stacked piles of cards were low-risk, low-gain. Those cards said things like "Win $100" or "Lose $50." If the person played consistently from those piles, the person would probably win money by the end of the game.

Antonio Damasio monitored people physiologically as they played his gambling game. Of most interest were their gut responses, which assessed the physiological tension in the gut that accompanied decision making. Because the people did not know what type of cards were in each stack, they usually began by turning over one card from each of the four stacks. Then they turned over a second card from each of the stacks. After two or three rounds of this, though, people began to gravitate toward different stacks. The experimenter sometimes stopped the participant as he or she reached for a card, asking "Why are you choosing that stack?"

The people in the study never learned consciously to distinguish among the four stacks. So people tended to say, "I just felt like turning over a card from that stack." Or they said, "Well, it's just that stack's turn," or "I'm turning over cards at random." The amazing thing, however, was that although people were not conscious of the reason they were reaching for a card, their gut knew. The sensors that monitored the gut spiked even *before* the person made a risky choice. The gut sensors were mellow when the person reached for a low-risk pile. All subjects got fluttery stomachs when they reached for the high-risk pile and none of the subjects realized that their stomachs were trying to warn the brain of risk.

Somehow, people without the damaged areas of the brain seemed to avoid the high-risk stacks as the experiment wore on, even though they never consciously figured out why. Most without the damaged brain area won some money. However, people with the brain damage kept pulling cards from the high-risk pile and lost money.

Antonio Damasio suggested that for people with damaged brains, these "gut feelings" were somehow unavailable to higher centers of the brain as it made decisions. The brain damage interrupted the signal from the gut to the moral decision-making center of the brain—the "working memory" within the left prefrontal cortex. Phineas Gage became immoral not because a center of moral reasoning was damaged. He became immoral because neurons (i.e., nerve cells) between the gut and the working memory weren't working. A crucial relay station was damaged—not the thinking, reasoning or moral judgment part of the brain. People took risks because their gut emotions could not warn them of risky decisions.

Combining Green's and Damasio's Research

From combining the footbridge problem with the Damasios's research, we find that different emotional centers in the brain can strongly affect the way that people make moral decisions. Moral decisions are not merely products of logical reasoning. Obviously, if we can't reason about right or wrong, we can't make good moral decisions. But even if we reason well about right and wrong, we might still make immoral decisions for many reasons.

Flexing Our Moral Muscle

Probably all of us struggle with the problem of self-control. Self-control can be related to our moral choices. We know that we shouldn't do something, yet we have trouble controlling ourselves and avoiding that behavior, or we know that we should do something but we have trouble making ourselves take that moral action. But self-control also involves issues that are not moral. Self-control involves exercising, eating healthy foods in moderation, not drinking alcohol to excess, giving up smoking, maintaining a healthy weight, controlling our sleeping times, disciplining ourselves to work, cutting down on television and a variety of other acts.

Roy Baumeister, a social psychologist, took the theorizing of Sigmund Freud seriously about some aspects of self-control.[4] Freud suggested a kind of conservation of energy was involved in self-control. Thus, for Freud, if a person used a lot of his or her intellectual and psychological energy to control himself or herself, then when presented with another self-control task, the person could not as easily exercise self-control on the second task. Baumeister likened self-control to a moral muscle. When we attempt to strengthen a physical muscle through exercise, it eventually tires, and we therefore will not have enough energy left in the muscle to meet a rapid demand on that muscle. Think how hard it is to do that fifth mile after running four. This is a physical analogy to Freud's conservation-of-psychological-energy analogy.

Baumeister set out to test this in the laboratory. He gave students back-to-back self-control tasks. These involved tasks like squeezing a grip-strength tester, trying to solve scrambled words, keeping their hands in ice water and the cookie experiment. In the cookie experiment, students skipped lunch and came to the laboratory at dinner time to participate in a study. Before students arrived, fresh chocolate chip cookies were baked. The smell wafted through the entire area. Students came into the lab smelling chocolate chip cookies and seeing a plate of cookies laid out before them.

Students were then assigned randomly to one of three conditions. In one condition, the student ate the chocolate chip cookies. In the second condition, the student was told by the experimenter, "Oh, I am sorry. You are in the radish condition." The experimenter then produced a bowl of radishes with a flourish. Then, the experimenter left the room and the student had to consume radishes while smelling and looking at the chocolate chip cookies. That difficult self-control task was thought to deplete the student's moral muscle. In the third condition—the control—students simply did the second task without eating anything.

People in the radish condition indeed did not do as well on a second self-control task, regardless of what that self-control task was, relative to people who ate the cookies and didn't have to exercise self-control. You might think that perhaps the chocolate made people stronger. But it turned out that the ones who ate the chocolate did not do better than the people who ate nothing.

To carry the moral muscle analogy a step further, Baumeister assumed that if people regularly exercised their moral muscle of self-control, they would strengthen that moral muscle, if the exercising was done slowly over time. That was analogous to working out three times a week. To test his idea, Baumeister brought students into the laboratory and gave one of two self-monitoring tasks. In one case they monitored some behavior that was not related to self-control, such as recording the number of people who smiled at them each day. In the other condition they monitored their posture. Every time they caught themselves slumping, they tried to correct their posture. When people were brought back after a week of self-monitoring, those who engaged in the high self-control self-monitoring did better on the self-control task than did those who did not exercise their moral muscle during the week.

These data suggest that people often want to make moral decisions, but different factors may affect their success. Both internal and external factors can affect success. Internal factors, such as the frequency that we exercise our moral muscle or our emotional passion about doing the right thing, can affect our morality. Mind and body both play a role in people's moral decision making.

Stanley Milgram's Obedience Experiments

But it isn't merely the internal factors that matter. Stanley Milgram, a Yale professor in the 1960s, was trained in the tradition of social psychology that studied the power of others to influence our judgments.[5]

In the 1950s, Solomon Asch (who trained Milgram) had invited students in a group to judge the length of lines.[6] When group members who were confederates of the experimenter intentionally gave the same incorrect judgment, the subject (who was not a confederate) often went along with the group. Asch found that people in groups influence us to make judgments that we might not make if we were alone.

Asch had been trained in the 1940s by the originator of social-influence research, Muzafer Sherif.[7] Sherif's research had led Asch to ask questions about the effects of groups. Sherif found that in very ambiguous situations, people looked to each other to make decisions.

Sherif placed individuals in a completely dark room, where they stared at a pinhole of light. The person's jiggling eyes caused the light to pass its image onto different places on the retina. Because the darkness allowed no point of reference, the light seemed to move. People viewed these "movements" within a group, so that they knew that each person was observing the same thing. The judgments about how far the points of light had moved converged over successive trials. Finally, agreement was reached within the group. People influenced each other's judgments.

Muzafer Sherif and Solomon Asch were the forerunners of Milgram. Milgram[8] was interested in why the Nazis in World War II had been capable of inflicting so much cruelty on Jews and Russians. Initially, Milgram sought to understand "the German personality," which he thought to be more highly responsive to authority than the independent American personality. He wanted to show that people with certain personality characteristics could more easily do evil acts.

Milgram's results surprised him. In a typical study Milgram asked two individuals to participate in a study of the effect of punishment on learning. The actual subject was "randomly" drawn to be the "teacher" in the study. The "learner" was in fact a confederate of the experimenter, and the "random drawing" was rigged. The "teacher" was required to give electric shocks of increasing intensity to the "learner" when the "learner" missed questions. The punishments were supposed to teach the "learner" to make correct responses. Unknown to the "teacher," no real shocks were actually given. The study was not about learning at all. The study was about the influences that experimenter and the experimental situation exerted on the "teacher" (i.e., the actual subject).

When people not in the study were asked to estimate how many shocks they would give to the "learner" (i.e., the confederate), they almost *never* estimated that they would give over 120 volts of shock.

When the experiment was really done, the "teacher" almost *always* gave over 120 volts of shock. Over half of the people gave as many as 450 volts of electric shocks (the maximum possible) to the "learner."

In a series of experiments summarized in his book *Obedience,* Milgram described how the presence of the closeness of the experimenter to the "teacher" strongly affected how many shocks the "teacher" gave. A "teacher," who was commanded by a mere audiotape recording to administer shocks, often would not obey. More obedience was obtained if the experimenter was in contact with the "teacher" by phone. Even more obedience occurred if the experimenter was in the same room as the "teacher." And the most obedience occurred when the experimenter stood close to the "teacher."

In addition, the distance between the "teacher" and the "learner" strongly influenced the outcome. If the "teacher" could not see or hear the "learner" and only the learner's responses were seen (such as lights indicating the "learner's" response), then the "teacher" tended to give the maximum numbers of shocks. If the "learner" could be heard but not seen, then fewer shocks were given. If the "learner" could be both seen and heard but was at a distance away, then still fewer shocks were given. If the "teacher" had to hold the hand of the "learner" onto a shock plate, the fewest shocks were given.

It is important to note that neither students nor experts accurately predicted these outcomes. Most said that they would not administer shocks (and if so, only a few). But in the experiment, they did. What people thought they *should* do and what they thought they *would* do was not what they *did* do.

This rounds out our picture of moral decision making. The *situation* has a large influence on a person's moral decisions. Sometimes situational pressures can be so strong that they overwhelm the power of even emotional decision making. We saw how powerful emotional decision making was in the footbridge problem. Just imagining putting one's hands on a person and pushing him to his death was seen as morally repulsive by most people.

Yet strong situations can overpower our natural inclinations. In Milgram's studies, some people still gave maximum shocks when they had to hold the confederate's hand down on a shock plate and give what they thought were near lethal shocks while the confederate screamed and pleaded for mercy. When situational demands are more ambiguous or weaker, then bodily processes and rational thinking have more influence on what a person decides in a moral dilemma.

SCRIPTURAL TRUTHS UNVEILED BY PSYCHOLOGICAL SCIENCE

Moral Development

The role of situations figures heavily in how, when, how often and under what circumstances we act morally. That suggests a strong role of learning in moral behavior. Yet that is far from the whole story. As Christians believe, people are intrinsically moral creatures because we bear the image of God. Though sin has corrupted the purity and strength of the moral motive, it has not blotted it out.

Melvin Lerner[9] has shown that people have an intrinsic justice motive. Furthermore, most people—unless they have hardened their hearts thoroughly—have a heroic justice motive. Lerner describes this motive as the strong energy that empowers behavior to defend the helpless, the weak, children and the defenseless. It takes powerful negative learning to snuff out that basic moral motive.

How did people develop their moral sense? Did they simply learn to write moral rules on a blank slate? The evidence is against that explanation. Rather, people seem to develop capabilities for moral reasoning and behavior as part of natural development. Sometimes their development is thwarted or bent because of this experience. Still there seems to be some evidence that children develop moral motivations—even when the content of what they are to consider moral has to be learned.

Kids and Adults Think Differently

We all know that children and adults think differently, but often that is treated like an adult mantra. We repeat it almost mindlessly without really understanding the extent of the differences. A specific example will reveal how differently children and adults reason.

Three-and-a-half-year-old Mary has been playing with Mother's valuable jewelry. Mother didn't know it. In Mother walks. Mary looks over her shoulder and sees the horrified look on her Mother's face. Immediately, she dips her head guiltily.

"You *should* be ashamed, young lady," says Mother. "You know better than to play with my jewelry. Come with me. You're going to have a time-out and think about your behavior. Then I'm going to have you put every one of those pieces of jewelry back where you got them." Then, thinking better of her strategy, Mother says, "No, instead, you're going to put these back in their boxes. Then, you are going to have a ten-minute time-out. Understand?" Mary nods. "You think about it. I'll be back," Mother says.

When Mother comes back in five minutes, Mary is sitting silently on the floor and the jewelry is where it was when Mother left. "Mary, you haven't obeyed at all! Pick my jewelry up, now." Mary begins to cry. Mother puts a ring in its box. "Put the rest away," she says. Mary begins to comply.

When the last earring is in its box, Mother says, "Now, you are going to have a ten-minute time-out. You sit on the floor and don't play with any toys. Just think about how you must not play with Mother's jewelry. Also think about obeying me when I tell you to do something." Mother leaves, confident that she is building good moral character in Mary. She is a bit worried, though, because Mary had indicated she understood the instructions, yet didn't obey. Perhaps, Mother fears, Mary is learning to lie and deceive.

What do you think? Should Mother have done anything differently? Let's see what psychological science might tell Mother.

Psychological Science Tells Mother That Mary Can't Easily Shift Rules

Imagine a bunch of plastic animals. Each animal is either red or blue. Each is either a bunny or a dog. There are each of the four combinations—red and blue bunnies and red and blue dogs. An experimenter says to Mary, "We are going to play a 'shape' game. Can you find a dog?" Mary does. "Put the dog in this tray." She does. "Can you find a bunny?" She does. "Put the bunny in this other tray." She does. "Now put all the ones of the same shape in the same tray." Mary successfully puts all dogs in one tray and all bunnies in the other.

The experimenter reshuffles the plastic animals and then says, "Now we are going to play a 'color' game. Can you find a red animal?" Mary does. "Put it in this tray." She does. "Can you find a blue animal?" She does. "Put it in this other tray." She does. "Now put all the *red* animals together in one tray and all the *blue* animals in the other tray." Mary puts all the bunnies in one tray and dogs in the other. She could not change from the original shape game to the new color game.[10]

Young children cannot easily shift rules. When Mary's mother directed her to have a time out and *then* put the jewelry away, but then changed the rules, Mother returned to find Mary sitting quietly on the floor (which we now can understand as Mary compliantly having a time-out). Mother was angry because Mary did not do the most recent sequence of rules. Mary was confused at Mother's anger and cried.

Mother had thought that her instructions were clear. She even asked Mary, "Understand?" Mary nodded. She understood as well as she could. But Mother might have found out about the misunderstanding before Mary "disobeyed" if Mother had read some studies by psychologist Daniel O'Leary.

Mother Could Have Had Mary Tell Herself Moral Rules

Daniel O'Leary[11] rigged a slot machine to look like a clown. The lever was the clown's arm. When the children pulled the arm, they received a marble. The children could redeem one to ten marbles for a small toy, and eleven or more marbles for a large toy. (In actuality, there was not enough time to collect eleven marbles, so all children received the same small toy.) With five-year-old children, O'Leary told all of the children the rule. "It's fair to pull the clown's arm when the green light is lit, but it's not fair to pull the clown's arm when the red light is lit." For one-half of the children, he repeated the rule. For the other half of the children, he said, "What's the rule?" They said the rule. So half heard the rule twice; the rest heard it once and said it once.

The result? Children who heard the rule twice cheated twice as often as those who heard the rule and repeated it. In a follow-up study, O'Leary[12] changed the game. He showed children a red or green light, but they could not pull the lever until the light turned off. At each trial, half were told to say the rule aloud. The other half knew the rule. They had demonstrated ten correct choices before the trials began. But they were not told to say aloud the rule. The half who said the rule aloud before every possible pull of the clown's arm cheated only 4 percent as often as those taught the rule but not required to say it aloud.

Psychological Science Could Have Told Mother That the Time-Out Might Not Work

Mary was directed to sit and think about her misbehavior and how she might comply in the future. Did the time-out help?

Some research by Becky Bailey[13] suggests that perhaps a time-out for the purpose of thinking might not work on a child only three-and-a-half-years-old. In a demonstration of early childhood thinking, Bailey laid out a line of seven objects. She and the child counted the objects aloud together and pointed to each object sequentially. After being sure that the child could count to seven, Bailey removed some (let's say two). She asked the child to tell her how many were there. The child counted aloud and pointed, and usually arrived at the correct answer.

Bailey repeated the task. This time she allowed the child to count aloud but not point. Again, most children got the right answer. On a third trial, she repeated the task, but the child could neither count aloud nor point. Virtually no child could get the correct answer. Children under four-and-a-half or five (and perhaps older) could not use internal speech to think and solve problems. However, they could think aloud and often direct their thinking that way. So Bailey's studies suggest that Mother will not succeed by directing Mary to sit silently and think. Mother should get her to talk about her behavior instead.

Speaking of Speaking Out Loud

In earlier research Don Meichenbaum,[14] the founder of cognitive-behavior modification, a type of psychotherapy, described how he realized he could help adults solve their personal problems. He was doing his dissertation research on schizophrenics. He tested the hypothesis that part of their problem-solving difficulties was not paying sustained attention to the task. One night he was listening to his own boy play.

He heard his child talking aloud to himself. "What do I have to do now? I must move this block here. Then I can move the other one." These weren't the exact words, but the concept struck Meichenbaum.

His boy was thinking, solving problems and keeping himself focused by talking to himself. Meichenbaum founded cognitive-behavior modification psychotherapy on the principle of helping people change their self-talk. He applied the method with anxious children, impulsive children and adults who struggled with depression, anxiety, anger, stress and pain. He helped people stop their fruitless attempts to control their problems. Next, he helped them become aware of their internal talk. Then he helped them focus on changing that speech by speaking aloud. Finally, the changed self-talk became private self-talk.

While adults could take the last step, turning their speech into thoughts, children—especially those younger than five—could not. Something in human development requires that children younger than five receive and use instruction from someone who can give wise advice. The ability to use language develops along a predictable course as long as the child receives encouragement and reward for reasoning. Yet below certain ages, children—regardless of how intellectually bright— simply are not capable of private internal speech.

So, in our example, Mother had a good heart. She wanted to help Mary learn good moral behavior. But she did not know some things that would help her discipline Mary effectively.

Was Mary Deceiving Mother?

In fact, Mother worried about the possibility that Mary was intentionally deceiving her. After all, Mary said she understood Mother's directions but didn't comply. Did she think she could fool Mother so easily?

Again, psychological science tells us some things that would help Mother be assured that Mary was not deceiving her mother. At three-and-a-half, most children have some sense of right and wrong. Jerome Kagan[15] demonstrated this by first making sure that children could follow directions. Kagan would have them pour purple dye from a cup to a bucket. He would then have them pick up a baby doll. Then he would say, "Pour the purple water on the baby doll." The children would get upset. They knew this was "wrong." They would look to Mother. Mother would say, "Go ahead. Pour the purple water on the baby doll." The child might cry. In one video clip of this demonstration, after the child poured purple water on the doll, she said to her mother, "Hug me, Mommy." The child had a sense of right and wrong. Pouring purple dye on the baby doll was wrong. In our example, Mary was probably too young to deceive Mother.

Standards Change with Age

What is understood to be right and wrong, and the degree of wrong for different transgressions, develop as children age and with teaching. For instance, a three-and-a-half-year-old like Mary would usually respond predictably if given the following problem.

"Let me tell you two stories, and you tell me which child did the worse act. A mother told two children, 'I just cooked some cookies. We'll eat them for dessert. Don't eat any now.' Mother went downstairs. She called one child. He came running, but he accidentally bumped into the cabinet and knocked over a bottle, which broke fifteen glasses." "That's this many glasses broken" (gestures by holding up ten fingers and then five). "When Mother went downstairs, the second child climbed up and ate some of the cookies. After Mother called, the second child was scared and knocked over one glass and broke it. That's how many glasses were broken" (gestures by holding up one finger). "Now which child did the worse thing?"

Below age five, most children immediately say, "The first boy." Why? "He broke more glasses."

After the turning point in mental development called the "5-to-7 shift,"[16] though, children immediately say, "The second boy." Why? "He disobeyed and was doing wrong when he broke a glass."

"Yes, but he only broke one glass."

"But it's worse to disobey than to have an accident. The first boy was doing what was right."

Development of Moral Reasoning

Most people are familiar with Lawrence Kohlberg's studies on reasoning about moral dilemmas.[17] Children were given difficult moral problems like the problem of Heinz: Heinz's wife became ill and was going to die. A druggist developed a medicine that could make her well. But the druggist would only sell it to Heinz for $1,000. Heinz asked the druggist to sell the medicine for less money, but the druggist said no. So Heinz broke into the druggist's store and stole the medicine. Do you think Heinz should have stolen the medicine? Why or why not?

Kohlberg was not interested in whether the child (or adults who responded to the same dilemma) thought the stealing was or wasn't justified. He was interested in the reasoning. People exhibited a predictable pattern of development in reasoning.

In the first stage, they reasoned according to consequences that might befall Heinz. Examples are these. "Heinz shouldn't steal because he might get caught and go to prison." "Heinz should steal because then his wife could be well."

In the second stage, social conventions dominated reasoning. Examples are "Heinz shouldn't steal because there are laws against stealing." "Heinz should steal because everyone would say he did a good thing to save his wife."

In the third stage of moral reasoning, a higher order of morality than social convention was appealed to. Examples are these. "Heinz shouldn't steal because the society depends on people obeying laws even if it is costly personally to do so." "Heinz should steal because love is more important than mere obedience."

Children who reason at stage one usually cannot understand the logic of stages two and three. When children begin to understand stage-two reasoning, they can understand stage-one reasoning but usually reject it as less important. Similar shifts occur when adolescents or adults reach stage-three reasoning.

One of Kohlberg's colleagues, psychologist Carol Gilligan,[18] challenged Kohlberg's justice-oriented moral reasoning. She argued that women often base their moral reasoning more on relationships than on principles of abstract justice. Still, both Kohlberg and Gilligan argued that children become more complex in reasoning through predictable stages.

Another Reason Mary Might Not Be Trying to Deceive

Recall that Mary nodded that she understood her mother's instructions but then did not carry them out. It isn't merely a level of development of moral reasoning that should suggest to Mother that Mary probably was not trying to deceive her. Another reason is that at three-and-a-half, Mary might not yet be capable of conscious deceit.

Imagine this scene: Mary watches as an experimenter involves a Barbie-like doll, a larger boy doll with removable boots and a mother doll in an acted-out story.[19]

Some muffins are in the corner of a room in a doll house. Flour in a fine (but visibly white) dusting is spread over the floor of the room. The experimenter holds the mother doll who looks at the brother and sister. The mother doll says, "Don't either of you eat any muffins while I'm gone. Suzie, are you going to eat any muffins?" The girl doll says no. "Johnny, are you going to eat any muffins?" The boy doll says no. Mother then goes away. (The experimenter puts the mother doll under the table where she cannot see.)

When she is gone, the Suzie doll says to Johnny, "Let me use your boots." She puts on the large boots over her small feet. The experimenter then walks Suzie across the floor, making boot-size tracks, and Suzie eats all the muffins. She walks back across the floor, leaving another trail of boot tracks. Suzie returns the boots to Johnny.

The mother doll is brought back. She is held directly over the place where the muffins were. She says, "The muffins are gone. Someone ate the muffins. I told them not to." The mother then looks at the tracks to and from the site of the purloined muffins. She examines the tracks very carefully. She follows the tracks, first toward the muffins and then away from them. She looks at Suzie's small feet and Johnny's flour-covered boots.

The experimenter asks the three-and-a-half-year-old child, "Who does Mother think ate the muffins?"

The child says, "Suzie."

The experimenter says, "Could Mother actually see who ate the muffins?"

"No."

The experimenter says, "Did Mother see Johnny's boots that made the tracks?"

"Yes."

"So, who will Mother think ate the muffins?"

"Suzie."

Apparently, at three-and-a-half, Mary thinks that because *she* saw Suzie eat the muffins, Mother must magically be able to know that Suzie did the dirty deed.

Here's another demonstration to the same effect. The experimenter shows a child a juice box.[20] "What do you think is in the box?" the experimenter asks.

"Juice," says three-and-a-half-year-old Mary.

"Watch this," says the experimenter. She pulls colorful ribbons from the box, then puts them back in.

"What do you think is in the box now?"

"Ribbons."

"What did you think was in the box at the beginning?"

"Ribbons."

A new child enters the room. The experimenter says, "This is Joan. She hasn't seen this box before. What do you think Joan will say if I ask her what is in the box?"

"Ribbons."

Mary thinks that what she knows, everyone must know. It is difficult in such a magical world for a three-and-a-half-year-old child to deceive. How can one deceive when one believes Mother knows what he or she knows?

When Deception Can Occur

Obviously, that doesn't last forever. Let's look at one demonstration that shows when the shift occurs.

Mary is introduced to Mean Monkey. "Mean Monkey likes stickers," three-and-a-half year old Mary is told. "He always gets first choice, and he always takes the one he thinks *you* like best. Mean Monkey is going away where he can't see now, but he'll come back in a short while."

Mean Monkey is put below the table. Two stickers, a flower and a house, are placed in front of the child. "Which sticker do you like best?" asks the experimenter. Mary points to the flower.

"Ok, here comes Mean Monkey." Mean Monkey is brought from under the table. The monkey says, "What pretty stickers! Which one do you like best?"

Mary points to the flower. "Good," says Mean Monkey. "I'll take the flower." He picks it up and leaves (under the table). Mary is stunned!

The same sequence is repeated with two other choices, with the same result. Mary tells the truth, suffers loss and is (you guessed it) stunned. Then, with Mean Monkey out of sight, the experimenter says to the child, "Mean Monkey always takes the one you like best. Can you think of a way that Mean Monkey won't take the one you like best? Here are two more stickers—a bird and a cow. Which do you like best?"

The child points to the bird.

"Okay, when Mean Monkey comes back, let's see if you can think of a way that he won't take the bird."

Mean Monkey comes back and says, "What pretty stickers! Which one do you like best?"

Mary points to—you guessed it—the bird. True to character, Mean Monkey takes it. (Shucks, he's mean. What can we say?) A three-and-a-half-year-old child apparently cannot believe that if she knows she likes the bird best, Mean Monkey doesn't also know.

By four-and-a-half, though, things are different. The first time Mean Monkey comes out, the child is shocked when Mean Monkey takes his or her favorite sticker. So the next time Mean Monkey comes, the child might lie when Mean Monkey asks, "Which one do you like best?" Even if the child does not lie during one of the early trials, the child *always* does so when the experimenter says, "Can you think of a way so that Mean Monkey doesn't take the one you like best?"[21]

Summary. Right is right. Wrong is wrong. Do right and please God. Do wrong and incur God's judgment. How hard can this be?

As we see, fascinating stories are told through looking at psychological scientific data. Clever scientists, seeking to read God's book of nature, reveal an enthralling, wonderful story of how morality develops. Morality develops as though a master storyteller is gradually unfolding a complex plot. In children, brain maturity limits and encapsulates development. But situations play a role. Adolescent brain development takes another spurt forward as the myelinization of neurons is completed. As the brain completes its wiring at about age nineteen, twenty or even later, the person is physically equipped for moral behavior as an adult. But by that time, experiences have accumulated to shape the personality toward different senses of morality and to guide the person into a choice among the many situations possible. Those *situations*, as we've seen by recalling Milgram's studies,[22] exert a larger effect on our behavior and on whether we choose moral or nonmoral acts than we sometimes wish were true.

Morality is not simply a matter of genes, early family environment, biological unfolding of a complex body-brain unit, situational influences, and choices of situations that we will allow to influence us. Morality also involves the hand of God, working through grace and mercy, to steer us in the way, the truth and the life.

But with sin in our nature—even though we are the image bearers of God—we all too often choose unwisely. Still, we see in the complex development of moral selves the hand of God at work within a universe that God imbued with free will. God superintends genetic transmission, but allows mutations both because the Fall introduced imperfection into the world and because God is a God of novelty and adventure who promotes change and growth. God directs biological development along a pathway that most people follow. Yet God allows novel situations, different family experiences and even natural life events to intrude. Those may bring pain, but they also discipline us (see Heb 12:5-8).

God creates orderly processes for human development—in particular moral development—but God neither imprisons us nor binds the divine hands through biological or genetic determinism. God is more than a God of order. God also loves humans. In the divinely created developmental plan to allow us to experience love, God allows freedom, novelty and spontaneity—all of which are necessary for a relationship characterized by love.

SUMMARY

These studies and demonstrations reveal fascinating aspects of human moral behavior that are not immediately revealed by Scripture. They reveal the complex mind and heart of the Creator who made us to reflect not just the relational nature of the Trinity but also the moral nature.

We certainly do not *need* the findings of psychological science to participate in eternal fellowship with God and other believers. Scripture is sufficient to lead us to a personal relationship with God. But knowing worldly philosophy made it easier for Paul to communicate on Mars Hill (Acts 17:16-33), and knowing Roman law helped him deal with Festus and Agrippa (Acts 25:1–26:32). Knowing music helped David find favor with King Saul, and practice with the slingshot helped him fell Goliath. Similarly, psychological science's findings can help people rely on Jesus when they face dilemmas similar to the self-control difficulties Paul lamented in Romans 7.

A child could be helped to practice self-control differently at age three-and-a-half or age six. An adolescent would react still differently. Even adults would be able to select different moral behavior in strong situations such as those in Milgram's obedience studies.[23] And *usefulness* isn't the only criterion for evaluating the benefits of psychological science. It can also tell us more about God and ourselves as we relate with God and others.

We learn from Scripture that we are moral creatures; we make moral decisions. Those decisions differ on the basis of our belief system. Belief systems such as Judaism, Roman Catholicism or Islam will prescribe and proscribe different behaviors in different situations. Nevertheless, Scripture tells us that in their heart-of-hearts people recognize an inner code of morality that God has put there (Rom 1:19; 2:15). We are all without excuse in regard to God's law.

We also realize from Scripture that the strength of faith, which is not merely intellectual assent to doctrine but involves our entire lives, can influence our behavior. People can embrace the same belief system but with different degrees of faith. It is clear from Scripture that there are situations in which moral behavior is more difficult than it is in others.

Psychological experiments have revealed some of the conditions under which moral decision making can be more or less difficult—such as making a deliberate decision to harm someone even if it would benefit others (e.g., scenario two in the footbridge problem[24] or situations like Milgram's obedience studies[25] where the social pressure is intense). Studies like these give new insight into what Scripture tells us.

Thus, we can learn several things from psychological science. (1) We are not self-sufficient, self-controlling people. We are morally needy. We depend on God's mercy and grace. We can either fight dependence on God or embrace it. (2) Psychology does not absolve us from making moral choices. We are without excuse. (3) On the other hand, we need to understand, empathize with and refrain from judging people who are placed in difficult situations and make immoral choices. We know that God commands us not to judge (Mt 7:1). By understanding psychological science, we may judge people less harshly because we (perhaps) can empathize more. (4) We need to be more cautious when we are placed in difficult situations. There, the temptation to choose immorally is strong—biology, situations and our fallen nature are strong. We are weak, so we must rely on God. (5) Psychological science doesn't replace scriptural truth. On the contrary, it enhances the truth and reveals more about what can be expected in applying scriptural truth today. (6) Psychological science stimulates wonder, and awe unfolds as we examine the experiments that progressively unfold God's general revelation.

PSYCHOLOGICAL SCIENCE
HELPS US LIVE MORE VIRTUOUSLY

THE LOVE OF CHRIST SHOULD PRODUCE a strong desire to live in a way that honors the triune God. Psychological science can not only help us understand moral behavior and how it develops but it can also show us how to live virtuously. Before we examine how psychological science can help us live virtuously, we will take a quick trip through moral development theory, classical virtue theory and moral identity theory.

MORAL DEVELOPMENT THEORY

Philosophy

Beginning with the Enlightenment and continuing until recently, philosophical approaches to ethics have been dominated by rational, rule-based theories of ethics. Western philosophy has produced many ethical rules, maxims and formulas for guiding "correct" behavior. Within this rational tradition we find philosophers like Immanuel Kant (the categorical imperative), utilitarians (the greatest good for the greatest number), equity theorists (economic cost-benefit analyses describe moral decision making) and evolutionary psychologists (moral decisions based on the most survival value). Philosophical approaches have most often asked "What should I do?" and answered with "What duty demands," "Whatever is not prohibited by the rules," "Whatever maximizes my net benefits" or "Whatever enhances my survival."

Psychological Science and Rational Morality

This rationalist understanding of moral psychology has, until recently, dominated psychological theorizing and research. Jean Piaget's,[1] Lawrence Kohlberg's[2] and their intellectual offsprings' models of moral development emphasize a stage-like development of formal problem-solving and rational judgments in explaining moral action. Even expanded theories that acknowledge the influence of cultural and emotional elements on moral action[3] still place most of their emphasis on context-sensitive moral analysis and judgment to define full moral maturity.

This emphasis on judgment and moral reasoning as the basis for moral action has been criticized.[4] Critics of cognitive-developmental theories argue that these theories neglect important emotional and motivational factors that lead people to act morally. Moral judgment is perhaps necessary but not sufficient for moral action.

AN ALTERNATIVE TO RATIONAL MORALITY: CLASSICAL VIRTUE THEORY

Greek Notion of Classical Virtues

Morality wasn't always thought to be so rational. In classical antiquity, philosophical approaches to ethics were dominated by the notion of *virtue*. For example, Aristotle thought that ethical behavior should be guided by ideal human traits that, when practiced, would bring about "the good life," "happiness," or "human flourishing."[5] Classical virtues, then, are desirable psychological traits. From classical virtue theory, they reflect merely the way people are raised.

We can learn virtues. Religious, educational and other social institutions promoted virtue. In the tradition of virtue theory, the central issue guiding action depends on the kind of person I want to be. Moral education was based primarily on learning virtue by imitating moral exemplars who provided a model of the desirable traits.[6]

Christian Virtues

Christian notions of virtue share more similarities with classical virtue theory than with rational moral theory. In classical theory the source of strength is thought to be oneself. One's community plays a role in defining "the good life," and the person is thought to act virtuously because of the way one is raised and the duties of community. For Christians the good is more God-centered than self-centered. People seek to please God, reflect God's or Jesus' character, and rely on God's strength through the indwelling Holy Spirit to yield fruit. A good starting place for Christian virtue is Galatians 5:22-23: "The fruit of the Spirit is love, joy, peace, patience, kindness, goodness, faithfulness, gentleness, and self-control."

Besides the fruit of the Spirit, another set of Christian virtues includes positive (virtuous) emotions: empathy, sympathy, compassion, gratitude, generosity, open-heartedness, peace and humility. Virtues are also found in the Gospels and the Epistles. These include truthfulness, justice, responsibility, accountability, forbearance, prudence and courage. Still others include faith, trust, hope, fidelity and religious commitment.

MORAL IDENTITY THEORY

In recent years the erosion of a Christian consensus (and the virtues) and the postmodern rejection of rationality have given rise to new ways of thinking about morality. One recent approach to bridging the gap between moral judgment and moral action is moral identity theory.[7] Here, psychological scientists define moral identity explicitly as a self-conception organized around moral traits. People think of themselves as moral creatures who have specific virtues. They may consider themselves, for instance, as caring, compassionate, fair, friendly, generous, hardworking, helpful, honest or kind as a primary trait. In some studies, psychologists found that people report positive associations of their virtuous traits with self-reported volunteering, donations to charity and moral reasoning.

Virtue Theory as a Moral Identity Theory

Virtue theory—drawing on classical and Christian virtues—can be seen as a version of moral identity theory. There are many similarities between trait-based moral identity theories and traditional virtue theory. In traditional virtue theory, socially valued traits are treated as ideals. Identity theorists refer to these as goal strivings.[8] Like many moral identity theories, virtue theory has stressed the importance of imitation of (and identification with) moral exemplars in forming moral character. The trait-centeredness of virtue theory makes it attractive to many psychological scientists.

Virtue theory has long-standing historical credentials. During the years driven by the moral reasoning approaches of Piaget, Kohlberg and Gilligan, virtue theory was rarely discussed. However, recently, within positive psychology, virtues are considered personality traits and have received a lot of attention. While in the moral domain, such traits have traditionally been referred to as "virtues," other terms, such as *human strengths*, have also been used in positive psychology. Chris Peterson and Martin Seligman developed a classification of twenty-one human strengths.[9] Six core strengths constitute the highest level of virtue: wisdom, courage, justice, humanity, temperance and transcendence.

In one attempt to study virtues collectively, Vincent Jeffries[10] proposed that the dispositions underlying altruism could be described in terms of the classic virtues. He developed a measure of the frequency of practicing the primary virtues cataloged by Thomas Aquinas (temperance, fortitude, mercy, justice and prudence). He found that Aquinas's primary virtues correlated highly with each other. Moreover, a composite scale of all the virtues correlated positively with an altruistic orientation. By now there is a substantial collection of virtues that have been studied by positive psychologists. There has been research on altruism,[11] forgiveness,[12] gratitude,[13] humility,[14] hope,[15] compassion[16] and other virtues.

Some psychologists[17] identified 140 virtues and found, through exploration factor analysis, that four factors undergirded the virtues. They were labeled "empathy," "order," "resourcefulness" and "serenity." They found that the four groups of virtues were positively associated with the big five personality factors of agreeableness and conscientiousness, and negatively associated with neuroticism. They found little relationship between the four virtue factors and moral development based on Kohlberg's model. They concluded, therefore, that virtues are a function of personality rather than of moral reasoning. This supports a classical virtue or Christian understanding of virtue more than a Kohlberg- or Gilligan-like rational analytic view of positive traits.

HOW PSYCHOLOGICAL SCIENCE
CAN HELP PEOPLE LIVE MORE VIRTUOUSLY

In Christianity, virtue is a fruit of the Spirit. That is, virtue is a manifestation of something inside, worked by the Holy Spirit, and it is part of Christian identity. The Scriptures tell us of the transformation of our character when we become Christians, and it assures us that the Holy Spirit can produce fruit (Gal 5:26) in our lives. But the Scriptures do not answer the *how* questions beyond relying on God, adhering to ethical teaching and drawing on the Holy Spirit for guidance, support and comfort when we fail morally. The Scriptures are meant to communicate to all ages, and are thus more general than science. Science pinpoints mechanisms for action and change. By its nature science is aimed at the present and will change with history, culture and situations. The Scriptures are not concerned with psychological mechanisms for how we develop and practice love, patience, self-control and the other fruits—just with whether we practice them. Psychological science can help us act virtuously in several ways.

Understanding Changing Moral Capabilities with Development

In chapter fourteen I described studies structured around a fictitious interaction between three-and-a-half-year-old Mary and Mary's mother. The studies and experiments aimed at revealing what Mary was capable of doing morally. An entire literature exists to help adults understand the ways that children's moral reasoning and behavior change at different life stages and ages. Such topics are not addressed in Scripture.

Obviously, as people move from childhood to adulthood, their moral reasoning and actions change. Early in a child's life, parents are well advised to teach the child obedience to moral rules.[18] As children reach the age of about four-and-a-half or five, though, they become capable of reasoning very differently than at younger ages. (Recall the shape game, Mean Monkey and Suzie-the-cookie-crook from the previous chapter.) They can thus control their behavior by understanding not only the rules for what to do and what *not* to do, but also the principles behind the rules. Parents can teach both rules and principles. As children begin to reason more abstractly (at age eleven and older), the parent becomes the moral coach. The child, in effect, plays the game of life and the coach (parent) provides advice and guidance about which principles might be applied in which situations. Parents ultimately want to help a young adult (eighteen and older) function within a moral framework to guide his or her behavior without needing to consult the parent except when desired.

There is a rough parallel between the way that the child is taught morality as he or she ages and the way that God unfolded divine revelation to humans. Early in the process God gave the law—the Ten Commandments and the Pentateuch. As the Israelites matured, though, principles became the focus of morality. The books of wisdom, the Psalms, and the major and minor prophets unfolded how God deals with people. Principles plus the law were the basis of morality. Jesus emphasized principled teaching, though the principles changed in emphasis and complexity. After the crucifixion and resurrection, Jesus left the Holy Spirit as the believers' "coach." In eternity we will interact with the triune God as mature beings within the moral universe of love and relationship.

How to Teach Rules Effectively to Children

Rules are provided by an authority figure who is wise enough to guide moral behavior and who is able to enforce obedience to the rules. We know much about how to teach rules effectively to children. They can be taught through presentation of propositional statements, such as "We don't hit people" or "Don't whine; ask for what you want." However, much learning occurs through copying models.[19] Thus, children who observe parents saying, "We clean our plate," will also watch to see what the adult does. Does the adult clean his or her plate? If not, then the child will copy the adult's behavior, saying, "We clean our plate," but in fact not cleaning the plate. Children's moral identity is often built around their relationships with those adult models.

Much of the learning during this stage occurs through stories. Reading Scripture or Scripture books to children, even from the earliest ages, delivers moral principles and their applications enjoyably. Fables have been a cherished form of moral education for centuries. Fables tend to end with "The moral of this story is . . ." Middle-childhood children learn the principle by deducing it or from having it verbalized. But also they identify with characters in a moral story and thus form their moral identity as well as learn principles.

Maxims, proverbs and wise sayings are often repeated by parents. Sometimes those sayings are repeated so often they become automatic. As adults we often surprise ourselves and others by bursting forth with one of the sayings that we heard from our parents. Repeating maxims, proverbs and wise sayings seem to work regardless of our age. An editor of a psychological journal once selected me to be featured as a research mentor. Michael McCullough, an excellent psychologist, was once a graduate student who studied under my guidance at Virginia Commonwealth University. We each wrote an account of our mentor-student relationship.[20] Without consulting each other, we both organized the article around sayings I repeated endlessly as Mike was becoming a world-class researcher. Of course, most of Mike's achievements are due to his sheer native ability; mostly, I tried not to interfere too much. I just told him a few things that would make his research easier. Those lessons, often repeated, stuck— even after he had become quite accomplished and had gone on far beyond what I could do.

In the same way, parents tell stories with moral implications about themselves and other people. Children overhear the stories and learn morality through hearing those anecdotes. They not only learn specific behavior and principles, but they also develop moral identities that govern later choices. Adolescents are often curious about what their parents were like when young. They listen and can learn much morality through those stories. The stories help adolescents solidify their own moral identities.

Helping People Internalize Fundamental Values
Remember that moral identity theory suggests that we have an internal moral identity and act morally to try to be consistent with it. A different twist on morality comes out of three social psychological

theories. First, Charles Kiesler[21] suggested a social psychological theory called *commitment theory*. It proposed that people who make a public commitment tend to live up to that commitment more often than do people who make the same commitment privately and tell no one. People internalize what they value, often, simply because they tell others their values or pray their values to God (rather than treasuring them unspoken in their hearts). Similarly, psychologist Daryl Bem[22] proposed *self-perception theory*. Bem argued that when people act, they observe their own behavior just as if it had been another person's behavior. People then make inferences about their internal states on the basis of their observed behavior. So, if a person acts kindly, the person might conclude, "I am a kind person." Note how this reverses the moral identity causality. Bem suggests we develop the moral identity because we act morally; we are not acting morally because we have an already developed identity. Finally, psychologist Leon Festinger[23] proposed *cognitive dissonance theory*. He showed that if a person held an unspoken attitude and was induced to behave contrary to that attitude (without coercion), the person would usually change his or her attitude to be more in line with his or her behavior. Thus, if a person grumpy by nature joins a church that is particularly friendly, the person begins to act friendlier. Before many weeks, the person no longer is grumpy.

Note that these three social psychological theories have in common something that might go against our usual assumptions about human behavior. Each says that our internal and private beliefs are strongly affected by what we see and do. We change our attitudes—often without thinking consciously about them—merely because we have acted differently. Internalization of morality, then, can be strongly affected simply by acting morally. The dark side, though, is that regardless of our avowed Christian beliefs and values, and even our moral identity, if we behave immorally, that will erode our beliefs, values and identity just as quickly.

We can learn a lesson from this. Each of the three social psychological theories has loads of evidence showing the conditions under which it works. In Western culture, we often assume an internal causality that is more in line with moral identity theory. And sometimes that explains our behavior. But sometimes what we do really matters in shaping who we are.

This is why we do not forsake meeting together with other Christians (Heb 10:25), because meeting as a body solidifies our identity as a Christian. We pray always (Eph 6:18), not just because we are Christians but to solidify our identity as Christians. We put on the full armor of God (Eph 6:11-17), not just because we are Christians and are involved in spiritual warfare but to solidify our commitment as Christians. Knowing that both moral identity theory and the social psychological theories of commitment, self-perception and cognitive dissonance are working is a great encouragement to us as Christians.

Understanding How We Struggle at Self-Control

A large literature has developed on understanding human struggles of self-control. In chapter fourteen, we examined some of the recent research by Roy Baumeister on the moral muscle. Let's take a trip farther back. In the 1970s, the behavioral self-control therapeutic approach studied reasons people failed to control themselves. Therapists then developed therapeutic techniques to help people attempt to overcome these self-control problems. One interesting approach was based on research by social psychologist Stanley Schachter[24] in a fascinating article titled "Some Extraordinary Facts About Obese Humans and Rats." Schachter reported a series of studies in which rats had received lesions (i.e., surgical brain damage) to the ventral medial hypothalamus—the part of the brain controlling the offset of eating. Those rats tended to wake up from the brain operation and begin to eat. They fell asleep in their food and woke up eating again. This dynamic phase of weight gain went on usually until the rat was obese. Schachter observed that the literature studying rats found that obese rats (1) ate more good-tasting and less bad-tasting food; (2) ate fewer meals per day, ate more per meal and ate more rapidly; (3) reacted more emotionally; (4) ate more when food was easy to procure and less when it was difficult; (5) did not regulate food consumption when preloaded with solids but did when preloaded with liquids; and (6) were less active than were rats whose brains had not been surgically damaged.

Schachter then set up experiments with obese humans and normal-weight humans to see whether similar findings occurred. For example, in a taste-rating task, humans drank more regular milkshakes than lousy tasting milkshakes—similar to rats (see 1). By observing people at restaurants, Schachter found that obese people ate more of their food and ate it faster than people of normal weight—again similar to the rats (see 2). Obese humans, like the rats, were more emotional (see 3). Obese humans reported more fears on a fear survey than did normal-weight humans (see 3). Schachter found that obese humans would not work hard for food (see 4). While doing a mindless task, people were given a bowl of nuts. In some cases the nuts had to be cracked and shelled. In other cases the nuts were ready to eat. Of twenty obese humans who had to shell nuts, only one ate nuts and nineteen didn't. Of normal-weight people, ten ate and ten didn't. When the nuts were already shelled, nineteen of twenty obese people ate nuts and again only about half of the normal weight people ate (see 4). Schachter also found similarities in whether obese humans would cut down the amount they ate if they drank water before a meal (they did cut back) but not if they ate food (like cheese and crackers) before a meal (they did not cut back) (see 5). Finally, like rats, obese humans were less active than normal-weight humans (see 6).

Faced with these parallels Schachter concluded that overeating that led to obesity might be due to sensitivity to the situation. A behavior therapist, Richard Stuart, helped turn those observations into the popular Weight Watchers program. However, a lot of Big Macs have passed through the alimentary canal since Schachter studied obese rats and humans in 1971. The optimism of weight-control programs has turned into pessimism as people, time and again, lost weight only to regain it. Most studies of self-control as applied to weight loss have shown how woefully weak we are in self-control.[25]

And it is not just with controlling eating that we persistently fail. If we set out to, by grit and by guts, defeat a problem in self-control, we usually fail. Succeeding is less a testimony to our self-control and more a testimony to God's grace or mercy. We need God.

Understanding How the Virtues Relate to Each Other

Jack Berry and I attempted to assess the value that people place on different virtues. We asked how many virtues there are, what relationships there are among the virtues, and whether there is an empirically based classification of virtues.

We defined virtues as the best of human character. When valued by an individual, the virtues can function as goals that shape an individual's self-concept and thus can motivate behavior judged to be consistent with this self-concept. Worthington, Berry and Les Parrott[26] have suggested that many traditional moral virtues can be organized into two broad, functional classes: *warmth-based* and *conscientiousness-based* virtues (see table 15.1 for a listing of each and their definitions). The warmth-based virtues, such as compassion, forgiveness, generosity and gratitude, facilitate the development of warm, affectionate bonds between people. The conscientiousness-based virtues, such as self-control, perseverance and justice, *inhibit* impulsive, selfish and antisocial behavior. This classification of virtues bears a resemblance to two mechanisms underlying socialization of children that have been frequently found in factor analytic studies: parental support and control.[27] These differential parental practices are potentially one means by which different moral identities are formed.

Warmth-based virtues are essentially affective traits involving the capacity for emotional commitments.[28] Conscientiousness-based virtues involve the capacity for what Frank[29] has described as contractual commitments. Warmth-based virtues, then, are backed primarily by emotion systems. Conscientiousness-based virtues are backed by capacities for rationality and self-control.

Daniel Gilbert[30] has suggested that virtues serve social functions. In our thinking, warmth-based virtues reflect ways of maintaining social networks of mutual affection, concern and emotional support. Conscientiousness-based virtues maintain social networks characterized by fair reciprocal exchange, justice and cooperation. Both sets of virtues, when they are valued by communities, serve as counterweights to unconstrained power wrangling and competition over resources.

Table 15.1. Virtues and Their Definitions

1. Justice: treating others with fairness according to what they deserve

2. Self-control: the ability to control our emotions, desires and actions

3. Forgiveness: replacing anger with positive feelings toward someone who hurt or offended us

4. Compassion: sympathizing with the suffering of others

5. Temperance: moderation or self-restraint in desires or actions

6. Courage: facing danger with confidence, resolution and firm control of oneself

7. Patience: ability to endure difficulties with calmness and understanding

8. Humility: lack of vanity, arrogance or self-righteousness

9. Honesty: being truthful and genuine

10. Prudence: wisely and carefully handling practical matters

11. Love: intense affection and warm feelings for others

12. Forbearance: the ability to refrain from acting when it is unwise or unwanted

13. Gratitude: thankfulness for the good things we have received in life

14. Generosity: willingness to give or share

15. Perseverance: persisting in a task, purpose or idea despite obstacles

16. Open-mindedness/docility: being open-minded and willing to learn from others

17. Gentleness: being mild, not harsh, severe or violent

18. Fidelity: being loyal, faithful and trustworthy

Used in studies by Jack W. Berry and Everett L. Worthington Jr., Virginia Commonwealth University; worth-based virtues are 3, 4, 7, 8, 11, 13, 14, 17 and 18.

Understand the Place of Virtue in the Social Order

Virtue implies goodness. But something or someone must define what is good. Psychological science tells us repeatedly that we often set our standards by consulting the behavior and norms set by other people we think are important. Thus, our perception of God, the family, the local church body and the work unit are important in shaping our moral behavior.

Because situations often differ drastically, they can make different demands on our behavior. The work group might require deadened compassion, power politics and self-promotion. The church might emphasize love, compassion, empathy and altruism. The extended family might be bathed in conflict and grudges, calling out justice. We might even see God as angry and vengeful. Life is inconsistent. When we get caught in inconsistent social groups, we feel uncomfortable and are upset. People tend to handle such discrepant emotions by building a wall around the discrepant group. If the church is in conflict, we try to isolate its influence from the rest of our lives. If work is full of conflict, we think, *It's just business.* Or people become miserable and believe they have become hypocritical. They struggle with negative feelings about themselves for their moral failures. They feel depressed, anxious or angry.

Virtue is not just something within us. It is something we measure ourselves against. As such, it depends on a community of faith and a faith tradition shaped by multiple Christian communities. Ideally, we should let God's virtue be our guiding light. We should strive to discern God's will through prayer and reading and studying the Scriptures in each situation. We should employ our rational analytic abilities and consider our community and ask whether warmth-based or conscientiousness-based virtues are called for. We should analyze our own personality and determine which of our possible actions would be most consistent with our moral identity. We should think about the principles of the faith, meditate on those principles, consult with wise mentors and peers, speculate about how our decisions might affect and be affected by the community of faith, and consult our own godly character. *Is my moral decision and my behavior,* we might ask ourselves, *Spirit-controlled or flesh-controlled? Will my actions be fruit of the Spirit or fruit of the flesh?*

Nevertheless, we will make mistakes. We will sometimes profane virtue. Yet if we are repentant, the Lord is merciful to forgive and restore us to loving fellowship.

SUMMARY

The triune God is relational and has created people to have relationships with each other and with God. As we reflect on morality, we marvel at the intricate influences that affect morality. Most of those influences occur in relationships. We learn from parents, who model moral behavior and read us stories. We listen to our parents' personal narratives and use those to shape our behavior and moral identity. We find that morality and virtue are defined by the communities in which we live and act. The more we make Christian communities our focus, the more likely we are to allow those values and beliefs to interpenetrate our lives and influence our decisions.

Even Scripture has come to us mostly in the form of narratives and stories about the ways people interact with each other and with God. We see the successes of human rationality and power. But more often we see the corruptness of rationality and power. Rationality can be turned into a club to beat our adversaries. Power is a snare that entraps the powerful.

Instead we need love as our guiding virtue. Then all the other virtues will fall into line. And even when they don't—and that occurs all too often—we know that the love of God is still our only recourse. We need God. When we finally realize the fruitlessness of self-effort and turn from it, we find Jesus directly behind us with open arms waiting to embrace us.

CAN PSYCHOLOGICAL SCIENCE
HELP US KNOW GOD BETTER?

IN 2005-2006, KIRBY AND I HAD wonderful adventures traveling in both Europe and Asia. Getting away from home has a lot to commend it. That grand adventure allowed us to spend a lot of time together. It dramatized the joys of marriage. We chatted, talked about mundane things, planned our next ten years (the Lord willing), and talked seriously about the things that matter to us in life. We enjoyed intimacy, just being together, and times when we could be comfortably apart.

Communication seems so easy when you are in love, yet there were a few days when we got our wires crossed. Maybe I didn't get my morning coffee and was grumpy. Maybe Kirby got lonely, missing her friends back home, and got clingy. When grumpiness or clinginess met love and support from the other person, our feelings were soon smoothed out. But when my grumpiness met her clinginess, we aggravated each other. It took some time to discuss what was happening and forgive each other. Thank the Lord that it happened only a couple of times, because misunderstandings are no fun.

You might think that after forty years of really good marriage, we would not misunderstand each other. That is why the infrequent misunderstandings are even harder to take. Yet we change as we age, and we don't always change in the same direction or at the same rate. If we didn't walk and talk together as much as we do, I don't know how we would keep up with the many ways we are changing. It would be very hard to maintain a viable marriage.

It is helpful that we have many common interests. We love to walk together. We have logged thousands of miles hiking through mountains, on city sidewalks, through local parks and around our neighborhood. We also learn from each other.

PSYCHOLOGICAL SCIENCE AND RELIGION ARE MARRIED

I'm not sure that science and religion ever really decided to get married. They seemed to drift into marriage like some people coast into deeper relationships. They were interested in similar topics, talked more about the topics as time went on, found common interests, discussed and debated, and eventually saw that many of the values and interests were similar. At times psychological science and religion, as disciplines, have marital spats, engage in a deep interchange or simply pass the time of day. Like Kirby and me, science and religion share intimacy, communicate, work on resolving conflicts, confess shortcomings and failures to each other, and seem committed to dialogue.

There were plenty of times—especially early in the relationship—when it seemed like the two disciplines would part company. (And some in-laws seemed focused on making that happen.) But like partners who couldn't live together or apart, they kept coming back into proximity. Now, the disciplines seem no longer bent on destroying or ignoring each other. They actually seem to be talking more often than not.

PSYCHOLOGICAL SCIENCE AND CHRISTIANITY IN RELATIONSHIP

Psychologists and theologians are at the threshold of studying each other's disciplines, so bilingual experts are available to serve as resources when issues arise. I am writing this book mainly to summarize for the public (and psychologists and theologians) some ways that psychological science can inform Christian theology. To a far lesser extent, I have tried to show how theology could provide research ideas for psychologists or psychologically minded laypeople. I also want to attract psychologists to study theology and theologians to study psychological science. I want to inspire young people to become psychological and theological experts, and to encourage established psychological scientists and theologians to increase their expertise in each other's field so they can be science-religion experts.

Relationships

Marriage is the intimate relationship in which two people commit to each other, invest their lives in each other and in their children, and increase their generativity through strength and mutual support.

Though I have dealt with many relationships in this book—most of it has been about the relationship between Christianity and psychological science. Worldwide, virtually every political conflict involves religion, and people look to science and technology as solutions for many of life's problems. It seems likely that the intersection of religions and psychological science will become increasingly prominent.

The Dance

I commend synchronized efforts. Both psychological science and Christianity help us see more clearly into the unseen world. Both help us respond to Jesus' call. We need more Christians who want to dance with psychological scientists and vice versa.

Through a Mirror Darkly

We now see spiritual things through a mirror darkly, says Paul. But in the end, we will see face to face. It is better to walk by sight—face to face—than by faith. But for now, we have only faith by which to walk. We need God, Jesus and the Holy Spirit to see into the unseen world. Psychological science is an exciting tool that inspires wonder, excites imagination and gives a sense of how orderly God's mind is and how fearfully and wonderfully made we are. Psychological science is a way to try to catch a glimpse of God.

Paul was writing to Greeks when he used the metaphor of seeing God as if through a mirror darkly. But it is not just the absence of light that Paul was referring to. It's far too easy to see our own reflection in a mirror and mistake it for God's.

Many of Paul's readers would have heard Paul's dark-mirror analogy and thought of Plato's cave of shadows. Plato suggested that what we see in the world is like a shadow on a cave wall. The real was obscured, and we could only get a distorted look at either God or nature.

But with apologies to Paul and to Plato, let me suggest another metaphor for viewing the world God created. Imagine looking for God's face through a stained-glass church window. Beams of light are refracted through the stained glass, flooding the building with color. We lift up our eyes to see beauty. We think about the Bible stories told in the windows. We see glimpses of God revealed by the art. We are warmed by the light and drawn to the windows' beauty and order. We marvel at the relationships among the colors and between light and observer. These metaphors—Paul's, Plato's and the stained-glass window—humble us as we seek to peer into the unseen world and see the face of God.

A Brief Excursion into Knowing God Better

Fraser Watts, a cognitive psychologist, ordained clergyman and professor at the University of Cambridge has written discerningly about religious knowing in his book *The Psychology of Religious Knowing.*[1] As Watts and his colleagues[2] reviewed the literature on cognition and motivation, they concluded that information-processing can be experienced as "hot" or "cold." Logical, rational and dispassionate reasoning is experienced mostly as cold head knowledge. Affective, intuitive and automatic reasoning is thinking influenced by hot emotion (often experienced by people as heart knowledge). The English language does not distinguish the two types in a single word—though head and heart knowledge capture the distinction. Other languages embed within them differences between knowing things and knowing people personally. For example, *wissen* and *kennen* (German, to know facts and to know people, respectively), or *savoir* and *connaitre* (French), or *saber* and *conocer* (Spanish) reveal the differences.

Religious knowledge is hot and cold. It is cold when we believe propositions about God, God's interaction with people and the church, and life among people as a consequence of God's existence and presence as an active agent. It is hot, however, when we respond to God emotionally during worship, experience God's presence during prayer or Christian meditation, sense God's presence through the beauty of nature or are filled with awe at the birth of a child. We react emotionally as we seek solace for disappointments, care for harms and wounds, aid in betrayals, and help for times when we feel helpless.

In *The Psychology of Religious Knowing*, Watts and Williams[3] suggest that religious knowing may be unlike other types of knowing (involving either hot or cold knowledge). It may not be simply a set of beliefs about God or simply an emotional experience of relationship with God, but it might involve different types of knowing as well. Religious knowing involves aesthetic knowing. To know beauty, we must simultaneously set aside enough rational analysis to appreciate actual beauty, yet retain enough analytic faculty to not simply dissolve into raw emotion. They liken this type of knowing to that experienced in meditative prayer. Such knowing can lead to insight *and* connection. They find, however, that likening religious knowing to aesthetic appreciation is also inadequate. After all, God is an active, personal agent who changes and interacts with people. But art is more static—or at least not interactive agentively. Second, our information about art comes directly through the senses, but God is incorporeal, and so direct knowledge about God may not be possible through the senses. Third, the consequences of knowing a painting or sculpture, for example, are quite different and relatively inconsequential in comparison to knowing God, who makes claims on our reverence, devotion, love and worship.

Watts and Williams[4] settle on psychotherapy as a helpful metaphor for religious knowing. Knowing in therapy is in many ways a good metaphor for knowing God. Therapy is not a matter of learning propositions about how we should act. It is about taking propositions to heart and experiencing them within an emotional context that motivates behavior, cognition and action.

> The contrast is between insight that is merely intellectual or neutral and a second type of insight that has been variously described as true, effective, dynamic or emotional. . . . Religious insight that, like therapeutic insight, has been chiseled out of experience will have more personal consequences than merely intellectual or "notional" religious insight.[5]

Therapy occurs within a healing context, and God's interaction with us is also within a healing context. Therapy involves an intimate experience of deep sharing. The relationship is among unequals—or at least equals who are in highly prescribed, limited and unequal roles.

We can see that religious knowing is born out of experience. It involves propositional, emotional and *relational* knowledge. It occurs within relationships.

What is the *best* metaphor to capture the relationship-based knowing of God? I'm not sure that psychotherapy is. First, our relationship with a therapist is centered on ourselves, yet our proper relationship with God is primarily centered on love of God. This is like going to therapy to focus most on loving the therapist. Second, the relationship of psychotherapy is limited by a narrow range of roles. The therapist provides care and guidance in healing for the patient. The relationship is not intended to get to know the therapist, so in some ways, a psychotherapeutic metaphor gets things reversed. The marriage metaphor that I've suggested is between equals, which is not accurate to our relationship with God either, but the range of roles we enact in marriage is much more reflective of our range of roles in our relationship with God. Third, while the psychotherapeutic relationship is all about our healing, our relationship with God is not *primarily* about our healing. In fact, even on earth, in our fallen state, the thrust of our lives with God is more about relating to God in every circumstance—healing being just one. We are created for life eternal with the triune God, which after life on earth ends, will not involve healing because tears, pain, conflict and hurts will be gone.

The Science-Religion Dialogue

Most of the writers in the science-religion dialogue have centered on knowing a subject matter—at best, knowing *about* God. The approaches have been mostly propositional. However, emotional connection is not excluded. But God is a God of beauty and order, and that knowledge should inspire awe and wonder, say the cosmologists. God is a God of mystery and novelty, say evolutionary theologians, and that should inspire a sense of adventure. God is a God of compassion, care and love for the sick and sad, say the clinical psychologists, and that should inspire gratitude.

I have tried to show that psychological science can examine the contrails of a God with whom we are in relationship—if we have the eyes to see. I hope that I have helped you see that we can see more of God in surprising ways as we discover more about humans through psychological science.

Some people approach the science-religion dialogue from bottom-up thinking and others from top-down thinking. Some approach it (bottom-up) from the stance of a scientist—with as much objectivity as they can muster. They cannot seek for a complete bottom-up approach. They must have some presuppositions, and those must be a priori and are not derivable from bottom-up scientific observations. For example, a belief that one can meaningfully understand reality by observing physical phenomena is not derivable from science. It is a presupposition to science. I have approached the science-religious dialogue directly and unapologetically as a Christian believer who experiences God as my lover and sees myself as God's committed devotee. From this Christian stance, I can provide an insider's (i.e., Christian) look at the relationships within human psychological functioning, and I hope to stimulate that insider's relationship between you and God.

I have sought to help you know more about people through my selection of studies from psychological science. I have purposefully chosen many of the studies in this book with a secondary goal in mind. I tried to show how unpredictable the results of scientific observations sometimes are. I have tried to help you learn *about* God through understanding some of the contributions of psychological science to theology and life. More important than that, I want to help you *know God better* through psychological science.

Sometimes, scientific explanations sound so impersonal and cold. But I hope you've found that psychological science does not necessarily take the mystery out of life or spiritual experience. Scientific explanations do not eliminate awe and wonder. Instead, they can provide other levels of mystery.

Our amazing abilities to conceptualize, talk to and think of ourselves in relationship with God do not disappear when we understand brain chemistry. They do not diminish when we understand the patterns of neuronal firing underlying consciousness. These new understandings give us something else to be awed at. Even more than a nineteenth-century person could possibly understand, we are indeed fearfully and wonderfully made.

Stanley Milgram's[6] shocking experiments and Roy Baumeister's[7] studies of moral muscle help us realize the frailty of moral will and heighten our sense that we do what we don't want to do and we don't do what we want to do. Thus we should be rightly inspired to redouble our reliance on God, for therein lies our only hope. For who will deliver us but God? In response to God, we also redouble our own effort, because God made us not passive but active agents.

The tools that extend the senses—brain scans, behavioral genetics and statistical methods—do not deaden our spirits. Like the first people to invent the wheel, our spirits are energized. We feel the same excitement as those who invented the telescope and the same wonder as those who invented the microscope. We feel the same intimacy with God as those who developed new spiritual disciplines, which extend people's abilities to experience God more closely and in different ways.

Understanding the power of the justice motive[8] and the different types of forgiveness—decisional and emotional forgiveness[9]—does not make us doubt the adequacy of Scripture. Scientific knowledge of justice and forgiveness add another layer of awe and wonder, understanding, and new, enticing and engaging mysteries. Those new mysteries enrich, not impoverish, life and spirit.

Psychological science does not constrict experiences. It can be an illuminating, informing and enlivening source of *spiritual* experiences which can help us know God the Father, Jesus and the Holy Spirit more deeply, and can add new dimensions to our relationship with the triune God.

Reflect back on the stories and psychological experiments I have described, and ask yourself: Could I have predicted these findings without psychological science, or were many of the findings truly surprising? For instance, could you have predicted that strangers spending fifteen minutes in a person's dorm room could predict the dorm resident's personality more accurately than his or her friends?[10] Nature, and particularly human nature, is God's dormitory room. God leaves signs that reveal some of the divine character, and often in different ways than even direct personal interaction does.

This is true also with marriage. Kirby has left signs, artifacts of her life and relationships in our living space that help me know her better and love her more. Could I love her as much if she hadn't drawn those pictures that hang on our wall? Could I love her as much without the fifty pictures of missionaries and our family members that adorn the refrigerator door that reveal her heart for others? If the house were absolutely sterile, I could live in it, but living with her orderliness and messiness helps me love her in ways that are far deeper than if we related only at the library, park and work. The living space is particularly revealing of her mind and heart.

We know and love each other more *because* we share living space of people and things, not in spite of sharing that space. We could turn a blind eye to noticing all the things within that shared space. But that would not be wise. Rather, we can know and love God's heart better because of the scientific study of humans in our world—that is, the study of God's living places. Psychological science is useful not just for learning about God's creatures and for learning about God, but also for knowing and loving God better.

NOTES

Introduction
[1]Charles E. Hummel, *The Galileo Connection: Resolving Conflicts Between Science and the Bible* (Downers Grove, Ill.: InterVarsity Press, 1986).

[2]Daryl H. Stevenson, Brian E. Eck and Peter C. Hill, eds., *Psychology and Christianity Integration: Seminal Works That Shaped the Movement* (Batavia, Ill.: Christian Association of Psychological Studies, 2007).

[3]Malcolm Jeeves and Warren S. Brown, *Neuroscience, Psychology, and Religion: Illusions, Delusions, and Realities about Human Nature,* Templeton Science and Religion Series (West Conshohocken, Penn.: Templeton Foundation Press, 2009).

[4]Jay E. Adams, *Competent to Counsel* (Philadelphia: Presbyterian and Reformed, 1972).

Chapter 1: Interesting Things About People
[1]John Mordechai Gottman, *What Predicts Divorce? The Relationship Between Marital Processes and Marital Outcomes* (Hillsdale, N.J.: Lawrence Erlbaum Associates, 1994).

[2]F. D. Fincham, J. H. Hall and S. R. H. Beach, "'Til Lack of Forgiveness Doth Us Part: Forgiveness and Marriage," in Everett L. Worthington Jr., ed., *Handbook of Forgiveness* (New York: Brunner-Routledge, 2005), pp. 207-25; Everett L. Worthington Jr., *Hope-Focused Marriage Counseling: A Brief Therapy,* rev. ed. (Downers Grove, Ill.: InterVarsity Press, 2005).

[3]Everett L. Worthington Jr., ed., *Handbook of Forgiveness* (New York: Brunner-Routledge, 2005).

[4]Scott M. Stanley, Thomas N. Bradbury and Howard J. Markman, "Structural Flaws in the Bridge from Basic Research on Marriage to Interventions for Couples," *Journal of Marriage and the Family* 62 (2000): 256-64.

[5]Malcolm Gladwell, *Blink: The Power of Thinking Without Thinking* (New York: Little, Brown, 2005). I am summarizing Gladwell's more extended and entertaining account on pp. 99-146.

[6]Ibid., p. 110.

[7]Cassie Mogilner, Tamar Rudnick and Sheena Iyengar, "The Mere Categorization Effect: How the Presence of Categories Increases Choosers' Perceptions of Assortment Variety and Outcome Satisfaction," *Journal of Consumer Research* 35 (2008): 202-15.

[8]Samuel D. Gosling, Sei Jin Ko, Thomas Mannerelli and Margaret E. Morris, "A Room with a Cue: Personality Judgments Based on Offices and Bedrooms," *Journal of Personality and Social Psychology* 82 (2002): 379-98.

[9]Marianne Bertrand, Dean Karlan, Sendhil Mullainathan, Eldar Sharfir and Jonathan Zinman, "What's Psychology Worth? A Field Experiment in the Consumer Credit Market" <www.princeton.edu/~rpds/downloads/Shafir_2006What's%2Psych %Worth_%20South%20Africa.pdf> described in Ori Brafman and Rom Brafman, *Sway: The Irresistible Pull of Irrational Behavior* (New York: Doubleday, 2008), pp. 85-88.

[10]Barry M. Staw and Ha Hoang, "Sunk Costs in the NBA: Why Draft Order Affects Playing Time and Survival in the NBA," *Administrative Science Quarterly* 40 (1995): 474-94.

Chapter 2: A Tale of Two Cities

[1]Charles Dickens, *A Tale of Two Cities* (New York: Signet Classics, 2007/1859).

[2]Augustine of Hippo, *Of the City of God,* translated by Henri Bettenson (London: Penguin Books, 2003/ca 410).

[3]Francis Schaeffer, *The Francis Schaeffer Trilogy: Three Essential Works in One Volume/ The God Who Is There/Escape from Reason/He Is There, He Is Not Silent* (Wheaton, Ill.: Crossway Books, 1990).

[4]Carl R. Rogers, *Client-Centered Therapy: Its Current Practice, Implications, and Theory* (Boston: Houghton Mifflin, 1951).

[5]Clyde M. Narramore, *The Psychology of Counseling: Professional Techniques for Pastors, Teachers, Youth Leaders and All Who Are Engaged in the Incomparable Art of Counseling* (Grand Rapids: Zondervan, 1960); Bruce S. Narramore, *No Condemnation* (Grand Rapids: Zondervan, 1984); Paul Tournier, *Escape from Loneliness* (Philadelphia: Westminster, 1962); James Dobson, *Dare to Discipline* (New York: Bantam, 1977); Gary R. Collins, *Effective Counseling* (Carol Stream, Ill.: Creation House, 1972).

[6]James R. Beck and Bruce Demarest, *The Human Person in Theology and Psychology: A Biblical Anthropology for the Twenty-First Century* (Grand Rapids: Kregel, 2005).

[7]Ibid., p. 397. Reproduced with permission.

[8]Ibid., p. 20.

[9]Jay E. Adams, *Competent to Counsel* (Philadelphia: Presbyterian and Reformed, 1972).

[10]Jay E. Adams, *The Christian Counselor's Manual* (Grand Rapids: Baker Book House, 1973).

[11]Lawrence J. Crabb Jr., *Basic Principles of Biblical Counseling: Meeting Counseling Needs Through the Local Church* (Grand Rapids: Zondervan, 1975); Lawrence J. Crabb Jr., *Effective Biblical Counseling: A Model for Helping Caring Christians Become Capable Counselors* (Grand Rapids: Zondervan, 1977).

[12]Schaeffer, *Francis Schaeffer Trilogy.*

[13]Everett L. Worthington Jr., *When Someone Asks for Help: A Practical Guide for Counseling* (Downers Grove, Ill.: InterVarsity Press, 1982); Mark R. McMinn, *Psychology,*

Theology and Spirituality in Christian Counseling (Wheaton, Ill.: Tyndale, 1996).

[14]Lawrence J. Crabb Jr., *Effective Biblical Counseling: A Model for Helping Caring Christians Become Capable Counselors* (Grand Rapids: Zondervan, 1977).

[15]John Carter and Bruce S. Narramore, *The Integration of Psychology and Theology* (Grand Rapids: Zondervan, 1979).

[16]H. Richard Niebuhr, *Christ and Culture* (New York: Harper & Row, 1951).

[17]Robert C. Roberts, *Taking the Word to Heart: Self and Other in an Age of Therapies* (Grand Rapids: Eerdmans, 1993).

[18]A. R. Damasio, *Descartes' Error: Emotion, Reason and the Human Brain* (New York: Putnam, 1994).

[19]Eric L. Johnson, *Foundations for Soul Care: A Christian Psychology Proposal* (Downers Grove, Ill.: IVP Academic, 2007).

[20]David Powlison, "Redeeming Psychology Means Learning How to Better Use the Bible in Psychological Work," *Comment*, June 2009, pp. 34-36.

[21]Crabb, *Effective Biblical Counseling*.

[22]Powlison, *Comment*, p. 35.

[23]Ibid.

[24]Ibid.

[25]Ibid., p. 36.

[26]Worthington, *When Someone Asks for Help*.

[27]William James, *The Varieties of Religious Experience: A Study in Human Nature* (Cambridge, Mass.: Harvard University Press, 1985). Original work published 1902.

[28]John Watson, *The Interpretation of Religious Experiences* (Glasgow, Scotland: Gifford Lectures: 1910-1912) <www.giffordlectures.org/>.

[29]John Dewey, "The Quest for Certainty" (Edinburgh: Gifford Lectures, 1928-1929) <www.giffordlectures.org/>.

[30]Malcolm A. Jeeves, *The Scientific Enterprise and Christian Faith* (Downers Grove, Ill: InterVarsity Press, 1969); Malcolm A. Jeeves, ed., *From Cells to Souls and Beyond: Changing Portraits of Human Nature* (Grand Rapids: Eerdmans, 2004); Malcolm A. Jeeves, *Human Nature at the Millennium: Reflections on the Integration of Psychology and Christianity* (Grand Rapids: Baker Books, 1997).

[31]C. Stephen Evans, *Wisdom and Humanness in Psychology* (Grand Rapids: Baker Books, 1989).

[32]David G. Myers, *Introduction to Psychology*, 9th ed. (New York: Worth Publishers, 2010); David G. Myers, *The Pursuit of Happiness: Who Is Happy and Why?* (New York: Avon Books, 1993).

[33]David G. Myers, "A Levels-of-Explanation View," in *Psychology and Christianity: Four Views*, ed. Eric L. Johnson and Stanton L. Jones (Downers Grove, Ill.: InterVarsity Press, 2000), p. 79.

[34]Fraser N. Watts, ed., *Science Meets Faith: Theology and Science in Conversation* (London: SPCK, 1998); Fraser N. Watts and M. Williams, *The Psychology of Religious Knowing* (Cambridge: Cambridge University Press, 1988).

[35]Watts, *Science Meets Faith*, p. 11.

[36]John Polkinghorne, *Science and the Trinity: The Christian Encounter with Reality* (New Haven, Conn.: Yale University Press, 2004).
[37]Ibid., p. 27.

Chapter 3: What Information Can I Trust?

[1]Alexander C. McFarlane and Rachel Yehuda, "Resilience, Vulnerability, and the Course of Posttraumatic Reactions," in *The Effects of Overwhelming Experience on Mind, Body and Society*, ed. Bessel A. Van der Kolk and Alexander C. McFarlane (New York: Guilford Press, 1996), pp. 165-81.
[2]George A. Bonanno, "Resilience in the Face of Potential Trauma," *Current Directions in Psychological Science* 14 (2005): 135-38.
[3]Bonanno, "Resilience in the Face of Potential Trauma," p. 136. Figure 3.1 reproduced with permission.
[4]George A. Bonanno, S. Galea, A. Bucciarelli and D. Vlahov, "Psychological Resilience After Disaster: New York City in the Aftermath of the September 11th Terrorist Attack," *Psychological Science* 17 (2006): 181-86.
[5]For a review, see Bonanno, "Resilience in the Face of Potential Trauma."
[6]George A. Bonanno, A. Papa, K. LaLande, M. Westphal, M. and K. Coifman, "The Importance of Being Flexible: The Ability to Both Enhance and Suppress Emotional Expression Predicts Long-Term Adjustment," *Psychological Science* 15 (2004): 482-87.
[7]Solomon Asch, "Forming Impressions of Personality," *Journal of Abnormal and Social Psychology* 41 (1946): 258-90.

Chapter 4: Why You Might Not Believe What You Don't Already Believe

[1]Barry M. Staw and Ha Hoang. "Sunk Costs in the NBA: Why Draft Order Affects Playing Time and Survival in the NBA," *Administrative Science Quarterly* 40 (1995): 474-94.
[2]Richard E. Nisbett and Dov Cohen, *Culture of Honor: The Psychology of Violence in the South* (Boulder, Colo.: Westview Press, 1996).
[3]Noah J. Goldstein, Steve J. Martin and Robert B. Cialdini, *Yes! 50 Scientifically Proven Ways to Be Persuasive* (New York: Free Press, 2008).
[4]Ibid., p. 22.
[5]Ibid., p. 24.
[6]David Powlison, "Redeeming Psychology Means Learning How to Better Use the Bible in Psychological Work," *Comment,* June 2009, p. 36.
[7]Daniel Gilbert, *Stumbling on Happiness* (New York: Vintage, 2006), p. 245.
[8]P. Cross, "Not Can But Will College Teachers Be Improved?" *New Directions for Higher Education* 17 (1977): 1-15.
[9]D. Walton and J. Bathurst, "An Exploration of the Perceptions of the Average Driver's Speed Compared to Perceived Driver Safety and Driving Skill," *Accident Analysis and Prevention* 30 (1998): 821-30.
[10]L. Larwood and W. Whittaker, "Managerial Myopia: Self-Serving Biases in Organi-

zational Planning," *Journal of Applied Psychology* 62 (1977): 194-98.

[11]J. Kruger, "Lake Woebegone Be Gone! The 'Below-Average Effect and the Egocentric Nature of Comparative Ability Judgments,'" *Journal of Personality and Social Psychology* 49 (1985): 1378-91.

[12]E. Pronin, D. Y. Lin and L. Ross, "The Bias Blind Spot: Perceptions of Bias in Self Versus Others," *Personality and Social Psychology Bulletin* 28 (2001): 369-81.

[13]Gilbert, *Stumbling on Happiness,* p. 253.

[14]Powlison, "Redeeming Psychology," p. 35.

[15]Ibid.

Chapter 5: The Methods of Disciplines

[1]C. S. Lewis. *Mere Christianity (in Christian Behaviour)* (New York: Macmillan, 1943), p. 79.

[2]Francis Schaeffer, *Escape from Reason* (1968; reprint, Downers Grove, Ill.: InterVarsity Press, 2006), p. 35. Adapted with permission.

Chapter 6: A Relational Model

[1]Roger W. Sperry, "A Modified Concept of Consciousness," *Psychological Review* 76 (1969): 532-36; Roger W. Sperry, "Bridging Science and Values: A Unifying View of Mind and Brain," *American Psychologist* 32 (1977): 237-45; Roger W. Sperry, "In Defense of Mentalism and Emergent Interaction," *Journal of Mind and Behavior* 12 (1991): 221-46.

[2]Michael Polanyi, *The Tacit Dimension* (Garden City, N.Y.: Doubleday Anchor Books, 1967); Michael Polanyi, "Life's Irreducible Structure," *Science* 160 (1968): 1308-12.

[3]C. S. Lewis, "The Laws of Nature," in Walter Hooper, ed., *God in the Dock: Essays on Theology and Ethics* (Grand Rapids: Eerdmans, 1970), pp. 76-79.

[4]Bernard I. Murstein, *Paths to Marriage* (Beverly Hills, Calif.: Sage Publications, 1986).

[5]Caryl E. Rusbult and Paul A. M. Van Lange, "Interdependence, Interaction and Relationships," *Annual Review of Psychology* 54 (2003): 351-75.

[6]Augustine of Hippo, *Confessions,* trans. Rex Warner (New York: Penguin Books, 1963).

[7]Ian G. Barbour, *When Science Meets Religion* (New York: HarperCollins, 2000).

Chapter 7: Understanding the Relational Partners

[1]S. I. Hayakawa and A. R. Hayakawa, *Language in Thought and Action,* 5th ed. (Orlando, Fla.: Harcourt, 1990).

[2]Hendrika Vande Kemp, "Dangers of Psychologism: The Place of God in Psychology," *Journal of Psychology and Theology* 14 (1986): 97-109.

[3]Michael Polanyi, *The Tacit Dimension* (Garden City, N.Y.: Doubleday Anchor Books, 1967).

[4]Karl Popper, *The Logic of Scientific Discovery* (New York: Basic Books, 1959).

[5]Thomas S. Kuhn, *The Structure of Scientific Revolutions,* 2nd ed. (Chicago: University of Chicago Press, 1970).

[6]Imre Lakatos, *The Methodology of Scientific Research Programmes: Philosophical Papers, Volume 1* (Cambridge: Cambridge University Press, 1978).

[7]Greg Allison, "Describing Theology," paper presented at the meeting of the American Association of Christian Counselors, Dallas, February 2005.

[8]E. P. Sanders, *Paul and Palestinian Judaism: A Comparison of Patterns of Religion* (Minneapolis: Fortress, 1977).

[9]Abraham Kuyper, Stone Lectures on Calvinism (Princeton University), pp. 130-32 <www.kuyper.org/main/publish/books_essays/article_17.shtml?page=all>.

[10]Malcolm A. Jeeves, *Human Nature at the Millennium: Reflections on the Integration of Psychology and Christianity* (Grand Rapids: Baker Book House, 1997).

Chapter 8: Dealing with Some Challenges

[1]John Carter and Bruce S. Narramore, *The Integration of Psychology and Theology* (Grand Rapids: Zondervan, 1979); Lawrence J. Crabb Jr., *Basic Principles of Biblical Counseling: Meeting Counseling Needs Through the Local Church* (Grand Rapids: Zondervan, 1975).

[2]Edward M. Smith, *Theophostic Prayer Ministry: Basic Seminar Manual 2007,* 5th ed. (Cambellsville, Ky.: New Creations Publishing, 2007).

[3]As a sampling, see Everett L. Worthington Jr., *When Someone Asks for Help: A Practical Guide for Counseling* (Downers Grove, Ill.: InterVarsity Press, 1982); Everett L. Worthington Jr., *Marriage Counseling: A Christian Approach to Counseling Couples* (Downers Grove, Ill.: InterVarsity Press, 1989); Everett L. Worthington Jr., *Forgiving and Reconciling: Bridges to Wholeness and Hope* (Downers Grove, Ill.: InterVarsity Press, 2003).

[4]Lawrence J. Crabb Jr., *Basic Principles of Biblical Counseling: Meeting Counseling Needs Through the Local Church* (Grand Rapids: Zondervan, 1975).

[5]Worthington, *When Someone Asks for Help.*

[6]Daniel Kahneman and Amos Tversky, "Choices, Values and Frames," *American Psychologist* 39 (1984): 341-50.

[7]Eric L. Johnson, *Foundations for Soul Care: A Christian Psychology Proposal* (Downers Grove, Ill.: IVP Academic, 2007).

[8]Ibid., p. 99.

[9]Ibid.

[10]Ibid.

[11]G. K. Chesterton, *Orthodoxy* (Chicago: Moody Publishers, 2009). Originally published by Dodd, Mead & Co., 1908.

[12]Johnson, *Foundations,* pp. 97-98.

Chapter 9: Psychological Science Provides a New Tool

[1]Thomas Kuhn, *The Structure of Scientific Revolutions* (Chicago: University of Chicago Press, 1996).

[2]Peter Galison, *Einstein's Clocks, Poincare's Maps: Empires of Time* (New York: Norton, 2003).

[3]Kuhn, *Structure*.

[4]Thomas Kuhn, *The Essential Tension: Selected Studies in Scientific Tradition and Change* (Chicago: University of Chicago Press, 1977).

[5]Galison, *Einstein's Clocks*.

[6]Martin E. P. Seligman and Mihaly Csikszentmihalyi, "Positive Psychology: An Introduction," *American Psychologist* 55 (2000): 5-14.

Chapter 10: Psychological Science Is Limited

[1]Everett L. Worthington Jr., "Progress in Physics and Psychological Science Affects the Psychology of Religion and Spirituality," in Lisa Miller, ed., *Oxford Handbook of the Psychology of Religion and Spirituality* (New York: Oxford University Press, in press).

[2]For a summary, see David G. Myers, *Social Psychology*, 9th ed. (New York: McGraw-Hill, 2008).

[3]Elizabeth F. Loftus and G. R. Loftus, "On the Permanence of Stored Information in the Human Brain," *American Psychologist* 35 (1980): 409-20.

[4]William Hirst, Elizabeth A. Phelps, Randy L. Buckner, Andrew E. Budson, Alexandru Cuc, John D. E. Gabrieli, Marcia K. Johnson, Cindy Lustig, Keith B. Lyle, Mara Mather, Robert Meksin, Karen J. Mitchell, Kevin N. Ochsner, Daniel L. Schacter, Jon S. Simons and Chandan J. Vaidya, "Long-Term Memory for the Terrorist Attack of September 11: Flashbulb Memories, Event Memories, and the Factors That Influence Their Retention," *Journal of Experimental Psychology: General* 138 (2009): 161-76.

[5]Ibid.

[6]Malcolm Jeeves and Warren S. Brown, *Neuroscience, Psychology, and Religion: Illusions, Delusions, and Realities about Human Nature,* Templeton Science and Religion Series (West Conshohocken, Penn.: Templeton Foundation Press, 2009).

[7]C. S. Lewis, "Transposition," *The Weight of Glory and Other Addresses* (Grand Rapids: Eerdmans, 1965). Originally published by The Macmillan Company, 1949.

[8]Edwin A. Abbott, *Flatland: A Romance of Many Dimensions* (New York: Dover Publications, 1952). Originally published under the pseudonym A. Square (London: Seeley & Co., Ltd., 1884).

[9]C. S. Lewis, *The Silver Chair* (New York: Macmillan, 1953).

Chapter 11: Psychological Science Strengthens Theological Claims

[1]Melvin J. Lerner, *The Belief in a Just World* (New York: Plenum, 1980); Melvin J. Lerner and G. Mikula, eds., *Entitlement and the Affectional Bond: Justice in Close Relationships* (New York: Plenum, 1994).

[2]Mihaly Csikszentmihalyi, *Flow: The Psychology of Optimal Experience* (New York: Harper Perennial, 1980).

[3]John Darley, "Just Punishments: Research on Retributional Justice," in *The Justice*

Motive in Everyday Life, ed. M. Ross and Dale T. Miller (New York: Cambridge University Press, 2002), pp. 314-33.

[4]Ernst Fehr and Klaus Schmidt, "The Economics of Fairness, Reciprocity, and Altruism—Experimental Evidence and New Theories," in *Handbook of the Economics of Giving, Altruism, and Reciprocity, vol. 1: Foundations*, ed. S.-C. Kolm and J. M. Ythier (New York: Elsevier Science, 2006), pp. 615-91; Ernst Fehr and Simon Gächter, "Altruistic Punishment in Humans," *Nature* 415 (2002): 137-40.

[5]Everett L. Worthington Jr., Andrea J. Lerner, Constance B. Sharp and Jeffrey Sharp, "Interpersonal Forgiveness as an Example of Loving One's Enemies," *Journal of Psychology and Theology* 34 (2006): 32-42.

[6]Steven G. Post, "Altruism, Happiness, and Health: It's Good to be Good," *International Journal of Behavioral Medicine* 12 (2005): 66-77; Steven G. Post, Lynn G. Underwood, Jeffrey P. Schloss and William B. Hurlbut, *Altruism and Altruistic Love* (Oxford: Oxford University Press, 2002).

[7]C. Daniel Batson, *The Altruism Question: Toward a Social-Psychological Answer* (Hillsdale, N.J.: Lawrence Erlbaum Associates, 1991).

[8]Stephen J. Pope, *The Evolution of Altruism and the Ordering of Love* (Washington, D.C.: Georgetown University Press, 1994).

[9]John M. Darley and Bibb Latane, "Bystander Intervention in Emergencies: Diffusion of Responsibility," *Journal of Personality and Social Psychology* 8 (1968): 377-83.

[10]Robert B. Cialdini, *Influence: Science and Practice*, 4th ed. (Boston: Allyn & Bacon, 2001).

[11]John M. Darley and C. Daniel Batson, "'From Jerusalem to Jericho': A Study of Situational and Dispositional Variables in Helping Behavior," *Journal of Personality and Social Psychology* 27 (1973): 100-108.

[12]Konrad Lorenz, *On Aggression* (Fort Washington, Penn.: Harvest Books, 1966).

[13]M. Scott Peck, *People of the Lie: The Hope for Healing Human Evil* (New York: Simon & Schuster, 1983).

[14]Robert Hare, *Without Conscience: The Disturbing World of the Psychopaths Among Us* (New York: Guilford Press, 1999).

[15]Roy F. Baumeister, *Evil: Inside Human Violence and Cruelty* (New York: Henry Holt, 2001).

[16]Julie J. Exline and A. Martin, "Anger Toward God: A New Frontier in Forgiveness Research," in *Handbook of Forgiveness*, ed. Everett L. Worthington Jr. (New York: Brunner-Routledge, 2005), pp. 73-88; Benjamin T. Wood, Everett L. Worthington Jr., Julie J. Exline, Ann Marie Yali, Jamie D. Aten and Mark R. McMinn, "Development, Refinement, and Psychometric Properties of the Attitudes Toward God Scale (ATGS-9)," *Psychology of Religion and Spirituality* 2 (2010).

[17]Mickie L. Fisher and Julie J. Exline, "Self-Forgiveness Versus Excusing: The Roles of Remorse, Effort, and Acceptance of Responsibility," *Self and Identity* 5 (2006): 127-46; Julie H. Hall and Frank D. Fincham, "Self-Forgiveness: The Stepchild of Forgiveness Research," *Journal of Social and Clinical Psychology* 24 (2005): 621-37; Julie H. Hall and Frank D. Fincham, "The Temporal Course of Self-Forgiveness,"

Journal of Social & Clinical Psychology 27 (2008): 174-202; Everett L. Worthington Jr., *A Just Forgiveness: Responsible Healing Without Excusing Injustice* (Downers Grove, Ill.: IVP Books, 2009).

[18]June P. Tangney, A. L. Boone and R. Dearing, "Forgiving the Self: Conceptual Issues and Empirical Findings," in *Handbook of Forgiveness*, ed. Everett L. Worthington Jr. (New York: Brunner-Routledge, 2005), pp. 143-58.

[19]Hall and Fincham, "Self-Forgiveness: The Stepchild of Forgiveness Research"; Hall and Fincham, "The Temporal Course of Self-Forgiveness."

[20]Terry D. Cooper, *Sin, Pride and Self-Acceptance: The Problem of Identity in Theology and Psychology* (Downers Grove, Ill.: InterVarsity Press, 2003).

[21]Carl R. Rogers, *On Becoming a Person: A Therapist's View of Psychotherapy* (London: Constable, 1961).

[22]Roy F. Baumeister, L. Smart and J. M. Boden, "Relation of Threatened Egotism to Violence and Aggression: The Dark Side of High Self-Esteem," *Psychological Review*, 103 (1996): 5-33.

[23]Morton Deutsch, "Cooperation, Conflict, and Justice," in *Advances in Field Theory*, ed. Susan A. Wheelan, Emmy A. Pepitone and Vicki Abt (Thousand Oaks, Calif.: Sage Publications, 1990), pp. 149-64.

[24]Roy F. Baumeister and Brad J. Bushman, *Social Psychology and Human Nature: Brief Version* (Monterey, Calif.: Wadsworth, 2008), p. 314.

[25]Richard E. Nisbett and Dov Cohen, *Culture of Honor: The Psychology of Violence in the South* (Boulder, Colo.: Westview Press, 1996).

[26]Linda Waite and Maggie Gallagher, *The Case for Marriage* (New York: Doubleday, 2001).

[27]Robert J. Sternberg, "A Triangular Theory of Love," *Psychological Review* 92 (1986): 119-35.

[28]Audrey R. Chapman and B. Spong, eds., *Religion and Reconciliation in South Africa* (Philadelphia: Templeton Foundation Press, 2003).

[29]Ed Cairns, Tania Tam, Miles Hewstone and Ulrike Niens, "Intergroup Forgiveness and Intergroup Conflict: Northern Ireland, A Case Study," in *Handbook of Forgiveness*, ed. Everett L. Worthington Jr. (New York: Brunner-Routledge, 2005), pp. 461-75.

[30]Ervin Staub, "Constructive Rather than Harmful Forgiveness, Reconciliation, and Ways to Promote Them After Genocide and Mass Killing," in *Handbook of Forgiveness*, ed. Everett L. Worthington Jr. (New York: Brunner-Routledge, 2005), pp. 443-59.

[31]Muzafer Sherif, O. J. Harvey, B. J. White, W. R. Hood and C. W. Sherif, *Intergroup Conflict and Cooperation: The Robbers Cave Experiment* (Norman: University of Oklahoma Book Exchange, 1961).

[32]Cairns et al., "Intergroup Forgiveness and Intergroup Conflict: Northern Ireland."

[33]Exline and Martin, "Anger Toward God"; Wood et al., "Development, Refinement, and Psychometric Properties of the Attitudes Toward God Scale (ATGS-9)."

[34]Viktor Frankl, *Man's Search for Meaning: An Introduction to Logotherapy* (Boston: Beacon Press, 1959).

[35]Dan P. McAdams and E. de St. Aubin, eds., *Generativity and Adult Development: How and Why We Care for the Next Generation* (Washington, D.C.: American Psychological Association, 1998).

[36]Ibid.

[37]Annette Mahoney, Mark S. Rye and Kenneth I. Pargament, "When the Sacred Is Violated: Desecration as a Unique Challenge to Forgiveness," in *Handbook of Forgiveness*, ed. Everett L. Worthington Jr. (New York: Brunner-Routledge, 2005), pp. 57-72.

[38]Gerald Edelman, *Wider Than the Sky: The Phenomenal Gift of Consciousness* (New Haven, Conn.: Yale University Press, 2004).

Chapter 12: Psychological Science Adds New Ideas to Theology

[1]E. P. Sanders, *Paul and Palestinian Judaism: A Comparison of Patterns of Religion* (Minneapolis: Fortress, 1977).

[2]James D. G. Dunn, *The New Perspective On Paul* (Grand Rapids: Eerdmans, 2007).

[3]N. T. Wright, *Justification* (Downers Grove, Ill.: InterVarsity Press, 2009). This perspective on Paul's writings has generated theological controversy and I recommend reading both Wright's and John Piper's takes on the issue. See also John Piper, *The Future of Justification* (Wheaton, Ill.: Crossway, 2007).

[4]Lewis B. Smedes, *Forgive and Forget: Healing the Hurts We Don't Deserve* (New York: Harper & Row, 1984).

[5]David Augsburger, *Helping People Forgive* (Westminster, Ky.: Westminster John Knox Press, 1996).

[6]L. Gregory Jones, *Embodying Forgiveness: A Theological Analysis* (Grand Rapids: Eerdmans, 1995).

[7]Miroslav Volf, *Free of Charge: Giving and Forgiving in a Culture Stripped of Grace* (Grand Rapids: Zondervan, 2005).

[8]Everett L. Worthington Jr., *Forgiving and Reconciling: Bridges to Wholeness and Hope* (Downers Grove, Ill.: InterVarsity Press, 2003).

[9]Everett L. Worthington Jr. and Fredrick A. DiBlasio, "Promoting Mutual Forgiveness within the Fractured Relationship," *Psychotherapy*, 27 (1990): 219-23.

[10]Fredrick A. DiBlasio, "The Use of Decision-Based Forgiveness Intervention Within Intergenerational Family Therapy," *Journal of Family Therapy* 20 (1998): 77-94.

[11]Everett L. Worthington Jr. and Nathaniel G. Wade, "The Social Psychology of Unforgiveness and Forgiveness and Implications for Clinical Practice," *Journal of Social and Clinical Psychology*, 18 (1999): 385-418.

[12]Worthington, *Forgiving and Reconciling;* Julie J. Exline, Everett L. Worthington Jr., Peter C. Hill and Michael E. McCullough, "Forgiveness and Justice: A Research Agenda for Social and Personality Psychology," *Personality and Social Psychology Review* 7 2003: 337-48.

[13]Everett L. Worthington Jr., *Forgiveness and Reconciliation: Theory and Application* (New York: Brunner-Routledge, 2006).

[14]Everett L. Worthington Jr., Joshua N. Hook, Shawn O. Utsey, John K. Williams and R. L. Neil, "Decisional and Emotional Forgiveness," paper presented at the

International Positive Psychology Summit, Washington D.C., October 5, 2007.

[15]Jacquelin Borg, Bengt Andree, Henrik Soderstrom and Lars Farde, "The Serotonin System and Spiritual Experiences," *American Journal of Psychiatry* 160 (2003): 1965-69.

[16]Karl Popper, *The Logic of Scientific Discovery* (New York: Basic Books, 1959).

[17]Michael H. Kernis, D. P. Cornell, C.-R. Sun, A. Berry and T. Harlow, "There's More to Self-Esteem than Whether It Is High or Low: The Importance of Stability of Self-Esteem," *Journal of Personality and Social Psychology* 65 (1993): 1190-1204.

[18]Roy F. Baumeister, L. Smart and J. M. Boden, "Relation of Threatened Egotism to Violence and Aggression: The Dark Side of High Self-Esteem," *Psychological Review*, 103 (1996): 5-33.

[19]Thomas L. Friedman, *The World Is Flat: A Brief History of the Twenty-First Century* (New York: Farrar, Strauss and Giroux, 2005).

[20]Kenneth Gergen, *The Saturated Self: Dilemmas of Identity in Contemporary Life*, 2nd ed. (New York: Basic Books, 2001).

[21]Dan P. McAdams and E. de St. Aubin, eds., *Generativity and Adult Development: How and Why We Care for the Next Generation* (Washington, D.C.: American Psychological Association, 1998).

[22]Colin E. Gunton, *The One, the Three and the Many: God, Creation, and the Culture of Modernity* (Cambridge: Cambridge University Press, 1993).

[23]Wolfhart Pannenberg, "Human Life: Creation Versus Evolution?" in Ted Peters, ed., *Science and Theology* (Boulder, Colo.: Westview Press, 1998), pp. 138-39.

Chapter 13: Psychological Science Addresses Theologically Hot Social Controversies

[1]Michael Scherer, Kathryn Cooke and Everett L. Worthington Jr., "Bibliography of Professional Articles on Forgiveness," in *Handbook of Forgiveness*, ed. Everett L. Worthington Jr. (New York: Brunner-Routledge, 2005), pp. 507-56.

[2]Mickie L. Fisher and Julie J. Exline, "Self-Forgiveness Versus Excusing: The Roles of Remorse, Effort, and Acceptance of Responsibility," *Self and Identity* 5 (2006): 127-46.

[3]Julie H. Hall and Frank D. Fincham "Self-Forgiveness: The Stepchild of Forgiveness Research," *Journal of Social and Clinical Psychology* 24 (2005): 621-37.

[4]Julie H. Hall and Frank D. Fincham, "The Temporal Course of Self-Forgiveness," *Journal of Social & Clinical Psychology* 27 (2008): 174-202.

[5]David G. Myers, *The Pursuit of Happiness: Who Is Happy and Why?* (New York: Avon Books, 1993).

[6]Robert M. Sapolsky, *Why Zebras Don't Get Ulcers: A Guide to Stress, Stress-Related Diseases, and Coping* (New York: Freeman, 1994).

[7]Michael Casey, *Fully Human, Fully Divine: An Interactive Christology* (Liguori, Mo.: Liguori Publications, 2004), p. 357.

[8]Christian Smith and Patricia Snell, *Souls in Transition: The Religious and Spiritual Lives of Emerging Adults* (New York: Oxford University Press, 2009).

[9]William James, *The Varieties of Religious Experience: A Study in Human Nature* (Cam-

bridge, Mass.: Harvard University Press, 1985). (Original work published 1902.)

[10]David Shenk, *The Genius in All of Us: Why Everything You've Been Told about Genetics, Talent and IQ Is Wrong* (New York: Random House, 2010).

[11]Roy F. Baumeister, E. Bratslavsky, M. Muraven and Diane M. Tice, "Ego Depletion: Is the Active Self a Limited Resource?" *Journal of Personality and Social Psychology* 74 (1998): 1252-65.

[12]Smith and Snell, *Souls in Transition*.

[13]Bill Bright, *The Four Spiritual Laws* (Orlando, Fla.: Campus Crusade for Christ, 1952).

[14]Donald E. Miller and Tetsunao Yamamori, *Global Pentecostalism: The New Face of Christian Social Engagement* (Berkeley: University of California Press, 2007).

[15]Randy J. Larsen and Ed Diener, "Affect Intensity as an Individual Difference Characteristic: A Review," *Journal of Research in Personality* 21 (1987): 1-39.

[16]Stanley Milgram, *Obedience to Authority* (New York: Harper & Row, 1974).

[17]Kenneth Gergen, *The Saturated Self: Dilemmas of Identity in Contemporary Life*, 2nd ed. (New York: Basic Books, 2001).

[18]Linda Waite and Maggie Gallagher, *The Case for Marriage* (New York: Doubleday, 2001).

[19]Andrew Cherlin, *Marriage, Divorce, Remarriage*, revised and enlarged (Cambridge, Mass.: Harvard University Press, 1992).

[20]M. Clements, "Sex in America Today: A New National Survey Reveals How Our Attitudes Are Changing," *Parade Magazine*, August 7, 1994, pp. 4-6.

[21]Michael W. Wiederman, "Extra-Marital Sex: Prevalence and Correlates in a National Survey," *Journal of Sex Research* 34 (1997): 167-74.

[22]P. R. Amato and S. J. Rogers, "A Longitudinal Study of Marital Problems and Subsequent Divorce," *Journal of Marriage and the Family* 59 (1997): 612-24.

[23]Smith and Snell, *Souls in Transition*.

[24]Everett L. Worthington Jr., *A Just Forgiveness: Responsible Healing Without Excusing Injustice* (Downers Grove, Ill.: IVP Books, 2009).

[25]Gus Martin, *Understanding Terrorism: Challenges, Perspectives, and Issues*, 3rd ed. (Thousand Oaks, Calif.: Sage Publications, 2010).

[26]Scherer, Cooke and Worthington, "Bibliography of Professional Articles on Forgiveness."

Chapter 14: Psychological Science Helps Us Understand Victorious Living

[1]Joshua D. Greene, R. B. Sommerville, L. E. Nystrom, John M. Darley and Jonathan D. Cohen, "An fMRI Investigation of Emotional Engagement in Moral Judgment," *Science* 293 (2001): 2105-108.

[2]Konrad Lorenz, *On Aggression* (Fort Washington, Penn.: Harvest Books, 1966).

[3]A. R. Damasio, *Descartes' Error: Emotion, Rationality and the Human Brain* (New York: Putnam, 1994).

[4]Roy F. Baumeister, E. Bratslavsky, M. Muraven and Diane M. Tice, "Ego Depletion: Is the Active Self a Limited Resource?" *Journal of Personality and Social Psychol-*

ogy 74 (1998): 1252-65.

[5]Stanley Milgram, *Obedience to Authority* (New York: Harper & Row, 1974).

[6]Solomon Asch, "Opinions and Social Pressure," *Scientific American* 193 (1955): 31-35.

[7]Muzafer Sherif, *The Psychology of Social Norms* (New York: HarperCollins, 1936).

[8]Milgram, *Obedience to Authority*.

[9]Melvin J. Lerner, *The Belief in a Just World* (New York: Plenum, 1980).

[10]D. A. Baldwin, "Priorities in Children's Expectations about Object Label Reference: Form Over Color," *Child Development* 60 (1989): 1291-306.

[11]K. Daniel O'Leary, "The Effects of Self-Instruction on Immoral Behavior," *Journal of Experimental Child Psychology* 6 (1968): 297-301.

[12]J. Monahan and K. Daniel O'Leary, "The Effects of Self-Instruction on Rule-Breaking Behavior," *Psychological Reports* 29 (1971): 1059-66.

[13]Becky A. Bailey, *Easy to Love, Difficult to Discipline: The Seven Basic Skills for Turning Conflict into Cooperation* (New York: HarperCollins, 2000).

[14]Donald H. Meichenbaum, *Cognitive-Behavior Modification: An Integrative Approach* (New York: Plenum, 1977).

[15]Jerome Kagan, *The Nature of the Child*, 10th anniversary ed. (New York: Basic Books, 1984).

[16]Arnold J. Sameroff and Marshall M. Haith, eds., *The Five to Seven Year Shift: The Age of Reason and Responsibility* (Chicago: University of Chicago Press, 1996).

[17]Lawrence J. Kohlberg, *The Psychology of Moral Development: The Nature and Validity of Moral Stages*, vol. 2 (San Francisco: Harper & Row, 1984).

[18]Carol Gilligan, *In a Different Voice: Psychological Theory and Women's Development* (Cambridge, Mass.: Harvard University Press, 1993).

[19]David F. Bjorkland, *Children's Thinking: Developmental Function and Individual Differences*, 3rd ed. (Monterey, Calif.: Wadsworth, 1999); see also John H. Flavell, "Development of Children's Knowledge about the Mental World," *International Journal of Behavioral Development* 4 (2000): 15-23.

[20]Flavell, "Development of Children's Knowledge."

[21]Joan Peskin, "Ruse and Representations: On Children's Ability to Conceal Information," *Developmental Psychology* 28 (1992): 84-89; Joan Peskin, "Guise and Guile: Children's Understanding of Narratives in Which the Purpose of Pretense is Deception," *Child Development* 67 (1996): 1735-51.

[22]Milgram, *Obedience to Authority*.

[23]Ibid.

[24]Greene et al., "An fMRI Investigation of Emotional Engagement in Moral Judgment."

[25]Milgram, *Obedience to Authority*.

Chapter 15: Psychological Science Helps Us Live More Virtuously
[1]Jean Piaget, *The Moral Judgment of the Child* (London: Kegan Paul, Trench, Trubner and Co., 1932).

[2]Lawrence J. Kohlberg, *The Psychology of Moral Development: The Nature and Validity of Moral Stages*, vol. 2 (San Francisco: Harper & Row, 1984).

[3]Carol Gilligan, *In a Different Voice: Psychological Theory and Women's Development* (Cambridge, Mass.: Harvard University Press, 1993).

[4]Lawrence J. Walker and Russell C. Pitts, "Naturalistic Conceptions of Moral Maturity," *Developmental Psychology* 34 (1998): 403-19.

[5]Solomon Schimmel, *The Seven Deadly Sins* (Oxford: Oxford University Press, 1997).

[6]Alasdair MacIntyre, *After Virtue*, 3rd ed. (South Bend, Ind.: University of Notre Dame Press, 2007).

[7]Karl Aquino and A. R. Reed, "The Self-Importance of Moral Identity," *Journal of Personality and Social Psychology* 83 (2002): 1423-40.

[8]Robert A. Emmons, *The Psychology of Ultimate Concerns: Motivation and Spirituality in Personality* (New York: Guilford Press, 2000).

[9]Chris Peterson and Martin E. P. Seligman, *Character Strengths and Virtues: A Handbook and Classification* (Washington, D.C.: American Psychological Association, 2004).

[10]Vincent Jeffries, "Virtue and the Altruistic Personality," *Sociological Perspectives* 4, no. 1 (1998): 151-66.

[11]Steven G. Post, "Altruism, Happiness, and Health: It's Good to be Good," *International Journal of Behavioral Medicine* 12 (2005): 66-77.

[12]Robert D. Enright and Richard P. Fitzgibbons, *Helping Clients Forgive: An Empirical Guide for Resolving Anger and Restoring Hope* (Washington, D.C.: American Psychological Association, 2000).

[13]Robert A. Emmons and Michael E. McCullough, eds., *The Psychology of Gratitude* (New York: Oxford University Press, 2004).

[14]Everett L. Worthington Jr., *Humility: The Quiet Virtue* (Philadelphia: Templeton Foundation Press, 2007).

[15]C. R. Snyder, *The Psychology of Hope: You Can Get There from Here* (New York: The Free Press, 2004).

[16]Paul Gilbert, ed., *Compassion: Nature and Use in Psychotherapy* (East Sussex, U.K.: Psychology Press, 2005), pp. 168-92.

[17]Michael J. Cawley III, James E. Martin and John A. Johnson, "A Virtues Approach to Personality," *Personality and Individual Differences* 28 (2000): 997-1013.

[18]R. Kirby Worthington and Everett L. Worthington Jr., *Value Your Children: Becoming Better Parental Disciple-Makers* (Grand Rapids: Baker Book House, 1996).

[19]Albert Bandura, *Social Learning Theory* (Englewood Cliffs, N.J.: Prentice Hall, 1977).

[20]Everett L. Worthington Jr., "Mentoring: Walking the Path of Life Together," *Journal of Psychology and Christianity* 19 (2000): 359-62; Michael E. McCullough, "Ev Worthington as Mentor: 'It'll Keep You Off the Streets,'" *Journal of Psychology and Christianity* 19 (2000): 355-58.

[21]Charels A. Kiesler and Joseph Sakumura, "A Test of a Model for Commitment,"

Journal of Personality and Social Psychology 3 (1966): 349-53.

[22]Daryl J. Bem, "Self-Perception: An Alternative Interpretation of Cognitive Dissonance Phenomena," *Psychological Review* 74 (1967): 183-200.

[23]Leon Festinger, "Cognitive Dissonance," *Scientific American* 207 (1962): 93-107.

[24]Stanley Schachter, "Some Extraordinary Facts About Obese Humans and Rats," *American Psychologist* 26 (1971): 129-44.

[25]T. Mann, A. J. Tomiyama, E. Westling, A.-M. Lew, B. Samuels and U. J. Chatman, "Medicare's Search for Effective Obesity Treatments: Diets Are Not the Answer," *American Psychologist* 62 (2007): 220-33.

[26]Everett L. Worthington Jr., Jack W. Berry and Les Parrott III, "Unforgiveness, Forgiveness, Religion, and Health," in *Faith and Health: Psychological Perspectives*, ed. T. G. Plante and A. Sherman (New York: Guilford Press, 2001), pp. 107-38.

[27]Diana Baumrind, "Current Patterns of Parental Authority," *Developmental Psychology* 4 (1971): 1-103.

[28]R. M. Nesse, ed., *Evolution and the Capacity for Commitment* (New York: Russell Sage Press, 2001).

[29]R. Frank, "Cooperation Through Emotional Commitment," in R. M. Nesse, *Evolution and the Capacity for Commitment* (New York: Russell Sage Press, 2001), pp. 57-76.

[30]Daniel Gilbert, *Stumbling on Happiness* (New York: Vintage, 2006), p. 245.

Chapter 16: Can Psychological Science Help Us to Know God Better?

[1]F. N. Watts and M. Williams, *The Psychology of Religious Knowing* (Cambridge: Cambridge University Press, 1988).

[2]Ibid.

[3]Ibid.

[4]Ibid.

[5]Ibid., pp. 72-74.

[6]Stanley Milgram, *Obedience to Authority* (New York: Harper & Row, 1974).

[7]Roy F. Baumeister, E. Bratslavsky, M. Muraven and Diane M. Tice, "Ego Depletion: Is the Active Self a Limited Resource?" *Journal of Personality and Social Psychology* 74 (1998): 1252-65.

[8]Melvin J. Lerner, *The Belief in a Just World* (New York: Plenum, 1980).

[9]Everett L. Worthington Jr., *Forgiving and Reconciling: Bridges to Wholeness and Hope* (Downers Grove, Ill.: InterVarsity Press, 2003).

[10]Samuel D. Gosling, Sei Jin Ko, Thomas Mannerelli and Margaret E. Morris, "A Room with a Cue: Personality Judgments Based on Offices and Bedrooms," *Journal of Personality and Social Psychology*, 82 (2002): 379-98.

Author Index

Abbott, Edwin A., 287
Adam, 91
Adams, Jay, 37, 40, 281-82
Alexander, Denis, 5
Allison, Greg, 286
Amato, P. R., 292
Andree, Bengt, 291
Aquino, Karl, 294
Aristotle, 83, 259
Asch, Solomon, 52-53, 192, 242-43, 284, 293
Augsburger, David, 290
Augustine (of Hippo), 31-32, 45, 101, 137
Bacon, Francis, 33
Bailey, Becky, 248, 293
Baldwin, D. A., 293
Bandura, Albert, 294
Barbour, Ian, 102, 285
Barkley, Charles, 57
Barrow, John, 5
Barth, Karl, 45, 124
Bathurst, J., 284
Batson, Daniel, 288
Baumeister, Roy, 187-89, 210, 241-42, 266, 288-92, 295
Baumrind, Diana, 294
Beach, S. R. H., 281
Beck, James, 35-36, 282
Bem, Daryl, 265, 295
Bentham, Jeremy, 183
Berry, A., 291
Berry, Jack, 268-69, 290, 295
Bertrand, Marianne, 282
Bjorkland, David F., 293
Boden, J. M., 289, 291
Bonanno, George A., 49-52, 131, 284
Boone, A. L., 289
Borg, Jacquelin, 291
Bowie, Sam, 57
Bradbury, Thomas, 17, 281
Brafman, Ori, 29, 282

Brafman, Rom, 282
Bratslavsky, E., 292
Bridgman, Percy, 160
Bright, Bill, 292
Brown, Warren S., 281
Brunner, Emil, 36
Bucciarelli, A., 51, 284
Buckner, Randy L., 287
Budson, Andrew E., 287
Bushman, Brad, 189, 289
Cairns, E., 289
Calvin, John, 32
Carter, John, 38, 283, 286
Casey, Michael, 291
Cawley, Michael J., III, 294
Chapman, Audrey R., 288
Chatman, U. J., 295
Cherlin, Andrew, 292
Chesterton, G. K., 136, 286
Cialdini, Robert, 63-65, 185-86, 284, 286
Clements, M., 292
Cohen, Dov, 61, 142, 184, 289, 292
Coifman, K., 284
Collins, Gary, 34, 282, 292
Comte, Auguste, 160
Cooke, Kathryn, 291-92
Cooper, Terry, 289
Cornell, D. P., 291
Crabb, Larry, 37-38, 40, 282-83, 286
Csikszentmihalyi, Mihaly, 286-87
Cuc, Alexandru, 287
Damasio, Antonio, 238-40, 283, 292
Damasio, Hannah, 238
Darley, John, 183, 186, 287-88, 292
Darwin, Charles,
Dearing, R., 289
Demarest, Bruce, 35-36
de St. Aubin, E., 290-91
Deutsch, Morton, 289
Dewey, John, 283

DiBlasio, Frederick A., 290
Dickens, Charles, 31, 282
Diener, Ed, 292
Dobson, James, 34-35, 282
Dunn, James D. G., 290
Eck, Brian, 281
Edelman, Gerald M., 195-96, 198-99, 201, 290
Emmons, Robert A., 294
Enright, Robert D., 294
Evans, Steven, 42, 283
Eve, 91
Exline, Julie, 187, 193, 219, 288-91
Farde, Lars, 291
Fehr, Ernst, 183-84, 288
Festinger, Leon, 265, 295
Fincham, F. D., 281, 288-89, 291
Fisher, Mickie, 219, 288, 291
Fitzgibbons, Richard P., 294
Flavell, 293
Francis of Assisi, 136
Frank, R., 295
Frankl, Viktor, 193, 289
Freud, Sigmund, 12, 35, 39, 48, 108, 131, 223, 241,
Friedman, Thomas, 212, 291
Gabrieli, John D. E., 287
Gächter, Simon, 288
Gage, Phineas, 237-38, 240,
Galea, S., 51, 284
Galileo, 11, 33, 83, 281
Galison, Peter, 150, 152-53, 287
Gallagher, Maggie, 190, 227, 289, 292
Gates, Bill, 21
Gergen, Kenneth, 212, 226, 291-92,
Gibson, Nicholas, 5
Gilbert, Daniel, 41, 66,

68-70, 143, 268, 284-85, 294-95
Gilbert, Paul, 294
Gilligan, Carol, 251, 261, 294
Gladwell, Malcolm, 19, 22, 142, 281
Goldstein, Noah J., 63, 284
Gosling, Samuel, 23-24, 30, 140, 142, 282, 295
Gottman, John, 17-18, 30, 142, 281
Greene, Joshua, 236, 292-93
Gulliford, Elizabeth, 5
Gunton, Colin, 213-14, 291
Haith, Marshall M., 293
Hall, Judith, 219, 281, 288-89, 291, 294
Hare, Robert, 186, 288
Harlow, T., 291
Harvey, O. J., 289
Hayakawa, S. I., 106, 285
Heap, Brian, 5
Hewstone, M., 289
Hill, Peter C., 281
Hirst, William, 287
Hoang, Ha, 30, 56-58, 142, 282, 284
Hood, W. R., 289
Hugo, Victor, 141
Hume, David, 160
Hummel, Charles, 281
Hurlbut, William B., 288
Iyengar, Sheena, 23, 30, 142, 281
James, William, 41, 223, 283, 291
Jeffries, Vincent, 261, 294
Jeeves, Malcolm, 41-42, 120, 281, 283, 286-87
Job, 91
Johnson, Eric L., 39, 124, 132-34, 138, 283, 286-87, 294
Johnson, John A., 294
Johnson, Marcia K., 287
Jones, L. Gregory, 290
Jordan, Michael, 57

Kagan, Jerome, 249, 293

Kahneman, Daniel, 286

Kant, Immanuel, 183, 258

Karlan, Dean, 29, 282

Kernis, Michael, 210, 291

Kiesler, Charles, 265, 294

Kirby. *See* Worthington, Kirby

Ko, Sei Jin, 282, 295

Kohlberg, Lawrence, 250-51, 259, 261, 293

Kohut, Hans, 127

Kolm, S.-C., 288

Kruger, J., 285

Kuhn, Thomas, 112-13, 150-53, 286-87

Kuyper, Abraham, 119-20, 138, 286

bin Laden, Osama, 22, 195

Lakatos, Imre, 54, 112-14, 134, 286

LaLande, K., 51, 284

Larsen, Randy J., 292

Larwood, L., 285

Latane, Bibb., 288

Lerner, Andrea, 288

Lerner, Melvin, 183, 245, 287, 290, 293, 295

Lew, A.-M. 295

Lewis, C. S., 45, 77-78, 93, 180, 285, 287, 290

Lin, D. Y., 285

Lorenz, Konrad, 186, 236, 288, 292

Lustig, Cindy, 287

Luther, Martin, 32

Luzio, Paul, 5, 9

Lyle, Keith B., 287

MacIntyre, Alasdair, 294

Mahoney, Annette, 195, 290

Mann, T., 295

Mannerelli, Thomas, 282, 295

Markman, Howard, 17, 281

Martin, Gus, 292

Martin, James E., 294

Martin, Steve J., 63, 284, 288-89

Maslow, Abraham, 209

Mather, Mara, 287

McAdams, Dan P., 194, 213, 290-91

McCullough, Michael, 264, 290, 294

McFarlane, 284

McMinn, Mark, 9, 283, 288

Meichenbaum, Don, 248-49, 293

Meskin, Robert, 287

Michelangelo, 141

Milgram, Stanley, 226, 242-44, 255-57, 279, 293, 295

Miller, Dale T., 288

Miller, Donald E., 292

Mitchell, Karen J., 287

Mogilner, Cassie, 281

Monahan, J., 293

Morris, Margaret E., 282, 295

Mullainathan, Sendhil, 29, 282

Muraven, M., 292

Murstein, Bernard, 100-101, 285

Myers, David G., 41, 43, 220-21, 283, 287, 291

Napoleon, 21

Narramore, Bruce S., 34, 38, 282-83, 286

Nesse, R. M., 295

Newton, Isaac, 33, 93, 151

Niebuhr, H. Richard, 38, 283

Niens, U., 289

Nisbett, Richard, 61, 142, 189, 284, 289

Nystrom, L. E., 292

O'Leary, Daniel, 247, 293

Ochsner, Kevin N., 287

Olajuwon, Hakeem, 57

Pannenberg, Wolfhart, 213, 291

Papa, A., 51, 284

Pargament, Kenneth, 195, 290

Parrott, Les, III, 295

Paul, apostle, 75, 81, 93, 98, 124, 137-39, 171, 177, 203, 218, 226, 232, 235, 256, 274-75

Peck, M. Scott, 186, 288

Peskin, Joan, 293

Peterson, Chris, 261, 294

Phelps, Elizabeth, 287

Piaget, Jean, 141, 259, 261, 293

Pitts, Russell C., 294

Plante, T. G., 295

Polanyi, Michael, 92, 112, 161, 169, 285

Polkinghorne, John, 5, 9, 44-45, 284

Pope, Stephen J., 288

Popper, Karl, 112, 161, 169, 286, 291

Post, Steven G., 288

Powlison, David, 40, 41, 65, 71, 283-85

Pronin, E., 285

Reed, A. R., 294

Roberts, Robert C., 39, 283

Rogers, Carl, 33, 35, 127, 188, 209, 282, 289, 292

Ross, L., 285

Rudnick, Tamar, 281

Rusbult, Caryl, 101, 285

Rye, Mark, 195, 290

Sameroff, Arnold J., 292

Samuels, B., 295

Sanders, E. P., 114, 203, 286, 290

Sapolsky, Robert, 221, 291

Sakumura, Joseph, 294

Schachter, Daniel L., 287

Schachter, Stanley, 266-67, 295

Schaeffer, Francis, 37, 45, 79, 80, 282, 285

Scherer, Michael, 218, 234, 291-92

Schimmel, Solomon, 294

Schloss, Jeffrey P., 288

Schmidt, Klaus, 288

Schwarzenegger, Arnold S., 223

Seligman, Martin, 162-63, 261, 287, 294

Sharp, Constance B., 288

Sharp, Jeffrey, 288

Shenk, David, 292

Sherif, Muzafer, 192, 243, 289, 293

Sherman, A., 295

Simons, Jon S., 287

Smart, L., 289, 291

Smedes, Lewis B., 290

Smith, Christian, 222-23, 232, 291-92

Snell, Patricia, 292

Snyder, C. R., 294

Soderstrom, Henrik, 291

Sommerville, R. B., 292

Sperry, Roger, 92, 285

Spong, B., 289

Stanley, Scott, 17, 281

Stannard, Russell, 5

Staub, Ervin, 289

Staw, Barry, 30, 56-58, 142, 282, 284

Sternberg, Robert J., 191, 289

Stevenson, Daryl H., 281

Stockton, John, 57

Stuart, Richard, 267

Sun, C.-R., 291

Tam, T., 289

Tangney, June P., 289

Tchaikovsky, Peter, 141

Tertullian, 137

Thomas Aquinas, 45, 119, 261

Tice, Diane M., 292, 295

Tomiyama, A. J., 295

Tournier, Paul, 34-35, 282

Tversky, Amos, 284

Underwood, Lynn G., 288

Vaidya, Chandan J., 287

Van der Kolk, Bessel A., 284

Van Riper, Paul, 19, 21-22, 30, 142

Vande Kemp, Hendrika, 111, 285

Vlahov, D., 51, 284

Volf, Miroslav, 290

Wade, Nathaniel, 205, 290

Waite, Linda, 190, 227, 289, 292

Walker, Lawrence J., 294

Watson, John, 41, 283

Watts, Fraser, 5, 9, 42-44, 275-76, 283-84, 295

Werner, Emmie, 49

Westling, E., 295

Westphal, M., 51, 284

White, B. J., 289

Whittaker, W., 285

Wiederman, Michael W., 292

Williams, M., 295

Worthington, Everett, 3, 4, 41, 268-69, 281-83, 286-92, 294-95

Worthington, Kirby, 10, 87, 95-98, 102-3, 105, 141, 214, 220, 272-73, 280, 294

Wright, N. T., 203, 290

Yamamori, Tetsunao, 292

Yehuda, 284

Ythier, J. M., 288

Zinman, Jonathan, 29, 282

Zwingli, Ulrich, 32

Subject

abnormal psychology, 162

accountability, 77, 192, 260

adolescent(s), 12, 162, 174, 194, 251, 255, 256, 264

agent(s), 57, 93, 275-76

aggression, aggressive, 61-62, 186-87, 189, 210-11, 236, 288-90, 292

algorithm, 174

altruism, altruistic, 98, 163, 182, 185-86, 192, 211, 221, 261, 270, 287-88, 294

anger, 27, 48, 75, 87,

187-88, 190, 193, 210-11, 230, 247, 249, 269, 288-89, 294

anthropological theology, 114-15, 128, 155, 209

anxiety, 27-28, 48, 234, 249

art(s), 45, 72, 77, 81, 83, 97, 115, 137, 140, 275-76, 282

association, 12, 56, 72, 198, 237, 286, 289, 291, 294

assume, assumption(s), 19, 39, 44, 49, 51, 54, 63, 119-20, 127-28, 130, 133, 138, 156, 172, 177, 188, 207, 209-11, 216, 226, 228, 231, 242, 265

attend, attention, 12, 21, 29, 32, 43, 45, 53, 57, 60-61, 63, 71, 74, 79, 85, 130-31, 143, 154, 163, 178, 197-98, 218, 222, 224, 229, 248, 261

attitude(s), 43, 56, 61, 95, 136, 206, 217, 265, 288-89, 292

attribution(s), 95

authority, authoritative, authorities, 24, 33, 37-38, 56, 111, 133-37, 144, 217, 233, 243, 263, 292-93, 295

availability heuristic, 174

behavior bias, behave, 27, 45, 73, 111-12, 129-31, 149, 162, 173, 193, 202, 212, 238, 265

behavior therapy, behavior therapist, 37, 127, 131, 267

belief bias, 84

belief perseverance, 84-85

belief(s), 19, 34, 38, 42, 51, 54-56, 74, 83-85, 100-101, 113, 125, 130, 135, 144, 163, 176-78, 183, 193, 211, 213, 219, 223,

226-27, 234, 256, 265, 271, 276, 278, 287, 292, 295

Bible, biblical(ly), 4, 34-35, 37-40, 43, 71, 77, 79-80, 83, 113-14, 117, 120, 133-34, 136-38, 142, 144, 154-55, 181, 185, 203, 207-9, 211, 216-17, 219-20, 227, 275, 281-84, 286

biblical theology, 113-14, 155

Big Five, 24, 261

biopsychology, 108, 125

canon, 79, 116, 169

catharsis, cathartic, 48, 51

cause, cause and effect, 32, 38, 92, 95, 106-7, 109, 152, 178, 185, 209, 224

certain, certainty, 17-18, 21, 46, 60, 85, 120, 135, 162, 177-78, 236, 243, 249, 283

change(d), changing, 10-11, 18, 45, 49, 54, 64, 71, 74, 78, 85, 93- 96, 98, 100, 102, 104, 108, 129-30, 134, 150, 152-53, 155, 158-59, 161-62, 164, 168-70, 172-73, 179, 188, 198, 203, 206, 208, 212, 214, 223-26, 228-30, 236-37, 247, 249-50, 255, 263, 265, 272, 276, 283, 292

charismatic, 70, 154

cheat(ed), 247-48

Christ, 13, 34, 38, 86, 98, 101, 105, 139-40, 142, 202, 224, 258, 283, 291

Christian, Christianity, 4, 9, 10-11, 13, 15, 17, 31-43, 45-46, 55-56, 62, 74, 77-79, 86-87, 89-90, 98, 101-3, 105-6, 114-17, 122-26, 128, 131-34, 137, 139, 143-45, 154-55, 163, 177-78,

180, 185, 190-91, 194-95, 207, 213, 217, 219, 222-25, 227, 232-33, 259-62, 265-66, 270-71, 273-75, 278, 282-86, 291, 294

church, 11, 32, 34, 43, 76-79, 85, 98, 115, 117, 134-35, 137, 154-55, 163, 169, 171, 181, 193, 195, 201, 203-4, 217-18, 222, 224, 232-33, 265, 269-70, 275, 282, 286

circuit(s), 198, 224

City of God, 31-32, 45, 282

clinical science, 10, 13, 55, 115, 125-26

cognition, 95, 130, 275-76

cognitive dissonance theory, 265

cognitive neuroscience, 162

cognitive psychology, 84

cognitive-behavior therapy, 37

commit, commitment, 43-44, 74, 89, 96, 101-2, 163, 179, 190-91, 194, 224, 227-31, 233, 260, 265-66, 268, 273-74, 278, 294-95

communication, communicate, 20, 22, 79, 81, 87, 89, 91-92, 95-96, 124, 140, 144, 180, 190, 208, 229, 233, 256, 262, 272-73

community, communities, 12, 28-29, 34-35, 59, 65, 74, 78, 115, 135, 141, 155, 163, 169, 190-91, 222, 230, 237, 259-60, 268, 270-71

compassion, 88, 92, 95, 98, 125, 132, 163, 191, 260-61, 268-70, 277, 294

confession(s), 38, 101,

135, 195, 285
confirmation bias,
confirm, 53, 84-85,
112, 130, 175-76
conflict, 18-19, 38-39,
43-44, 87, 101-4,
115, 118-20, 122,
131, 144, 156,
190-92, 221, 270,
274, 277
conscience, 186, 188,
234, 288
conscientiousness-
based virtues, 268,
270
conscious(ness), 19, 42,
60, 170-72, 174, 179,
196-201, 213, 223,
252, 278, 285, 289
consensus, consensual,
135-36, 260
conservative, 34, 133,
207, 216
control, 23, 51, 62,
64-65, 74-77, 81, 94,
102, 109, 125, 127,
138, 160, 171, 173,
222-23, 225, 227-29,
235, 238, 240-42,
249, 256, 260, 262,
266-70
cope, coper, coping, 48,
52, 221, 223, 291
correlational methods,
108-9
cortisol, 61-62, 110,
157, 221
cosmos, 120, 208
counseling psychology,
counseling
psychologist,
counseling,
counselor, counsel,
12, 18, 33-35, 37, 39,
55, 98, 115, 125-32,
137, 152, 154, 161,
168-70, 192, 281-83,
286
courage, 10, 68, 144,
260-61, 269
craft(s), 111, 149, 153,
156
creation, 13, 30, 36, 76,
79-80, 83, 87-89, 91,
93-94, 99, 120, 136,
138-41, 143, 149,
153, 160, 166, 187,
215-16, 226, 282,

286, 291
creation, 13, 30, 36, 76,
79-80, 83, 87-89, 91,
93-94, 99, 120, 136,
138-41, 143, 149,
153, 160, 166, 187,
215-16, 226, 282,
291
Creator, 79-81, 136,
141, 166, 256
creed(s), 135, 180
crime, 60, 64, 158, 210,
213
crisis, 151-52
cultural psychology,
158, 163-64
culture, cultural, 20,
38, 45, 59-62, 74,
115, 117, 142,
154-55, 158-59,
163-64, 189, 194,
203, 207-10, 212,
214, 218, 220,
223-26, 259, 262,
265, 283-84, 289-91
dance, dancing 70,
97-100, 119-22, 136,
195, 274
data, 12, 20, 27, 30,
39-43, 45, 53-55, 57,
65, 72-74, 81, 88-90,
104, 106, 108,
111-12, 114-19,
125-27, 130, 136,
143-45, 150-53, 157,
159-60, 174, 176,
179, 190, 200, 202,
211, 214, 217, 219,
234, 242, 254
decisional forgiveness,
decision to forgive,
206
defense, defensive,
defensiveness, 21, 48,
57, 210, 285
degeneracy, 198
depression, 27, 48, 152,
249
desecration, 183, 195,
289
determined, 42, 53,
173, 207, 210
developmental
psychology, 42, 108,
125, 161, 164, 293,
295
dialogue, dialogue
model, 9, 11-12, 15,

32, 43, 86, 89, 102-4,
137, 273, 277-78
discern, discernment,
18, 26, 48, 51, 54,
76-77, 79, 81-82, 87,
95, 121, 135-36, 177,
203, 270
disciplinary matrix, 73,
150, 152
discipline, disciplines,
disciplinary, 7, 13,
35-37, 44-46, 73,
75-77, 79, 82-90, 99,
101-2, 121-24, 132,
137, 144-45, 150,
152, 154, 156, 161,
165-66, 201, 203,
222, 241, 249, 255,
273, 279, 282, 293
disconfirm, 54, 176,
208
discover, 12, 79, 82-84,
95, 100, 108, 150,
166, 169-70, 193,
199, 202, 208,
213-15, 217, 226,
278, 285
distress, 98, 101, 109
diversity, 195, 214, 233
divine image, 80-81,
87
divine revelation, 76,
81, 263
divorce, 190-91,
227-32, 281, 292
earthly city, 31-32, 45
emotion, emotional,
11, 19, 21, 24-27, 39,
48, 50-52, 62, 67, 85,
91, 95-96, 105,
127-29, 155, 158,
162-64, 170-71, 174,
178-80, 183, 192-93,
197-98, 205-6, 209,
221-22, 224-25,
237-38, 240, 242,
244, 259-60, 267-70,
275-77, 279, 283-84,
290, 292-93, 295
emotional forgiveness,
205-6, 279, 290
empathy, empathic,
91-92, 98, 131, 171,
185-86, 190, 260-61,
270
empirical, empirical
method, 44, 83,
108-9, 127, 151, 160,

188, 288, 294
enemy, enemies, 20, 21,
86, 104, 122, 185,
234, 287, 290
environment,
environmental, 9, 20,
40, 79, 89, 115, 157,
169, 198, 223, 255
epistemology, 108, 135
ethics, 258-59, 285
ethnic, ethnicity,
ethnicities, 19, 163,
207, 216, 232-33
evil, 171, 185-87, 243,
288
evolve, evolution,
evolutionary, 40, 94,
98, 134, 136, 150-51,
154-55, 168, 185-86,
198, 216, 224, 258,
277, 288, 291, 295
exegetical theology,
113-14
experiment, 12, 25, 52,
54, 61, 84, 88, 104,
109, 114, 140, 151,
163, 172-73, 182,
194, 199, 202,
240-42, 244, 257,
262, 267, 279, 282,
287, 289
experimental methods,
109, 173
explain, explanations,
28, 36, 41-43, 62, 65,
69, 89, 91-95, 106-7,
113-14, 120, 123,
15053, 159, 180, 196,
199, 245, 266, 278,
283
fair, fairness, 183, 192,
218, 247, 260,
268-69, 287
faithful, 158, 231, 269
fall, fallen, 9, 13, 21,
25, 31, 80-81, 83, 91,
93, 100, 119-20, 132,
136-37, 141, 182,
185-90, 193-94, 201,
208-9, 211, 213, 223,
234-36, 255, 257,
271, 277
filter model, filter
theory, 15, 35, 37-39,
41, 116-17, 124, 132,
137, 144
findings, 13, 15, 38,
40, 43, 46, 49, 51, 68,

73, 82, 88-89, 102,
111-13, 132, 134-35,
153-55, 158, 161,
169, 178-79, 192,
201-3, 207, 214, 236,
256, 267, 279, 288
flow, 93, 104, 121, 154,
160, 183, 196, 198,
287
forbear, forbearance,
260, 269
forgive, forgiveness,
forgiving, 59, 75, 92,
104, 139, 144, 163,
187-88, 192, 195,
204-6, 214, 218-20,
230, 234, 261,
268-70, 279, 281,
286-92, 294-95
free, freedom, 9-10, 34,
56-57, 94-95, 107,
122, 133, 158, 164,
172, 179, 201, 209,
221, 227, 235, 255,
284, 290, 294
free will, 94-95, 107,
122, 164, 172, 201,
255
fruit of the Spirit, 223,
260, 262, 270
game, game theory, 19,
21, 27, 30, 56-57, 62,
67, 69, 93, 142, 158,
183-84, 189, 195,
221, 239, 246-47,
262-63
gene(s), genetic, 40, 94,
157, 223-24, 255,
279, 291
generalize, generaliza-
tion, 72, 110, 125-26,
131, 202-3
general revelation, 11,
13, 36, 38, 76-77, 81,
101, 124, 133,
138-41, 234, 257
generosity, 10, 260,
268, 269
goal(s), 42, 79, 100,
104, 129, 152,
192-94, 260, 268,
278
God, 7, 10-14, 31-32,
36, 38, 40-41, 44-46,
55-56, 60, 65-66,
75-83, 85, 87-89,
91-94, 97-99, 101-2,
104-9, 115-16, 118,

120-126, 131-144,
149-50, 153-56, 160,
164-66, 171, 177,
179-83, 185, 187-88,
190-91, 193-96, 201,
205-6, 208-9,
213-15, 217, 219-22,
225-26, 232, 234-35,
245, 254-58, 260,
262-63, 265-67,
269-80, 282, 285,
288-89, 291
gratitude, 144, 163,
193, 208, 260-61,
268-69, 277, 294
grace, 13, 75, 92, 109,
123, 164, 185, 192,
213, 255, 257, 267,
290
group(s), 21, 49, 50, 61,
67-69, 77, 121-22,
131, 141, 154-55,
159, 163, 169, 178,
190, 192-93, 198,
201-2, 216, 231-34,
237, 242-43, 261,
270
happy, happiness,
17-18, 30-31, 43, 66,
68, 163-64, 220-22,
229-30, 232, 259,
283, 285, 287, 291,
294-95
hardiness, 51
health psychology, 108,
125
heart, 32, 66, 81, 96,
105, 110-11, 131,
136, 138-39, 157,
165-66, 223, 245,
249, 256, 275-76,
280, 283
helping, 38, 55, 108,
120, 125-27, 129,
131, 163, 192, 194,
249, 264, 282-83,
288, 290, 294
helpful, 11, 24, 36, 48,
77, 82, 84, 125, 180,
195, 260, 272, 276
heuristics, 53-54, 84,
174
historical theology, 114
Holy Spirit, 75-76, 82,
106-7, 133-34,
138-39, 142, 171,
235, 260, 262-63,
274, 279

honest, 260, 269
honor, 59-60, 62,
74-75, 136-37, 142,
189, 258, 284, 289
hope, 10, 13, 17, 31, 41,
55, 67, 81, 89, 108,
118, 129, 132, 139,
143, 150, 156,
163-65, 183, 193-94,
201, 215, 220,
260-61, 278-79, 281,
286, 288, 290,
294-95
humanities, 9, 45, 81,
83, 87, 115, 161, 215
human, humans,
humanity, 13, 23, 27,
30-32, 35-37, 39-43,
45-46, 52, 54-55,
65-66, 72-73, 76-83,
87-91, 94-96, 98,
104-5, 107, 115-40,
143-44, 149, 153,
156-57, 160-66,
171-72, 174, 179-80,
182-90, 193, 195-96,
199, 201, 205-6,
208-9, 211-12,
215-16, 220, 226-28,
234, 249, 255-56,
259, 261, 263,
265-68, 271, 278-83,
286-92, 294
human nature, 13, 23,
27, 30, 35, 39-40,
42-43, 46, 52, 54-55,
77, 87, 90-91,
118-20, 122, 124-26,
128-31, 133, 138-40,
143-44, 166, 195,
208, 211, 215, 227,
279, 281, 283, 287,
289, 291
humble, 30, 45, 75-76,
124, 132, 134,
136-37, 165, 168,
178, 219, 275
humility, 43, 46, 119,
123, 132, 134, 136,
144, 163, 178,
260-61, 269, 294
hypothesis, hypotheses,
hypothesize, 54, 83,
88, 108-9, 112-14,
150-51, 171-72,
175-76, 185, 202,
204, 206, 208, 248
identification, 57, 261

identity, 35, 47-48,
163-64, 192-94, 214,
225, 258, 260,
262-66, 270-71, 288,
291-92, 294
image of God, image,
divine image, 13,
80-81, 85, 87, 97,
136-37, 139-40, 166,
182-83, 185-86, 194,
197-99, 201, 243,
245, 255
individual(s),
individualism, 35,
40, 65, 69-72, 78, 81,
96, 111, 120, 128,
131-32, 134, 151,
163-64, 169, 172,
186, 189, 192,
197-98, 201, 204,
209-13, 218-19, 222,
225, 227, 230, 232,
235, 243, 268, 291,
293-94
implicit associations
test (IAT), 206
infidelity, 231
influence, 30, 32,
41-42, 59, 65, 74, 89,
103, 117, 127, 130,
132, 158, 163-65,
170, 174, 187, 217,
242-45, 255-56, 259,
270-71, 275, 287-88
in-group(s), 122, 193
integration, integrate,
10, 12-13, 15, 32-35,
37-39, 41, 43, 45-46,
55, 58, 102-4, 114,
124-28, 131-32, 194,
197-200, 225, 283,
286, 293
interpret, interpreta-
tion, 74, 81, 89,
114-18, 134, 136,
138, 144, 149,
153-54, 161, 169,
173, 182, 203, 209,
211, 215, 217, 225,
227, 283, 294
interview, 18, 28-30,
51, 78, 160
intimacy, 87, 100,
102-3, 190-91, 212,
229-30, 272-73, 279
Jesus, 13, 34, 36, 56,
60, 75-77, 80, 94,
107, 110, 117, 122,

125, 132, 134, 137,
139-42, 144, 164,
177, 180-81, 205-6,
208-9, 211, 219,
224-25, 235, 256,
260, 263, 271, 274,
279
judge, judgment,
23-25, 29, 31, 33, 37,
46, 57, 73, 75, 82, 85,
91, 132, 137, 170,
174, 185, 196, 218,
239-40, 242-43, 254,
259-60, 268, 284,
292-93, 295
just, justice, 59-61,
121, 178, 182-85,
192, 195, 207, 209,
234, 245, 251,
260-61, 268-70, 279,
287, 289-90, 292,
295
kindness, kind, 92, 98,
260, 265
kingdom of God, 137,
225
know, knowledge,
knowing, head
knowledge, heart
knowledge, 7, 10-11,
13, 18, 21, 24-28, 30,
33, 36-37, 40, 44, 46,
54, 56, 60, 65-66,
69-71, 75-83, 87, 89,
91-93, 95-98,
100-101, 103, 105-8,
115, 120-22, 124-25,
132-44, 149, 152-56,
158, 161-63, 165-66,
168, 171, 173-74,
180-82, 185, 187,
195, 198-99, 201,
208, 214-15, 223,
225, 228, 230,
234-35, 239-40, 243,
245-46, 249, 253-54,
256-57, 259, 263,
266, 271-73, 275-80,
283, 293, 295
law, 36-37, 41, 43, 60,
93, 138-39, 202-3,
224, 251, 256, 263,
273, 285, 291
leader, leadership, 32,
70, 95, 120, 137, 211,
226, 282
levels-of-explanation,
level(s), 14-15, 23, 37,

42-43, 47, 50, 61-62,
88, 92-95, 100,
111-12, 172, 179,
194, 200-201, 210,
218-21, 227, 229,
232-34, 252, 261,
278, 283
lie, 186, 246, 254, 288
life, life sciences, 9,
11-14, 28, 30-32, 34,
43-45, 47, 51, 55, 65,
67, 70, 72-77, 83,
86-87, 91, 94, 96-97,
104, 107-8, 115, 121,
123, 129-30, 132-34,
137, 140, 149,
152-53, 155, 157,
159, 162, 165,
170-71, 173-74, 177,
179-80, 190-91,
193-94, 196, 201-2,
208, 211, 213, 216,
220, 222-23, 225-26,
228-29, 231, 234-35,
255-56, 259, 262-63,
269-70, 272, 275,
277-80, 287, 291,
294
literature, 12, 23, 32,
72, 74, 154, 188-89,
192, 217, 226, 262,
266, 275
logic(al), 48, 54, 72, 84,
86, 98, 111, 160, 171,
172, 237, 240, 251,
285, 290
Lord, 13, 82, 91, 165,
193, 270, 272
lordship, 56, 134, 137,
141, 144, 224-25
love, loving, 11, 50, 52,
55-56, 70, 75-77, 81,
84, 87-88, 92, 95-98,
101-2, 105-7, 122,
127, 131-32, 136-37,
139, 141, 145, 160,
163-65, 182, 187,
190-91, 208-11,
214-15, 230, 234,
251, 255, 258, 260,
262-63, 269-72,
276-78, 280, 287-90,
293
map, 20, 45, 106-7,
111-12, 118-19, 157,
170
marriage, marriage
model, 11, 17, 28,

86-87, 90, 95-96,
101-5, 119, 123, 145,
176-77, 190-91, 195,
217-18, 227-32,
272-74, 277, 280,
285-86, 289, 292
materialist, materialis-
tic, 39, 44, 89, 106-7,
120, 196
meaning, meaningful,
12, 51, 73, 81, 92, 95,
111, 113-14, 124,
134, 143, 166, 170,
180, 182, 193-94,
201, 205, 213, 221,
231, 278, 289
measure(ment), 38, 42,
49, 54, 65, 73-74, 89,
106-8, 110-12, 116,
126, 143, 149-51,
156-57, 159-61, 168,
171-73, 186, 199,
206, 217, 225, 228,
261, 270
memory, 104, 158, 177,
178, 196-98, 240,
287
mercy, 75, 92, 94, 121,
123, 185, 192, 245,
255, 257, 261, 267
metaphor, 45, 60, 86,
88, 90, 95, 98, 195,
218, 224, 232,
274-77
method, 7, 17, 33, 35,
40, 42, 45, 66, 72-77,
79, 81, 83-90, 99,
104, 108-9, 111-15,
119, 121, 125, 127,
129, 133, 143,
149-51, 153-61, 163,
166, 169-73,
mind, 18, 24, 31, 33,
53, 58, 79, 83, 89, 91,
93, 121, 124, 129,
130, 137-39, 141,
143, 154, 156, 162,
170, 177, 180, 183,
186, 196-99, 202-3,
215-16, 222, 224,
227, 242, 245, 256,
269, 273-74, 278,
280, 285
mindfulness, 143, 154
miracle, miraculous,
94-95
model, 7, 15, 37-39,
41-42, 74, 86, 90, 98,

100-108, 111-12,
114, 116-18, 124,
132, 135, 137,
144-45, 156-57, 159,
162, 183, 194-97,
201, 219, 224, 238,
259, 261, 263, 271,
282-83, 294
modernity, 211-13,
226, 291
moral action, 240, 259,
260
moral development
theory, 258
moral dilemma, 236,
245, 250
moral judgment, 240,
259-60, 292-93
moral muscle, 81,
240-42, 266, 279
moral, morality,
morally, morals, 20,
66, 75, 81, 93, 139,
161, 179, 181, 183,
187, 213-14, 217-18,
222, 229, 235-38,
240-42, 244-47,
249-52, 255-66,
268-71, 279, 292-94
motive(s), motivation,
79, 93, 95, 101, 121,
131, 136, 140, 155,
158, 164, 166, 170,
183-86, 194-95,
223-24, 234, 245,
259, 268, 275-76,
279, 287, 294
mystery, mysteries,
143, 215, 233, 277-79
narrative(s), life
narrative(s), 34, 157,
170, 194, 213, 217,
293
natural law, 41
natural philosophy, 76
natural theology, 41
nature, 13, 23, 26-27,
30-32, 35-36, 39-43,
46, 52-55, 65, 76-77,
80-81, 87, 89-91,
93-95, 97, 102,
111-12, 115, 118-20,
122, 124-26, 128-31,
133-40, 142-44, 149,
155-56, 160, 166,
195, 201-4, 208, 211,
213, 215, 227, 235,
237, 255-57, 262,

274-75, 279, 281,
283-87, 289, 291,
293-94
neurons, 143, 162,
196-201, 240, 255,
278
noetic effects of sin,
noetic, 137-39, 145
normal science, 150-52
obey, obedience, 205,
244, 246-47, 250-51
objective, objectively,
objectivity, 205, 226,
233, 242, 244,
246-47, 250-51,
256-57, 262-63,
292-93, 295
observational methods,
44, 108-9
ontology, ontologically,
93, 182, 214
out-group(s), 122, 193
paradigm, 111-13,
150-53
parent, 26, 59, 67, 94,
97, 103, 136, 174,
201, 228, 232,
262-64, 268, 271,
294-95
partner(s), 7, 13, 95,
98-100, 106, 119,
121, 123-25, 132,
158, 177, 184,
191-92, 228-32, 273
pastor, 48, 82, 102,
126, 219, 282
pastoral care, 115, 125,
131, 137
patience, 10, 260, 262,
269
peace, 13, 29, 31, 60,
90, 109-10, 145, 192,
206, 211, 221, 226,
260
Pentecostal, 79, 225,
291
perception, 53, 56, 73,
85, 89, 131, 155, 170,
176-78, 197-98, 200,
219, 265-66, 269,
281, 284, 294
persona, 212, 214
personal, 14, 22, 26,
42-44, 51, 66, 73-74,
79-80, 88, 98-102,
109-10, 117, 124,
129, 131, 152-54,
159-60, 162, 164,

185, 187, 189, 215,
218-19, 234, 248,
256, 271, 276, 279
personality, 23-25, 27,
29-30, 39, 42, 57, 76,
86, 97-98, 105, 108,
125, 127, 130-31,
133, 141, 162, 164,
166, 187, 194, 209,
212, 225-26, 233,
243, 255, 261, 270,
279, 281, 284, 288,
290-95
person-centered, 127
perspectival,
perspectivalisit, 15,
42
PET, 156, 184, 208
philosophical theology,
114-15, 155
philosophy, 35, 37-38,
71-72, 76, 83, 86,
115, 149-50, 152,
160-61, 226, 232,
256, 258
physical science(s), 87,
215
politics, political,
11-12, 20, 32, 77, 86,
117, 120, 158, 163,
168, 216-17, 226-27,
232-34, 270, 274
positive psychology, 43,
144, 162-64, 261,
290
postmodern,
postmodernism,
211-13, 226-27, 260
power, 11, 19-21, 31,
38, 64, 73, 94, 120,
139, 142, 163, 165,
171, 219, 227,
234-35, 242, 244,
268, 270-71, 279,
281
practical theology, 115,
124-25, 131, 153
praise, 31, 142, 154,
208, 221
prayer, pray, 14, 22, 34,
77-79, 87, 94, 107,
109-10, 154, 208,
223, 230, 265-66,
270, 275-76, 286
preach, preaching, 30,
37, 135, 137
pride, 30, 73, 75, 91,
93, 166, 181, 187-89,

211, 288
principle(s), 13, 37-38,
43, 63, 71, 93, 95,
120, 173, 198, 203,
230, 235, 249, 251,
262-64, 270, 282,
286
probabilistic,
problem, 29, 34, 38, 48,
53-55, 67, 79, 92,
95-96, 99, 127, 129,
132-33, 150-52, 159,
161, 163-64, 174-76,
181, 188, 192, 196,
202-3, 209-10,
221-23, 229, 231,
235, 237, 240, 244,
248-51, 257, 259,
266-67, 274, 288,
292
progress, 48, 149-51,
168, 179, 208-9, 211,
226, 286
proposition, 136, 182
prudence, 260-61, 269
psychoanalytic, 108,
127, 223
psychodynamic, 127
psychology of religion,
86, 88, 108, 144,
163-64, 286-88
psychology,
psychological
science, 7, 9-15,
17-18, 22, 27-28, 30,
32-46, 52-53, 55-56,
62-63, 65-69, 71-90,
92, 95-96, 98-99,
101-6, 108, 113,
115-19, 121-22,
124-28, 130-34,
136-37, 142-45,
149-50, 153-73,
179-83, 185, 187-88,
190, 195-96, 201-11,
213-19, 221, 223-24,
226-30, 233-35, 242,
245-46, 248-49,
256-58, 261-62, 269,
273-76, 278-95
psychotherapy, 12, 35,
38, 42, 46, 48, 88,
127, 129, 132, 149,
164, 168, 209, 222,
248-49, 276-77, 288,
290, 294
PTSD, 47-49
punish, 60, 121,

184-85
rational, rationality, 28,
36-37, 44, 82, 160,
175, 237, 245,
258-61, 268, 270-71,
275-76, 283, 292
reason, reasons, reason-
ing, 19, 45, 47, 56,
63, 66, 70, 72, 74,
83-84, 93, 98, 105,
111, 120, 127, 131,
134-35, 140-41,
161-62, 173-74, 204,
208-9, 220, 223-25,
228-29, 231, 237,
239-40, 245, 249-52,
259-63, 266, 275,
282, 285, 293
reconcile, reconcilia-
tion, 37, 192, 199,
205, 234, 286, 289,
290, 295
redemption, redeem,
13, 31-32, 91, 120,
132, 135-39, 160,
164, 194, 213, 217,
226, 235, 247,
283-85
reduce, reducing,
reductionism,
reductionistic,
reductionist, 39, 42,
143, 180, 219, 221,
234, 285
relational, 7, 15, 80, 86,
90-91, 98, 104, 106,
118-19, 124-25,
131-32, 137, 144-45,
160, 164, 182, 190,
192-93, 195-96, 201,
213, 218, 232, 270,
277
relationship,
relationship model, 7,
11-15, 32, 35, 41,
44-45, 49, 51, 66,
75-76, 79-80, 83, 86,
88-90, 95-96,
98-109, 111, 115,
119, 120-24, 133,
141-42, 145, 152-54,
159-61, 164-65,
171-73, 177, 179,
190-93, 195-96,
198-201, 204,
213-15, 227, 229-34,
251, 255-56, 261,
263-64, 268, 270-71,

273-81, 285, 287, 290
religion, religious, 9, 11-13, 19, 33, 35, 38, 41-44, 74, 86, 88, 100-104, 107-8, 111, 120, 136, 144, 152, 155, 161, 163-64, 179, 193-95, 222, 231-34, 259-60, 273-78, 281, 283, 285-89, 291, 294-95
remorse, 219, 288, 291
repress, repression, repressive, 48, 51-52
research, 9, 12, 17-18, 24, 40-41, 48-49, 51-52, 61-62, 64, 68-69, 75, 82, 111-13, 115, 125-26, 128, 131, 133, 137, 157-59, 168-71, 174, 177-78, 182-83, 185-95, 201, 203-4, 206, 209-10, 213, 220, 223, 229-34, 237-38, 240, 243, 248, 259, 264, 266, 273, 281, 285, 287-88, 290-92
research design, 158-59, 171
research programs, 51, 112-13, 131, 195, 285
resilience, resilient, resiliency, 48-52, 54, 131, 142, 284
responsibility, 192, 213, 219, 227, 260, 288, 291, 293
resurrection, 163, 180, 207, 263
reveal(s), 13, 25-27, 36, 40, 46, 48, 52, 62, 71, 76-77, 80-82, 93-98, 101, 107, 115, 120, 125, 129, 131, 133-34, 137-39, 141-44, 150, 154-57, 160, 162-67, 169-72, 180, 183-84, 186, 188, 190, 194, 206-7, 215, 235, 245, 255-57, 262, 275, 279-80, 292
revelation, 11, 13, 36, 38, 40, 44, 71, 76-78, 81, 101, 120, 124,

133-35, 138-42, 144, 154, 166, 195, 215, 234, 257, 263
revenge, 189, 234
revolution, 33, 134, 150-53, 224, 285
right, 19, 28, 54, 59, 63, 77, 85, 120, 127, 188, 196, 199, 209-10, 213-15, 218-20, 235, 240, 242, 248-50, 254
rule(s), 19, 37, 53, 54, 72, 83, 85-86, 128, 132, 136, 174-76, 223, 245-48, 258, 262-63, 292
sacrament, 32
sacred, 136, 166, 183, 195, 289
saint(s), 78
salvation, 66, 77, 124, 134-35, 139, 143, 224
sample, sampling, 12, 49-50, 54, 72-73, 78-79, 109-11, 126, 129, 217-18, 230, 286
science, 7-13, 15, 30, 32-33, 36, 39-46, 54-55, 63, 65, 69, 71-83, 85-90, 92, 94-96, 98-99, 101-8, 111-26, 130, 132-38, 142-45, 149-73, 175, 177, 179-83, 185-91, 193, 195-97, 199, 201-11, 213-19, 221-25, 227-35, 245-46, 248-49, 256, 259, 262, 269, 273-74, 277-90, 292, 294
scientific, 10, 12, 15, 17, 23, 32-33, 40, 42-45, 47, 54-55, 63, 65, 70, 73, 79, 81, 86, 89, 94-95, 104, 106-7, 111-14, 117-18, 120, 125, 133-35, 143, 202, 204, 206, 208, 211, 217, 227, 254, 278-80, 283-85, 290, 292, 294
scientific method, 40, 45, 79, 83-86, 112, 114, 142, 156, 163, 169, 208

Scripture, 15, 23, 27, 30, 32, 35-38, 40-41, 46, 54, 56, 62, 66, 76-78, 80, 82, 85, 88, 92-94, 104, 114-19, 132, 134-36, 138-39, 141-42, 144, 149, 154-55, 171, 177, 180, 187, 195, 202-8, 211, 214, 217-18, 221, 227, 235, 256-57, 262-63, 270-71, 279
self, selves, 24, 51, 53, 72, 75-77, 81, 84-85, 107, 111, 114, 127, 130-31, 138, 163, 173, 176-77, 179, 181, 187-89, 208-14, 218-20, 222-23, 225-27, 234-35, 238-42, 249, 255-57, 260, 262, 265-71, 283-84, 288-95
self-condemnation, 188, 218-19
self-control, 75, 77, 81, 138, 222-23, 235, 238, 240-42, 256, 260, 262, 266-69
self-esteem, 176, 188-89, 209-11, 289-90
self-forgiveness, 188, 218-20, 288, 291
self-love, 208-9, 211
self-perception theory, 265
self-sacrifice, 208, 234
self-serving bias, self-serving, 84-85, 130, 173, 177, 179, 181, 211, 284
self-sufficient, 257
self-talk, 249
sex, 191, 216-18, 231-32, 292
sin, sinful, sinfulness, 13, 31-32, 36, 73, 80-81, 116, 122, 124, 127, 135-41, 144-45, 165-66, 182, 186-87, 201, 205, 208, 219, 235, 245, 255, 288
single parent(ing), 228, 232
situation(al), 24-26, 40, 51, 54, 71, 108-9,

125, 129, 131, 136, 139, 142-43, 156, 158, 161-62, 164, 183-87, 189, 197-98, 212, 216, 224, 226-27, 237, 239, 243-45, 255-57, 262-63, 267, 269-70, 288
social psychology, 86, 108, 125, 155, 162-64, 185, 190, 242, 281, 284, 287-92, 294-95
social science(s), 36, 76, 81, 87, 115, 153, 168, 210
society, societal, 12, 33-34, 163, 190-92, 194, 204, 211, 218, 220, 222, 227-28, 232-34, 251
Son of God, 142, 234
soul, 39, 42, 46, 132, 220, 226, 283, 286, 291-92
sovereign, 32, 76, 88, 94, 129, 142, 201
special revelation, 36, 38, 76-77, 124, 133, 135, 139, 142, 154, 234
spiritual, spirituality, 9, 34, 37, 45, 77, 79, 82, 107, 110, 149, 153-54, 160, 164, 180, 187, 191, 208, 219, 221-22, 224, 266, 274, 278, 283, 286-88, 290-91, 294
spiritual disciplines, 77, 154, 222, 279
statistics, statistical, 56-58, 73-74, 126, 159, 172-73, 229-31, 279
story, stories, 11, 18-19, 25, 59, 61, 72, 88, 91, 99, 119, 140, 152, 159, 178, 185, 194-95, 211, 224, 235, 245, 250, 252, 254-55, 263-64, 271, 275, 279
strengths, 52, 100, 103, 131-32, 163, 233, 261, 294
stress, 33, 47, 70, 110,

129, 157, 212,
221-23, 225, 233,
249, 291
strong situation(s), 129,
244, 256
study, studies, 12, 17,
22-23, 27, 29-30,
32-33, 42, 47, 49,
51-53, 56, 58-59, 62,
66-69, 72-74, 76-77,
79-83, 85, 87-88, 97,
104, 108-11, 113-15,
121, 125-26, 128,
136-38, 140-44, 151,
153-55, 157, 160-61,
163-64, 169, 171,
173, 177, 179, 181,
183-87, 189-90, 192,
194, 199-201, 205-8,
210-11, 219-20, 226,
228, 234, 237-39,
241, 243-44, 247-48,
250, 255-57, 261-62,
267-69, 273, 278-80,
283, 288-89, 291-92
subjective, subjectivity,
subjectively, 42, 73,
85, 111-12, 125, 131,
161, 169, 180
suffer, suffering, 72,
91-92, 125-27, 158,
164-65, 174, 220,
234, 238, 254, 269
supernatural, 39,
93-95, 120
suppress, 51, 138, 284
sympathy, 92, 131, 260
systematic theology,
114, 155, 215
teach(ing), 13, 26, 32,
37-38, 49, 69, 77, 97,
102, 121, 127, 132,
135-37, 142, 154,
177, 212, 216,
243-44, 250, 262-63,
282, 284

tempt, temptation, 93,
175, 234, 236, 257
territory, 106, 112,
118-19
terrorism, terrorist, 19,
50, 233-34, 284, 287,
292
theology, theologian,
theological, 7, 10-15,
23, 30, 32, 35-41,
43-46, 53-56, 65, 72,
74, 77-79, 82-90, 96,
98-99, 101-6, 111,
113-28, 131-38, 142,
144-45, 147, 149-50,
153, 155-56, 163,
166, 170-71, 173,
177-79, 182, 185-87,
189-90, 193-96,
200-220, 222-27,
234-35, 237, 273,
277-78, 282-83,
285-88, 290-91
theory, theorize,
theoretical, 10, 27,
34-35, 37, 39-42, 52,
54-55, 72-73, 79, 83,
100-101, 106-8,
111-14, 127-31, 135,
150-53, 158-59,
161-62, 183, 185,
188, 191, 198, 201-2,
211, 214, 241,
258-61, 265-66, 282,
287, 289, 293-94
therapy, therapist, 33,
35, 37, 42, 49,
127-32, 183, 193,
224, 229, 267,
276-77, 281-83, 288,
290
translate, translation(s),
108, 116-17, 204-5,
225, 282
trauma, traumatic,
47-52, 54, 126, 131,

142, 284
Trinity, 190, 195, 213,
215, 286, 284
triune God, 31, 76, 98,
123, 139, 142, 160,
195, 213-14, 258,
263, 270, 277, 279
truth, true, 13, 15, 34,
36-38, 42, 44-48, 52,
54-56, 63, 71-73, 77,
79, 81-84, 89, 92,
94-95, 101, 106, 108,
111-13, 115-20,
125-28, 132-35, 138,
141, 160, 163, 166,
168-70, 173, 177-79,
182, 189, 192, 202-3,
205, 207-8, 211,
213-14, 219, 231-32,
245, 255, 257, 276,
280
understood, 45, 139,
143-44, 170, 185,
217, 246-47, 249-50,
252
union, unitive, unity,
101, 194, 213-14
universal, 130, 203,
207-8, 215
value, values, 15,
33-35, 42, 45, 56, 71,
74, 83, 97, 100, 118,
124-28, 131, 144,
151, 169, 194, 209,
220, 228, 230-31,
258, 264-65, 268,
271, 273, 285-86,
294
variable(s), indepen-
dent variable,
dependent variable,
62, 73-74, 89, 107-11,
158-59, 171-72, 288
virtue(s), virtuous,
virtuously, 7, 13-14,
31, 50, 56, 71, 81, 98,

137-39, 163, 235,
258-62, 268-71, 274,
293-94
war, warfare, warfare
model, 11, 19-22,
29-30, 59, 70, 86,
104, 193, 209, 226,
233, 243, 266
way, 13, 15, 24-28, 30,
40-42, 44-45, 53, 59,
62, 65, 68, 71, 73-74,
76, 80-81, 83, 87-88,
91, 94, 97, 100,
106-8, 110, 114-15,
120-22, 124-25,
129-31, 133, 135,
137, 139, 141,
143-45, 150-53, 155,
158-60, 171, 173,
177-79, 186, 188-89,
193, 196-97, 205,
207-8, 211, 218, 223,
225, 227, 234, 237,
240, 248, 254-55,
258-60, 263-64, 274
wife, 10, 81, 87, 95,
105, 201, 251
wisdom, 23, 30, 33, 48,
77-78, 179, 192, 194,
261, 263, 283
wonder, 30, 99, 107,
165, 229, 232, 257,
274, 277-79
Word, God's Word, 76,
87, 116, 134-35,
139-40, 142
worship, 34, 78, 92,
101, 138, 142,
154-55, 165-66, 208,
275-76
wrong, 23, 29-30, 63,
65, 83, 88, 113, 116,
188, 219, 235, 240,
249-50, 254, 291